BANANAS IN
BORDEAUX

Bananas in Bordeaux

Self-sufficiency for dreamers

LOUISE FRANKLIN CASTANET

ISBN
1 901253 29 5
First published May 2002

Published by:
Léonie Press
an imprint of
Anne Loader Publications
13 Vale Road, Hartford,
Northwich, Cheshire CW8 1PL
Gt Britain
Tel: 01606 75660   Fax: 01606 77609
e-mail: anne@aloaderpubs.u-net.com
Website: www.anneloaderpublications.co.uk
www.leoniepress.com

Printed by:
Anne Loader Publications

With many thanks to the *Bristol Evening Post* and *France Magazine* where some of this material was first published.

Contents

Acknowledgements

With all my love to Eric ... and the boys.
Special thanks to Lucienne for all the baby-sitting
while I was writing this...
Huge hugs for Audrey and Romain and to all my family.

Louise

Louise and Eric on their wedding day

About the author

Louise Franklin Castanet was born in Somerset. She moved with her family to the very North of the country (Cumbria) before moving to Bordeaux in 1980. In 1982 they returned to the West Country, settling in Bristol. Louise attended Bristol Grammar School and was a 6th form pupil at Colston's Girls' School. She achieved the John James award for Academic Success in 1990, and then went on to read French at University College London, where she graduated with a first class honours degree in 1994.

She met her future husband, Eric, in Bordeaux during her year-out from university, and settled in France permanently in 1994 once her degree was completed. Eric and Louise married in 1995, and still live happily together in the Bordeaux area with their TWO little boys, Benjamin and Hugo.

MARS

Bordeaux. Home. Sunday, 16th March.

It's time to start a new diary. *Au revoir* chic Chevignon filofax! You were just the thing for a working woman (albeit an English one) in France, but I have filed you away for a year or so. My new *journal intime* is completely plain – at twenty-five I feel I am starting a new era and I'm not sure what to expect. It is also going to be the first diary I have ever shared. This diary is for my baby who is just about to be born, and for the Mummy I am just about to become.

Home. Monday, 17th March.

I have three weeks left to get used to the idea of being a Mum. I must admit the whole thing has not been entirely stress free. My first twinges of anxiety started way back, when I began the ante-natal classes in Bordeaux. I had been warned that these are like sitting in a car and trying to prepare for a head-on collision, nevertheless I was looking forward to being a part of the Big Bump and Beanbag Brigade. I suppose that my main problem was intimidation. In France the midwife is called a *sage-femme*, literally a wise-woman, and my one certainly managed to make me feel like a complete idiot. Worse, although I have been scouring books on the ultimate B&B (Birth and Babies – I gathered early on that you can forget about Bed and Breakfast in this game) my confidence and new-found knowledge were swept away by the need to be liked and fit in. It was worse than starting a new school. Maybe it was just because this was my first bash at giving birth, and that it was not happening in

1

Old Blighty.

Of course, Bordeaux is my home. When I was just a child my family moved from England to a village near the city for a two-year sabbatical, and it almost seemed as though we were discovering a magical land, my Narnia. How beautiful it all was, the golden sandstone houses... the carved lions on the front of our house, sculpted at the time of Richard of Lionheart but to a child's eyes Aslan and his family.

And how blisteringly hot it was in summer, when I splashed with my sister and brothers in the cool water drawn from the ancient pump on the square... And the shock of the winter, how we shivered as we went to the *boulangerie* to buy those long French loaves, and hugged the oven-hot *baguettes* to our bodies as we walked home. Even now just the smell of baking bread makes me feel warm. There are so many images of that time which I treasure – like our pine cone and driftwood fires in the huge fireplace... Or how our big brother turned some of that hard, white drift-wood into beds for us, the only beds in the world to have pearly ship worm casts and sea shells in their bedposts. The most precious moments of my childhood were spent here, and since I returned and married Eric, it has seemed more than ever my home. But, well, I hadn't quite realised what having a baby involved out here. It may seem ridiculous, but these things are NOT the same the world over.

As I said, my problems started in the first ante-natal class. The other Mums in my group looked unutterably *élégantes*, despite being about to pop. I could feel them eyeing my low-slung leggings from the start. What's more I hadn't realised how hot it was going to be, and had to take off my reasonably decent sweatshirt to reveal an old outsized painting tee-shirt of Eric's. The paint stains sizzled with embarrassment. And then there were the holes in my socks... Still, refusing (initially) to be crushed, I decided to dazzle them with my Intelligent Questions. After all, I had done my homework and was aware that the perineum is *not* a room in a Roman villa. So I got my dwindling courage together, and asked about pain relief: Could we have access to pethidine or gas and air?

This was greeted by a weighty silence. The midwife sighed heavily, gave me a patronising smile, and explained that in France (or at least in this clinic) a woman either has an epidural or must rely on her *forces intérieures*. Yeah, OK, like I HAVE seen "Star Wars" and am perfectly aware of the power of The Force, but I was somewhat alarmed to learn that here the solution to pain management was all or nothing – what's more, with not a beanbag on the horizon *"rien"* really meant *"rien."* To help us decide to go for the epidural, we were then shown a Video Nasty made by a pharmaceutical company just to show how thumpingly marvellous their invention is. It featured two women giving birth. Woman Number One had the epidural (although we never caught a glimpse of The Dreaded Needle, quite large enough to vaccinate rhinos). Anyway, she did it all very serenely; relaxed, beautiful and smiling up at her handsome husband right until the babe was born, when she sat up and sipped Champagne. Woman Number Two, epidural-less, screamed, howled and fainted with pain. At the end we were asked whether we'd made our minds up...

I thought I shouldn't swallow it all hook, line and sinker, so I asked what birthing positions we could learn to make things easier if we didn't opt for the Pharmaceutical Solution. "In France," explained the midwife with a thin smile, "giving birth is done in the same way as conceiving a child: lying down." I chickened out of saying that neither point was necessarily true.

Never mind. I sat through all the classes, which were really just hourlong sessions to tell you that you have to stay still while the needle goes in. The Big Day is not far off, and I'm sure I'll survive. It will definitely give me something to write about in my diary.

Home. Tuesday, 18th March.

These last few days have been difficult. My tummy feels so enormous that it is like trying to lug an overfull suitcase around with me all the time. You know, the sort of case that is so full that at any moment its zip could split and its contents burst. Braxton Hicks contractions are all very well, but at the moment it feels like I have stitch, severe back ache and that my insides are about to fall through my pelvis. I can't take much more of this. Still, twenty more days to go. (Groan, groan...)

Bordeaux, Maternity Unit. Wed, 19th March.

He's here! A little early, but perfectly cooked. *At last* – God, eight and a quarter months can seem a long time! It seems so strange that the Mysterious Little Hero of Shadowy Scans is now lying beside me, looking so peaceful after what must have been BIG trauma. For both of us. I did try (honest) to do it all anaesthetic-less, but the pain was like having

3

a bulldozer driven back and forth over the lower half of my body. It made period pain seem like a joke – a mosquito bite compared to having your pelvis chewed up by a crocodile. What's more, when I eventually decided that my pain could be contractions and went to the maternity unit with Eric last night, it suddenly seemed a caesarean was in the offing. My hips, though obviously built for childbearing on the outside, are oddly boyish on the inside. On X-ray I am the spitting image of Kate Moss. I can't say I felt much like a supermodel when I was sent in to Radiology. I stood in front of Supremely Gorgeous Radiologist in my knickers and bra, vaguely wondering if the aforesaid matched. It didn't take me long to realise that as I couldn't even see my knickers over my bump it probably didn't matter if they matched or not.

After my worrying (if flattering) pics I was sent to the *maternité*. I was initially a little embarrassed, as I have had so many contractions over the last few days I wasn't sure I was actually in labour. The midwife told me to take off everything below the waist and to lie down on the couch and wait. I wasn't expecting the warmest of welcomes, but she could have done a bit better. She looked like Frankenstein as she strapped the electrodes to my tummy. After a few minutes she grunted that the *travail* was starting. This was Labour. Ten minutes later the crocodile started chomping, and then I was sure.

I thought the pain was bad, but the midwife told me (reassuringly) it was going to become a thousand times worse. What's more, with the monitoring whatnot strapped to me she said I couldn't move. She suggested I think about an epidural.

A few hours of labour later, as the midwife was wanting me to give an intelligent opinion about her daughter's difficulties learning the English preterit, it all became too much. I remembered the video, the calm relaxed woman (despite having been stuck with the rhino needle) and her happy husband. Eric was there holding my hand, but this was looking more like a scene from a disaster movie than the cosy, loving labour of the video. I found myself yelling for the rhino needle and a rhino's dose. A grumpy anaesthetist turned up at around 1.30am, groaning that he was exhausted and totally incapable of doing *anything* (the mind boggles) at that time in the morning. On his third attempt at the epidural he accused me of having a twisted spine, but suddenly (Thank God) the pain was replaced by a warm and blissful numbness. I was very, very glad I couldn't feel much when a Bic razor was produced a few minutes later,

4

minus shaving cream, and I was given the most radical bikini-line shave ever. Playboy, eat your heart out.

Everything went very quickly after that, and when I first set eyes on the best product that European Union has ever produced, the down side of the whole affair was swept away. Bébé Benjamin arrived with a yell but no cricket bat or string of onions. Looking at his wrinkly, wonderful face I know it was all very worth it.

I'm going to try and have a rest now. Benjamin is fast asleep and Eric has dashed off to the photographer's to get the first photos developed. One hour delivery... if only babies could be that quick!

Bordeaux, Maternity Unit. Thursday, 20 March.

I can't believe it – I think I have got the world's first ever non-crying baby. He just snuggles into my arms and sleeps. This does seem to be causing a problem amongst the nursing staff. One elderly nurse has told me three times this morning that a baby's brain only grows while it's asleep, and that if I keep picking him up to cuddle him I will be stopping his brain from growing. I never saw this in any of the baby books. Can too much cuddling during babyhood *really* relate to a low IQ? Well, I have put him down for a bit while I write my diary, so let's hope those brain cells have a growth spurt. God, he looks so gorgeous – not even a whimper. Makes me want to pick him up again. Just a quick hug then...

The breast-feeding is going well, but apparently I should be getting some kind of milk-rush in the next day or two. We'll see...

3pm. Mum and Dad came over from their house on the Bassin d'Arcachon to meet their first grandchild. Thrilled to bits. Mum reassured me about the cuddling while sleeping – it's ok. Have decided to believe her, as she was a paediatrician. She also looked a bit sceptical about the non-crying baby idea. Let's hope she's wrong about that.

Bordeaux, Maternity Unit. Friday, 21st March.

Mum was right. Benjamin can cry. Loudly. Apparently the first couple of days are a kind of honeymoon period, Nature's way of making sure babe and mother bond. The bonding lasts but the peace doesn't. Ben has been proving that to me by howling all night. I sang "Baa Baa Blacksheep" to him for two hours in English AND French between 3 and 5 am, until we both fell into an exhausted slumber. Nurse woke me up at

6am to take my temperature, *la garce!* She said that I was just looking for punishment, breastfed babies wind their Mummies around their little fingers. Ben needed a bottle and some discipline.

Fell asleep and missed breakfast. Awoke to find ROCKS in my bed. Rocks are attached to me!!! Gone are the post-partum joys of being able to lie on my front again, the milk-rush has swollen my cleavage to proportions that make Pamela Anderson's breasts look like bee-stings in comparison. I have Real European milk mountains.

Eric came to visit this afternoon. Ecstatic about my new breasts. "Will they last?"

Ben is nonplussed by the latest developments. His feeding has taken a turn for the worse. He latches on, and then wrenches his head from side to side, spluttering and soaked in milk. He does seem to be getting gorgeous Cleopatra-like skin, but not much sustenance. Mum rang and said not to worry, the milk flow will slow, and Ben won't drown. In the meantime the mini gauze circles I've been given to absorb the excess milk (that would otherwise be pouring down my front) are utterly drenched. With the addition of a few chives I could deep-fry them to make Pringles.

(*Last thing – hopefully – for tonight*). Evil nurse just came in and gave me a bottle of baby milk and a Meaningful Look. *Merde!!!!!*

Bordeaux, Maternity Unit. Sat, 22nd March.

Night was a little better, but still better not to think about it, I think. God, I can't think or write straight. How can 3kgs of baby govern me so entirely??? He is looking meltingly soft this morning. How can I have called him the Demon of the Night?

Had a shower while babe dozed. Have given up on gauze and was trying to shove a Pampers into each side of my bra when visitors arrived. I was half in my underwear and half still in a bath towel when they charged in – ten of them!! In France EVERYONE visits the *maternité* (and often, it seems, at the same time) and there is no one to stop visitors from coming straight in. They told me my state of undress was not *"grave"*, *they* didn't mind. Bloody cheek. The mayor of the village we used to live in was there plus some colleagues, and they all seemed to be staring at my bra. I suppose I could say the visit was worthwhile – embarrassing but Ben got some yummy presents. Nothing for me, oh well.

Bordeaux, Maternity Unit. Sunday, 23rd March.

Hooray, home tomorrow! I'm sick of this place. Can't wait to get Ben home and take him out in the pram – get some AIR! It is stunningly sunny outside, really hot, and here we are stuck in this tiny room with the heating full on. I am not even allowed to open the window (draughts, or *"courants d'air"* are considered to be Very Dangerous in France. They can give you anything from a common cold to rheumatism. I guess they might even keep you cool, but never mind.)

Paediatrician came to do Ben's leaving-the-unit check. WOKE HIM UP!!! What about his BRAIN?!!!!? I'll never know what the doctor said as Ben was yelling so much. He did say that it was *pas normal* that he had no identity bracelet. The nurse took him away to bath him, and he came back with the Missing Article – a cutesy bracelet. Unfortunately upon examination I saw it had 'Elodie Hauffman' written on it. It was definitely Ben though. Called the nurse who looked embarrassed; good to see her looking uneasy for once. Took the bracelet away. Wonder where Elodie is??

Gynaecologist popped in to talk about post-natal contraception. So tired suddenly I was brimming with tears and (of course) bra was over-flowing again. Managed a hollow laugh.

HOME!!Sweet Home!!!!!!!!! Monday, 24th March.

It is SO good to be home. Felt a bit wobbly when we set off, especially as there are no district nurse visits here. We are home alone! Still, regained confidence on the journey back from the hospital. Ben filled his nappy in the car, and I told Eric that I am now quite capable of changing his nappy in transit – or in our 2CV, as the case may be. I set the changing equipment out on the bonnet, and laid Ben on its gentle slope. Good thing we haven't got a Mercedes or Rolls-Royce that have got those spiky things on the front. Anyway, Ben must have felt relaxed because he produced another plump spurt of yellow poo, which dripped down the front of the car and onto the bumper. I took a deep breath, reassured a panicked Eric that I could cope, and cleaned up both car and baby with cotton wool and baby lotion. I don't think Virginie the 2CV has ever felt as cherished.

Eric dropped us off in our flat in the centre of Bordeaux, and went back – reluctantly – to work. Decided to take Ben straight out – it was a

BEAUTIFUL day and the fridge was MOURNFULLY empty. Guess I hadn't realised that most of the weight you lose after you have a baby is just due to being too disorganised to eat anything.

Strode off down the main pedestrian way, the Rue St Cathérine. GORGEOUSLY warm and sunny, full of pigeons, little kids and street artists. It is Europe's longest pedestrian way, and the way back certainly felt like a bloody long way. Wheel fell off the pram!!!!!! Maybe not pram's fault: perhaps due to the hundredweight of shopping in the basket underneath. Ben was safely tucked in, but had to retrieve ridiculous quantities of rolling fruit. Fixed wheel back on with a good kick.

6pm. *Merde!* Forgot to get Ben's first prescription. The hospital doctor gave me a list of potions, creams and powders as long as my arm (or at least Ben's arm). Rang Mum for her advice. It took me five minutes just to read the list. She laughed at the end of it and said it's no wonder France has a big hole in its health service. She thinks that as he has no nappy rash and seems perfectly content, just lashings of love and warm milk are all he needs. Maybe I'll trust her on this one.

Self-satisfied glow when Eric got in. Had a good dinner, lacking only candles. Ben slept like a, well, like a baby. Severe morale blow at bedtime. Eric remarked that lots of his favourite bits of me were now wrapped in inch-thick cotton wool, when would I be *normale* again? Charming. Can't believe Ben looks so peaceful, I am sure he'll sleep well now he's home.

Home. Tuesday, 25th March.

Not bloody likely. Too knackered to write anything today.

Home. Wednesday, 26th March.

Things not much better. Ben woke at 1am for a feed. At 2.30am woke again, and would only be comforted by sucking my finger. As I slept-walked back to bed, Eric tried to ask me how it was going, and was a little bemused when I dopily shoved my finger into his mouth and told him to be quiet.

Ben's dawn chorus at 5 am. Our own breakfast time saw us both sitting there, shell-shocked, scarcely able to pour the coffee into the right hole. As Eric was leaving for work Ben, at last, fell soundly asleep. With one arm around Teddy and the other thrown carelessly skywards he turned our exhausted hearts to the sweetest, gooiest *crème caramel*. Baby magic does work. OF COURSE we are the luckiest parents alive.

Spent all day getting Ben in and out of nappies and babygros. At least the feeding is going brilliantly – no messing about with bits of plastic and sterilizers and teats and INDECENTLY expensive milk powder. Nope, we have the best stuff on offer at anytime. What's more it's cheap, sterile, portable and comes in the most beautiful of containers.

Rang Mum and Dad for advice about the sleeping. Spoke to Dad. He said most children have a good sleeping pattern by the time they're eighteen years old.

Home. Thursday, 27th March.

Ben slept a million times better, but we still had a dreadful night. After his 1am feed we were all nicely asleep when someone crashed his car into the front wall of our flat – it's a good thing these 18th century walls are sturdy! Not much damage done except to our sleep. Lay awake worrying, have just read a Feng Shui article that explains what area of your house corresponds to what part of your life – the car crashed into the FAMILY corner! Let's hope it's a load of codswallop. Especially as now I think about it I can see what is in the wealth corner. The toilet.

Home. Friday, 28th March.

Lovely day today. Eric had his Friday off, and we all went out together. All four of us; Eric, me, Ben and... Dog. Poor Dog has been having a hard time recently. Instead of running free she has been firmly tied to the pram for every walk. Still, she has been enjoying the restful afternoons when Ben sleeps, and she stretches out in the warm spring sun in the courtyard. Today she was delighted to go on an amble with all of us.

We wandered through the maze of tiny cobbled streets – the houses are so beautiful with their tall windows, sculptured stone fronts and imposing street doors. Many of the houses in the Old Quarter are empty; modern Bordelais prefer to trade in charm and elegance for brand new flats. Eric pushed the front door of the house where his Mum was born and brought up. It creaked open to reveal the ancient interior – the cobbled yard where the family cooked, washed, dried washing and reared chickens, and the sandstone staircase curling up around it, reaching up to the upper storeys. Now it is derelict, but children used to play on the

9

stairs, and sausages and hams used to hang from the oak beams. His Grandfather worked in the abbatoirs and used to bring home scraps to make *saucisson*. Just a street away is the river, the Garonne, where they used to go to buy fish straight from the boats. Fresh *Alose* in April, and huge slabs of dried salted cod in February.

We decided to go down to the quays ourselves. The ornate stone façades of 18th century houses, bourgeoises and very Bordeaux, flank the river as far as you can see. Between the houses and the river there are the cobbled quays which are quite deserted and where Dog can run. It's strange to think that this place was once so bustling with activity, ships from every port: coal from England, cloves and spices from the East, pineapples and bananas from the French colonies in the Caribbean. The quays smelt of vanilla and of lands beyond the sea. Cruise ships from Africa and Brazil used to berth here, giving people a glimpse of another world. Today the port is further seawards at Bassens, but there is still one huge ship moored here – a warship called *Le Colbert*. It's Eric's ship – well, the one he was on when he did a four-year stint in the navy. (Not a brilliant career choice. Eric gets motion sickness on any form of transport whatsoever, and especially in boats. He was sick every day throughout his entire naval career. He is also a Pacifist and a teetotaller, which don't go down too well in the navy.) Yup, *Le Colbert* is here but it is now – and Eric was a bit nonplussed about this – a museum.

We sat on a bench in the sun and watched the river slip past. The Garonne is nicknamed the *'fleuve d'or'* and the sun CAN turn its muddy brown to gold. Dog chased pigeons and Ben slept – it is daytime after all, and the poor chap has to catch up on all the hours he missed in the night. Gulls wheeled and called, and traffic roared in the city behind us. Amazing that a pin dropped in the night will wake Ben, but the noise of a city centre doesn't trouble his dreams. Babies are Unfathomable Creatures.

Home. Saturday, 29th March.

Ben had one less feed today! We're getting there. Let's hope he drops the night feed(s) soon.

Home. Sunday, 30th March.

Went out to a little pavement café for lunch. Felt good in the bright sunshine, Ben dozing and Eric and me sipping our Monacos and watching the pedestrians. Food itself was a little disappointing. Eric was happy with his pasta, but I was half way through my ham salad when I realised it was full of hair, and of the thick, black variety. The manager tried to reassure me, saying that there was *pas de problème* as the hair belonged to the pig that made the ham. Unconvinced, I asked him what kind of pig has long, black hair. I mean I know flying pigs are few and far between, but so are pigs with fly-away hair problems. Another salad (minus keratin) was produced, and I nibbled cheerfully as Eric dug into a rich dark chocolate cake. Felt quite rested and replete. Ah, *la vie est belle!* (Except, possibly, if you're a pig.)

Home. Monday, 31st March.

Eric is back at work. He is looking very disgruntled. He hates being a salesman about as much as he hated being a sailor. He loves meeting people and all the human side of it, he just dislikes conning people into buying office equipment they don't want or need and that is too expensive for them anyway. Mind you, he is never allowed to think of items as too expensive, the company can always sort out HP facilities with repayments over the next fifty years...

Took Ben out for a long walk. It's Easter time so the tourists are arriving in droves. It's so EMBARRASSING to be English sometimes. Not because of our views on the EEC or Mad Cow Disease, but because of how AWFUL Brits look on holiday. WHY the 'orrible shorts left over from school PE? Why the ugly long white sports-socks – with SANDALS, for godsake? And WHY can't they tan properly? That pink, peely skin and general boil-in-the-bag appearance is so UNAPPEALING. (They have even been spotted with knotted hankies on their heads in a desperate attempt not to get frazzled.) *Mon dieu.* Worse still is when you see them on their preferred holiday territory – Le Camping. They always seem to be red and sweaty, whether they be holding barbecue tongs or their beloved badminton racket. WHY can't the Brits just SIT DOWN and BE COOL?

Moaned to my neighbour about how maladroit the English are sometimes. She shrugged and remarked that the English aren't **that** bad. The Germans are worse.

AVRIL

Home. Tuesday, 1st April.

Eric launched into a conversation tonight about a news item he'd heard on the radio. A giant truffle has just been discovered in Périgord – it weighs several tons and is the largest specimen ever found. He was just describing how it was going to be extracted using a hi-tech hydraulic crane (the very same one they used to tip the Titanic in the film) and a complex cradle harness when I asked him what the date was today. Suddenly he looked very embarrassed – well, I guess he looked like a real April Fool.

Home. Wednesday, 2nd April.

Decided to do something about my Horrible Hair this morning. I was spurred on by an article I read last night about Seducing Your Husband. I was halfway through it when Ben, who was dozing on my shoulder, threw up all over me (and the article, which was probably what it deserved). Then Eric walked in and just, well, LOOKED at me. I should say I was wearing unattractive leggings and a much worn white(ish) top. I was braless as all my maternity bras are in the wash, but maybe the wet tee-shirt (wet with vomit) wasn't too sexy. And I must admit I haven't been bothering with make-up – I mean I need more than powder to disguise the bags under my eyes, I need six months solid sleep and maybe surgery. Anyway, I resolved to improve my image by tending to my locks.

I thought I'd try one of the new Bordeaux All-Day salons. Yes, these

are open ALL DAY! That's rare in this country. Banks, shops, business-
es, government buildings, gyms, EVERYTHING closes at lunchtime
here. If you ever want to invade France do it between midday and two,
the place is deserted.

I was hoping to find that PERFECT hairdresser, someone that would
know how to create that classy yet wildly tousled sexy look, The Lady
and the Tramp effect. It's the kind of style that is a little daunting to
explain to the hairdresser, like trying to tell a surgeon how to take your
tonsils out or something. I had high hopes that I had found *la coiffeuse
idéale* when I went sat down and she ran her fingers through my hair. She
tweaked it about a bit and suddenly it looked GREAT, like with no cutting or anything. I wasn't sure she could be persuaded to pop around to
the flat every morning to ruffle it into shape, so I just let her go ahead
with the cutting. Casting caution to the winds I told her to use her own
judgement and do anything she liked.

She sighed and hummed and haaed a bit and informed me I needed
degrading. I was somewhat alarmed, but she explained that a *'degradé'*
just means having your hair layered through. And it *had* to be shorter. I
closed my eyes as the scissors descended. Ben had decided to drop off in
his pram, and I went off to join him in Nod Land. I awoke as the hair-
cutting finished. The hairdresser was grinning inanely and encouraging-
ly in the mirror at someone with a haircut like a crash helmet. I can't
quite describe that crushing feeling as I realised that someone was me.

Blinking back tears as she showed me my pinhead from every angle,
I stammered it was *magnifique*, then paid and fled. All the way home my
reflection in shop windows tormented me. Ben gazed up at me from his
pushchair in silent wonder – what was that strange thing on Mummy's
head? Yup, exactly like a crash helmet, but worse as I can't take it off.
It's the kind of cut that might look OK on a Sixties urchin who pouts all
the time and peers at other people through thick mascara. Tried the lowered head and peering through lashes approach when I got home and discovered Eric back for lunch. He managed not to laugh at the hair, and
was even quite sympathetic. He was just a bit phased by my new posture
– had I hurt my neck or something?

Will buy a copper rinse tomorrow. Maybe it will look better if it's a
funkier colour.

Home. Thursday, 3rd April.

I now have a bright red crash helmet.

Home. Friday, 4th April.

Old friends dropped in. Lots of jokes about whether my hair was an April Fool's day joke. Laughed about it. Cried in the kitchen.

Home. Saturday, 5th April.

Shaken out of my misery by a HORRIBLY traumatic experience. Eric left early this morning to spend the day cycling with his pals, and I had planned a quiet day at home. As is the way of all the best-laid plans, it was not to be.

It all went wrong when I put Ben down for a sleep at tennish. I took off my pyjamas and popped into the bathroom for a quick shower, and as I closed the door (I am still mentally scarred by the 'Psycho' shower scene and can't bear to leave the door open) the doorknob came off in my hand and the other handle and the rest of the lock fell off on the other side. The noise woke Ben, who started howling. For a second I was just numb, and then panicked. It wasn't just being shut in, but Ben being shut out.

There is no window in our bathroom, and no screwdrivers or anything remotely useful for opening doors. What's more our bathroom door is really old and heavy. Me trying to break it down was like trying to tickle my way past a quarterback.

Closing my ears to Ben's desperate sobs I tried to think logically of a way to get out. Three walls are 18th century foot-thick stone, and the other is brick. Just waiting five hours or so for Eric to come home and leaving Ben to howl was too awful to contemplate, so I climbed up onto the toilet cistern and started attacking the plasterboard ceiling with determined fists.

It look a long time to bash through the plasterboard, and when it finally broke an avalanche of thick dust and fibre glass fell on my head and into my contact lenses. Happily, through my tears, I got a glimpse of what I was hoping to see – the floorboards of the upstairs flat. Praying that they'd be in I yelled for help at the top of my voice.

Fortunately for Ben and myself our neighbour *was* in, and quite a Superman to boot. As my front door was locked, he had to jump from his first floor window into our courtyard – Dog's Lair. She is fierce at the best of times, and Ben's screams and my shrieks had done nothing to calm her. Somehow he managed to get past her without losing any limbs, and then broke our French windows to get into the flat. Then he made for the bathroom door, where he reassembled the handle and let me out. Suddenly I felt pretty stupid, standing on the loo wearing only a hand towel, a silly haircut and a thick coating of dust. Still, I was so grateful that I leapt down and threw my arms around Superneighbour and gave him a huge hug. Then Eric – back early due to a puncture – walked in.

Time seemed suddenly to be moving in slow motion, as I saw Eric take in the hanging ceiling, the fibre glass, a howling baby and the broken glass of the French doors. And his (practically) naked wife in the neighbour's arms. "What the f**k is going on here?" was his sympathetic response to my awful experience.

Well, sympathy did come later, and even a few laughs. I suppose one can laugh about days like today – once they are well and truly over.

Bassin d'Arcachon. Sunday, 6th April.

We set off early to visit Mum and Dad on the coast today. Not much fear of us oversleeping though – Ben is an incredibly accurate 5.30am alarm clock. We were expected at nine-ish, so we walked Ben around the block in his pram a few times. Guess what – the streets were crowded with pram pushers! Heads bowed we followed the flow, trundling through the last shadows of the night into the grey misty morning. All these parents had the same haunted look; these are people who have seen the dawn far too many times to find it beautiful. Some returned our smiles, but most were too far gone to even notice us. Maybe their prams were remote controlled and they were just tagging on behind.

After an hour's walking we went back to the flat. We were like the living dead, but Ben was bright and perky. We ate a little breakfast and then loaded mountains of baby gear into the car. I have this feeling that the size of the baby is inversely proportional to the amount of equipment it needs – 50cms long and he requires a cubic metre of brightly coloured plastic objects. I tried to explain to Eric that lots of the things in the pile were educational toys to stimulate our wee babe. Eric muttered darkly that he would prefer something that would send the little s*d to sleep.

Well, he did (eventually) drop off in the car. Cars are such wondrous things for curing babies' insomnia that I'm sure there would be a good living to be earned by running an all-night driving service for newborns.

We drove about thirty miles through the outskirts of Bordeaux and then through pine forest to the coast. The Bassin d'Arcachon is a huge roundish bay of salt water, connected to the Atlantic by a relatively narrow passage. It is sparklingly clean – big tides wash it out twice a day and also bring in from the open ocean tiny particles which oysters feed on. Oyster rearing is one of the mainstays of the area's economy.

The traditional flat-bottomed oyster fishing boats rub shoulders (or bows or whatever) with posh yachts here, and it's good to see that tourism and tradition can happily co-exist. Oyster-rearing means carefully monitored, unpolluted water and gastronomic delights for tourists, and a healthy tourist industry ensures good trade for fishermen.

It is paradise for boating fans, with acres and acres of calm water sheltered from the strong currents of the Atlantic. The water is clear and warm – fabulous for snorkelling. The beaches are gently sloping and covered with deep soft white sand, just right for when you want to come ashore and picnic. It is a rare and special place. Like so many French children, Eric and I used to spend our summers here; we didn't meet until I came to France for my university year-out when I was twenty, but for years and years we had both camped in the pine woods that grow right down to the water. We met inland, but fell in love at the Bassin d'Arcachon. We came here every weekend during our first winter to repaint a battered old fishing boat that we'd adopted in its retirement. It was unseasonably warm and sunny, and we were in shorts and jerseys as we brandished our paintbrushes. Swans relaxed on the beach beside us when the tide was out, all big feet and heavy wings and squabbles for scraps – then suddenly sublimely elegant as the tide washed in, gliding serenely on the perfectly smooth water. Each rising tide brought its orchestra of sounds: the gentle hiss of the sandbanks filling, the tiny crackling noise of thousands upon thousands of shellfish popping open to drink from the fresh tide and the deep bass boom of an ancient wreck on the sand-bank filling with water. It was clear and still and beautiful; it wasn't hard to see why so many artists have chosen to paint the place. Our painting was less successful. Water based paint is not ideal for painting a boat... every weekend the wood looked barer. In the end we abandoned our DIY and took to wandering along the deserted beaches and through the woods. We both knew the Bassin well, but that winter, when the tourist season was months away, it felt like it belonged to us. It was our *chez-nous*.

This morning we didn't have the energy to reminisce, but we did hold hands in the car, which was romantic if a little dangerous. We got to Mum and Dad's at 9.30am, four hours into our day. Mum smilingly remarked that we must have had a nice early start. Maybe she doesn't realise that her grandson is practically nocturnal.

Ben settled down for a doze in his pram (it was daytime so he could let himself go) and we sat out in the garden. Mum is an enthusiastic gardener and made Eric and me go for a 'bud count', examining every tree and shrub to check on its progress. Their garden is a little strange, their wombling tendencies are even stronger than their gardening ones, and the entire garden is filled with peculiar objects they have found while beachcombing. Bamboo poles hang from the fence, fishing nets adorn the trees, lobster pots and buoys are nailed to the front wall. Flowers push up through piles of beach wood and shells. Eric said it was all *charmant*, except possibly for the pile of dead(ish) oysters which were exuding quite a meaty smell in the morning sun.

We sat in the garden and chatted, and just, well, admired Ben. His toes fanning out in the sun, his tiny arm above his head, stretching out in sleep to touch-but-not-quite the top of his head. His every movement bringing its rush of love, his every sleepy sigh a miracle.

It was a wonderful spring day. A warm day. A family day.

Home. Monday, 7th April.

Ben was up at 5.30am again. I decided to let Eric get ready for work, so I had a bath with junior and quickly got ready to go out. The Capucin market opens at daybreak, and I thought I'd stroll down there with the pram and get our day's supplies.

It was lovely ambling through the old streets to the market; the sun was slanting in and making the cobbles shine grey, deep red and pale orange. The houses took on a golden glow. Despite the fact that is was so mind-numbingly EARLY I found myself humming a little song and feeling positively cheerful. Little Ben peeped up at me with gleaming eyes, his expression seeming to say "there you are, I knew you'd love it once you were up." Our quarter was quiet, but as we got nearer to the market the air was alive with the bustle of the traders getting ready. The fresh morning air was suddenly perfumed with the scent of fruit, bread and the salty smell of seafood; Bordeaux's best and at the best prices.

I started off with the fruit and veg, buying beautifully ripe avocado pears from a traditional wooden barrow stall – five for ten francs – and tomatoes, potatoes and radishes for another twenty. The lady that served me looked at me a little oddly, but perhaps she was a bit surprised about having her first customer before 6am. Next I set off in search of protein, heading for the free-range chicken stall and the fish market. Well, the bloke also looked at me strangely, but sold me several pieces of chicken – enough for lunch – for just fifteen francs. With another twenty francs *en poche* I wheeled the pram to the nearest fish stall to find something for tea. That is what is so great about the market, you can get great food for under a fiver a day. I eat so much better here than in England, and the fish is best of all...

The *poissoniers* (fishmongers, not poisoners) are legendary figures. They are renowned for their rudeness, but despite the poor service people still flock (or shoal?) to their stalls. Fish sells like, er, hotcakes.

Shining and firm it always looks as though it has only just leapt out of the water.

Most of the fish is from the Atlantic or from the Gironde Estuary, but some comes from the region's rivers, such as the mighty Garonne and the Dordogne. I love the *alose,* or shad, which is traditionally eaten in the springtime. It is absolutely succulent grilled and flavoured with sorrel and bay leaves. Today however, I was struck (not physically, never fear) by some huge greyish long fish, with mouths closely resembling mops. They were also very much alive, and slithering about in a big tank they looked like a mass of knotted, quivering intestines. These guys were SERIOUSLY unappetising.

I was pleased to discover that the fishmonger was not at all rude – in fact she was very chatty and just dying to tell me everything I ever wanted to know (or not) about her weird fish. She was a little baffled that I had no idea what these eely creatures were, as they are really famous in Bordeaux. She obviously thought I needed educating and set about teaching me the basics.

They were, it turned out, lamprey. They are caught in the same way as the *alose*, in a big square net called a *carrelet*, which is lowered into the river from a cabin on the bank. Catching the lamprey is the easy bit, and even that is quite hard. The preparation is where it gets really tricky.

Firstly, she explained, you need to put your lamprey into a rough pine case of wine. Yes, obviously, it DOES have to be empty. Next you pour boiling water over your lamprey (her eyes began to sparkle at this point) and the fish writhe around in agony, scraping off their nasty, slimy skin on the scratchy sides of the box. I felt I had heard enough and tried to make a getaway, but now she had me by the arm and was grinning wildly and generally looking more psychopathic by the second. After the de-sliming (she was so into it now that tiny bits of spit were flying as she talked), you have to hang them up on a hook and skin them. Alive. The rest is a bit of a blur but it involved bleeding and collecting the blood for a sauce – in any case I'm sure it was worse for the lamprey than for me. I only vaguely remember something about marinating the dead(ish) fish in Bordeaux wine. Eventually, I managed to blurt something out about baby needing a feed, and bolted for home. There were eggs in the fridge after all. Omelette seemed like a less bloody option.

When I got in I glanced in the mirror. I had two, thick black semicircles of mascara that had run down onto my cheeks. I am just not used to wearing the vast quantities of Rimmel that my impish haircut compels me to wear. *That* was why I got those funny looks in the market – except from the fish lady, who was barking mad and therefore not fit to judge my makeup. My early morning pallor and black eyes made me look, well, a bit like a corpse. And like a very unhealthy corpse at that.

10pm. Just about to settle down for the first part of the night – until Ben's squawk at 2-ish. Maybe it was my corpse impression this morning, but I have been thinking morbid thoughts all day. What if death IS the end? Or worse, what if there is such a thing as reincarnation? I mean I might get to come back as a lamprey...

Home. Tuesday, 8th April.

Ben got up at the same time but I didn't mind. He SMILED at me today! His first smile was the most beautiful thing I have ever seen. Even if it was at 5.30am.

Home. Wednesday, 9th April.

It's the long Easter weekend coming up. Hooray! Eric, like everyone else in France, gets Easter Monday off. Yes, I know that with little Ben we won't get to have a lie-in, but it will be nice to spend three whole days together. We have vague projects but these don't go much further than deciding not to do anything too energetic.

I have an appointment to take Ben to the doctor's for his one month check at two this afternoon. I'm a week or so early, but the doctor is away all next week (he is taking the entire Easter week off) so I have to slot his visit in somewhere. Every French baby must see the doctor every month for the first six months, and then at various strategic points during his/her development. I am dying to see how much Ben weighs and what his height is – although perhaps 'height' isn't the right word as it's measured when the baby is lying down; a kind of horizontal height.

We don't risk being arrested if we miss the visits, but apparently we could lose our Family Allowance if we slip up – this amounts to some hundred quid a month for the first three years of a little one's life, regardless of income. It helps out with the shopping and with buying nappies. Sales are slow at the moment for Eric, and as he is on commission we are all suffering. For the past month or so I think Eric's main food source has been his finger nails.

I have got to get Ben dressed and my paperwork together before we go to the Doc's. In medicine as in all things, France LOVES bureaucracy. It is hardly surprising that it's a French word. France has the largest artificial forest in Europe – more than a million hectares in the Landes – and I'm sure that its main function is to provide enough paper to keep the bureaucratic beast alive.

Adults were issued with a *'Carnet de Santé'* – a health book – a couple of years back, which we were supposed to take with us whenever we visited the doctor. The idea was that the patients would be in charge of their own records. Unfortunately, most of these brightly coloured booklets were mistaken for advertising fliers and thrown away. I plead guilty. Next we got a computerised card, but most doctors don't have the computer system which goes with them. Most people's cards have now vanished into desk drawers, glove boxes and other Dark and Mysterious Places. The result of all this expensive faffing is that we all go to the doctor's as we did before, armed with a cheque book and only a vague idea of when we last had an X-ray or a tetanus jab.

Once you have children the administration changes gear. You need to take the child's health book with you, and papers from two separate government departments. You also have to take your cheque book, although babies' consultations are completely reimbursed by the *Sécurité Sociale*. (I'm not sure why they can't let you off paying up front, as the consultation is going to be 100% reimbursed anyway, but then France's government workers do have to have something to shuffle around.) If you decide to go to the S.S. building (my abbreviation, but I have found that it doesn't go down well here) to get your money back more quickly, you need to take your S.S. card and Identity Card or Resident's Permit. Yup, even EEC residents need the latter, and it's a NIGHTMARE to obtain. Beware all ye who enter France.

Well, got to get organised. Will say how it all went tomorrow.

Home. Thursday, 10th April.

Ben has grown!!!!!!!!!! He has put on less weight than I would if I so much as sniffed a cream cake, but he's definitely on the up. Hooray! My milk is obviously Good Stuff.

The visit was all right. I was pretty pleased as I set off to the surgery with my Highly Organised Paperwork and my Delicious little boy. My confidence took a knock when the wheel fell off the pram as we bumped along the cobbled street. The road surface in the Old Quarter of Bordeaux is not kind to suspensions. With a bit of emergency mechanics I managed to fix it back on again – I pushed a nappy pin through the hole in the axle where the king pin had sheared off, and greased it with a generous squirt of Baby Oil. *Voilà!*

The surgery waiting room was bursting at the seams. I could see we were going to have plenty of time to contemplate the new posters. One of them left me a little bemused: 'Protect France's Healthcare System: Stop it being reduced to the kind of service they have in England.' As I shuffled three and a bit kilograms of baby and six kilograms of admin around on my lap, I couldn't help wishing that certain aspects of Healthcare could be cut back a bit.

The other people waiting were reading the French equivalent of 'Hello' magazine, and the braver ones were scanning the leaflets about all the diseases that you could catch if you hung around in the waiting room long enough. In general French people like talking about illnesses as dramatically as possible. The 'flu is usually called *'la crève'*, which simply means Death. Any gastric complaints are discussed (even at the best of tables) from one end of the intestine to the other. Health threats are lurking around every corner, especially if the corner is a draughty one. Draughts, as I said before, are guaranteed to dispatch even the healthiest of people – they can give you arthritis, conjunctivitis and, of course, *'la crève.'*

We waited for an hour – a fairly noisy hour as Ben doesn't like reading yet. Another Mum with a new baby came in and we got chatting. She had chosen the big general hospital to have her baby, and it had gone splendidly. She had to give birth in exactly the same way (beached-whale stuff), but at least everyone on team was friendly and caring. The *maternité* staff was very pro-breastfeeding, so she got lots of help and support. It sounded so great that I decided there and then that if there is a next time I will opt for the hospital rather than the smaller Utterly Beastly clinic.

Eventually we were called into the consulting room. Ben made me glow with pride as he gave the doctor a big smile. She asked me how he was feeding, and I could honestly say really well. Next she asked about sleeping, and I was a bit stumped there. She gave me a rather tired smile, and said that if I find anything that works can I tell her, as she has a four-month-old little boy who is still nocturnal. I'm not sure there are any easy solutions to this sleeping thing.

Next she measured his head. I did remark that I don't mind so much how big it is now it doesn't have to go through my pelvis any more. Still, it's good to know his brain is growing... Then we checked his 'height' – we measured three times and got three different measurements, so there is some guesswork involved. Fifty two centimetres and a lot of 'ish.'

His weight was the stickiest thing to check. When I took his nappy off he smiled a mischevious smile and produced a Huge Quantity of gungy yellow poo. It took ages to get him clean enough to go on the scales. If he'd have waited a few more minutes I'm sure he would have weighed in a good 500 grams heavier.

After that we set about the paperwork. I have to send forms to the *Sécurité Sociale* and to the *Allocations Familiales*. I also have to pick up a prescription for his first vaccination.

So now we can relax until next month's check – unless one of us is poorly. Heaven forbid! I can just about cope with all the paperwork when we're fit and well. Going to the doctor's when actually ill doesn't bear thinking about.

Home. (Good) Friday, 11th April.

Easter is here. It is BIG in France – in some villages statues of the Virgin Mary are paraded through the streets, and all over France the churches are full. Religion is allowed to mix tastily with France's culinary traditions; Easter is the time of year when the *chocolatiers* can really show off. When I wandered to the shops this morning with Ben I was amazed by the hand-crafted eggs that would rival any Fabergé number, by the bunnies so lifelike that their noses seem to twitch and by the astonishing variety of chocolate fish, from delicate baby sardines to a chocolate whale swallowing Jonah. This isn't cooking, this is sculpture.

Parents are terribly important when it comes to re-inforcing the shaky link between this chocolate fantasy and the religious side of things. The church bells are silent from Good Friday until Easter Day, and we are supposed to tell our little ones that this is because the bells have flown to Rome. The story goes that the bells fly over France, dropping chocolate eggs in their flight. On Easter Day (once the bells are safely back in their belltowers after their foreign holiday) they ring once more. It's the signal for children to rush into their gardens and hunt for the eggs their parents hid before they woke up. It seems like a likely tale to me, except for that last bit about children waking up later than their parents.

My Mum and Dad, for some unfathomable reason, have never been into Easter eggs. Every Easter we would receive everything but. I have a lovely collection of Easter beachtowels, Easter mugs and Easter books, but no memory of eggs. I remember one year waking up when it was still dark and making out the shape of a gloriously huge egg next to my bed.

I went back to sleep again, happily dreaming of my egg. When I finally woke up I leapt up to unwrap my egg, only to discover a giant coconut.

Little Ben is too tiny for chocolate (or, indeed, for coconut), but I would like to make him something special for Easter.

6pm. Ha! The joys of daytime TV! While Ben had his afternoon nap I switched on the telly and saw a hobbies program which was all about, yup, EASTER PRESENTS. It gave me a fab idea. I got six eggs from the fridge and emptied them, and then dyed them with natural colourings – boiling them in onion peel for ochre, red cabbage for blue and red cabbage and vinegar for red. When they were dry and varnished with clear nail polish the marbled colours on the shell shone with rich colour. I was very pleased with my work. It was tricky threading cotton through them and suspending them from a coathanger, but worth it. Ben on Easter Day will have a STUPENDOUS mobile above his bed. Not bad, eh? Well, better than a coconut, anyway.

Home. Saturday, 12th April.

Eric and I had resolved to spend the weekend together, but I couldn't resist his offer of looking after Benjamin this morning so that I could have a couple of hours to shop for some cooler clothes. Not 'cooler' as in funkier than my present wardrobe (maternity bras, SEXY!) but as in more suitable for the heat wave we're having. It is unseasonably hot, more like summer.

Set off in high spritis but it was dead weird not having Ben with me, like I'd come out without my right leg or something. Still, shopper's habits die hard, and I soon got stuck in. My body shape is difficult to adjust to – I'd just got used to looking like an overripe pear, and now I have changed again. My bump has gone but my chest-size is Enormous. At least I have plenty of milk. My D cups runneth o'er.

In the end found a couple of tee-shirts and a skirt. Nothing very nice as I'm sure my current shape won't last forever. It was just lovely to have two hours for me, and it felt great going back to the flat to find Ben fast asleep in his cot and lunch on the table. There was a reassuring smell of Baby Lotion and warm bread rolls. Maybe Eric's sales figures are down at the moment, but he is a wonderful father and a fabulous cook. And a *magnifique* husband.

A field. Easter Sunday.

It is difficult but quite delightful to write in your diary when there are caterpillars and all manner of insects busying their way across its pages. Eric and I are stretched out on a blanket in a meadow, quietly soaking up the sun. Wildflowers are exuding the most complex of pefumes in the heat; lavender and thyme, fennel and the heady scent of ripening grass. It seems to have worked like a general anaesthetic for Ben, who is sound asleep beside us. Somebody ought to market the formula.

I hung his Easter mobile over his car seat this morning and we drove off for a picnic. When the weather is this glorious it's a shame to stay in the city.

Virginie the trusty 2CV bowled through the countryside to an idyllic spot a little to the North of Bordeaux. The landscape is gorgeous, green and rolling. There are vineyards here but not *too* many, chestnut and oak woods and fields of creamy-coloured cows add variety. It is not hard to find a good spot for a picnic.

We got our hamper out in a meadow by a little brook. The sun was hot enough to have set a whole percussion band of crickets and grasshoppers clicking and whirring. Every blade of grass was pinging with life. Other animals were also enjoying the sun – after a few moments two coypu came out of their riverbank burrow and swam off downstream. Coypu are large and beaverish, and were introduced to the area from America to reduce the amount of vegetation in the marshland around Bordeaux prior to a construction project. They adapted beautifully to foreign climes, munching their way as predicted through the marshes, and then (not unsurprisingly) went on to discover the yummy crunchiness of surrounding cornfields and other cereal crops. These guys have no predators apart from the French, who turn them into *pâté* (coypuke *pâté*?) and *terrine*. Most of them spend their time outwitting the hunters – which isn't too much of a challenge – and rearing large families in burrows along the banks of France's rivers, which are now suffering from terrible erosion. It's odd that coypu are seen as environmental criminals and not the people who introduced them in the first place. Anyway, our two looked innocent enough.

We settled down to our picnic, which, I'm happy to say, did not include anything made of coypu. We had salad and goats' cheese and crusty *baguettes*. Ben had his favourite – yes, milk. He fell asleep before we even started on our dessert. We devoured a punnet of fresh strawberries in Utter Tranquility.

Now I have a little time to write my diary in peace. On the other hand I could lavish some Love and Affection on Eric, who has been looking a bit dejected of late. Between the difficult nights with Ben and his bad sales figures I think it hasn't been easy for him this last month. I could always write tomorrow.

Lundi de Pâques.

Hooray, another day with Eric. This *Jour Ferié* business is splendid. It is fabulous to wake up thinking 'Wow, what shall we do today?' Holidays are always so much more inspiring than working days. Eric is actually BEAMING this morning. I think we'll make another beeline for the country. Yesterday we missed some great things that were going on: in one village they made an Easter omelette out of 3000 eggs, enough for everyone in the entire village. Perhaps we'll be able to find something fun today. Even if there is nothing going on, I'd still exchange traffic fumes for wildflowers anyday.

Oops, Ben is waking up and Eric is coming out of the shower, so it seems like our departure is imminent. More later.

(Bedtime.) Home now after another Big Trip. We had a slight hiccup at the beginning – as we set off to the countryside a Smell from Hell filled the car. Never has Virginie smelled so foul. We inspected Ben's nappy, but he was innocent. After that we accused each other for a few miles, before we eventually tracked down the culprit. The egg mobile. I hadn't been quite thorough enough in my washing, and some of the eggs had started to ferment. As the car got warmer and warmer and they jiggled more and more on the country roads their Pong became all Powerful. Sadly, we had to abandon my contraption by the roadside. I'll try and make something better next year. Or then again, maybe he might get a Real Easter Egg, you never know.

We drove to the Entre Deux Mers, East of Bordeaux. It's a well-known wine area bordered by two rivers (the *mers*), the Dordogne in the North and the Garonne in the South. Créon, where I lived as a child, is the ancient capital of the region. We chose to explore a neighbouring village; La Sauve. It is tiny but breathtakingly delightful, perched up on a high hill looking over the rolling acres of vineyards. The summit of the hill is crowned by a stunning 11th century abbey, now in ruins but still impressive. I'm sure even Ben appreciated the architecture.

We took a long time to look around the abbey. The graceful stone arches of the interior are surrounded by collosally thick walls which in turn are protected by steep banks. These are now covered in soft daisy-strewn grass, but would have looked a lot more forbidding in the Middle Ages. We paid a few francs to enter the interior courtyard (it really is a lot easier to gain admittance these days), where red and black chickens peck busily in the dust. The stonework inside was marvellous – the walls are alive with sculpture; centaurs gallop, mermaids swim and gargoyles – er, oh dear – do their gargoyly thing. There are also many local images, like ferns and even pinecones. When we looked carefully at the walls – although I must admit Ben had nodded off by that stage – we saw that between the carved creatures were real animals, fossils of sea creatures from the age when the Entre Deux Mers was a sea and La Sauve an island. This stone was so full of life, carved or fossilised, that I'm sure that with a good squeeze it would have produced blood.

As dusk was falling we returned to Bordeaux. It looked welcoming, warm evenings are nice in town, too. The *terraces* were full of people relaxing with cold drinks after a hot and sticky day, and jugglers in the pedestrian ways were drawing crowds. Still, Eric had a lot of preparation to do for work tomorrow, so we had to head for home. His tension began building up as soon as he opened his briefcase, and Ben, who is a stress-barometer, started wailing almost immediately. It is now ten o'clock and he's been crying on and off for the last two hours. It does not feel like a fitting end to such a lovely day.

Home. Tuesday, 15th April.

Awful argument last night. Ben wouldn't stop howling, even after we went to bed. Tried all known remedies to little avail. When there was a five minute gap in the cries and we were trying to get some sleep I suddenly had a panic about whether the front door was locked. I had a Horrible Image of someone letting themselves in and stealing Ben from his cot in the living room. Eric said nastily that I must be joking, nobody would be mad or masochistic enough to steal Ben. Tensions rose and Ben started crying again. Seconds later, and in a Most Theatrical Fashion there was a clap of thunder and an almost simultaneous flash of lightning. The heavens opened as the storm broke – gallons and gallons of hot rain poured into our courtyard and under our French windows. Eric went to let Dog in, and I strode after him, still cross and yelling. Next thing I knew I was on my shoulderblades. The pool of rain on our floor tiles had upended me in the midst of my fury. Eric (unsupportively) collapsed laughing, while I writhed about on the floor, looking like a cross between an upturned beetle and a breakdancer having a fit.

Fortunately the fight was forgotten, and we went back to bed. Ben snuggled in between us, blissfully content to be in with us. As the storm died away his tired whimpers turned into soft, sleepy sighs and he finally slept.

Home. Wednesday, 16th April.

Eric gave me a huge hug this morning. The row and the storm have cleared the air. He went off to work with a spring in his step, and returned late this evening with a broad grin. He managed to pull off three big sales in one day – a record in his company. Now I know we'll be able to pay the rent things are rosier.

Tomorrow Ben and I can go with Eric to deliver one of the copiers he's just sold. The buyer is a small wine *château* in the village where his cousin Jean-Pierre lives, so I'll be able to introduce him to Ben. It'll also be nice to have the ride out into the country again. Can't wait.

Home. Thursday, 17th April.

Rather a mixed meeting with Jean-Pierre. When Ben and I knocked on his door (he lives above a beauty parlour where the local women go for their Wash and Wax) he appeared looking pale. He managed a smile and trying to sound nonchalant announced, "You're lucky to find me, I've only just got out of prison."

My heart sank. Jean-Pierre was rather short-changed when the family brains were handed out, and for some time Eric has had to watch over him. It's hard work.

We found him a job feeding horses in the local riding school, but as the horses grew skinny he wasn't kept on. At thirty he has no other work experience except from National Service and has no qualifications or diplomas whatsoever, except his blood doning certificate. Well, at least there he got an A+. We once encouraged him to 'enhance' his CV a little to get a job. A trifle ambitiously, he said his first job had been a 'professional race-horse breeder' and in the other interest section – inspired by his favourite Bruce Lee film – he put himself down as a karate black belt. The job centre immediately stopped sending him offers about jobs he might have done, and when he went to his one and only job interview he found himself face to face with a real black belt who only wanted to talk about advanced moves. Unfortunately bluffing isn't his thing, and he wasn't offered the job.

I have asked him what his dream is, and he said he'd like to be a Hero, to save dolphins and, as an afterthought, women. Well, only the pretty ones. Sadly he'd never seen a job ad for a hero.

He has been surviving by doing odd jobs for his landlady. As jobs go they have been decidedly odd. His first effort was to build a decorative wall around her garden. It went crumbly when the first rain fell on it, and the 100% cement mix killed all her flowers. The whole wall finally keeled over when someone tried to prop their bike up against it. His next job was putting up a curtain rail, which he fixed at such a slant that the curtains stayed permanently pulled, plunging the flat into total darkness. Undeterred his landlady asked him to fit the new carpet while she was on holiday. Her saintliness was sorely tested when she came home to find that he hadn't emptied the flat before laying the carpet, but had just unrolled it inch by inch, cutting holes around the furniture as he went. He had even cut a big hole under her coffee table in the middle of the lounge. She hasn't asked him to do anything since, and smiles rather thinly when he jokes about early retirement.

And now prison. It turned out that his best friend's cousin's girlfriend's brother (the relationship was so complicated that I suspect the local police gave up trying to fathom it out) had robbed the local bank over the Easter weekend. Not being a Bright Spark either, he was disappointed to discover only the £200 float and a Large Quantity of fluffy chick Easter decorations. He spent all Saturday night hunting for ingots whilst being filmed from every angle by security cameras.

On Tuesday, once the shops were open after the long Easter weekend, the Mastermind of the break-in got his friends together to see who would be willing to buy beer in the village shop with his "winnings." They all voted for Jean-Pierre, who was flattered. As he usually puts his shopping on the slate, the shopkeeper's suspicions were somewhat aroused when he asked for £200 of *bière blonde*. The police had circulated the numbers of the missing notes just in case anyone would be daft enough to try and spend them locally. Someone like Jean-Pierre.

Well, the shopkeeper called the police and they searched his flat. Jean-Pierre started getting worried when they found his prize collection of hand grenades that he'd kept as a souvenir of his army days. He got even more frightened when he was handcuffed and taken to the police station.

He was asked to explain everything from A to Z, but the alphabet never has been his strong point. He launched into such a confused and rambling story that the police soon gave up their questioning. He was given lunch in a cell and driven home.

I tried to sympathise, saying it must have been quite traumatic. "Oh no!" grinned Jean-Pierre, "it was brilliant!" he explained that he'd had the best lunch he'd had in a month of Sundays, and what's more, the robbery was in all the newspapers. "You see," he said triumphantly, "I've finally done it, I'm a hero!"

As if that wasn't bad enough he rang me up just a few minutes ago. He said Ben and myself had made him see the light and take a decision about what to do with his life. I was a bit baffled, and asked him if either Ben had been talking to him about careers, because I certainly hadn't said anything. "No," he replied' "But I've been thinking of what I really want to *be*. Well you two have helped me to decide. I want to be a father."

Home. Friday, 18th April.

Ben is going to be ONE MONTH old tomorrow! It feels like he's been here for ever (and that I haven't had a good night's sleep for even longer than that.) I'll have to plan something to celebrate – though he is a bit young for a cake, and I think a birthday candle stuck in my bra might be a bit dangerous. Oh well, perhaps we'll just sing *Joyeux anniversaire*. He is certainly looking very jolly – he's obviously all excited about his birthday.

Eric is also cheerful – another big sale today. He is putting in horrendously long hours but has already made half of the sales figure he supposed to make in the month in just four days. Hooray, maybe we'll be able to pay our overdraft off.

Things are looking up in the Castanet household.

Home. Saturday, 19th April.

Ben is one month old today! It was all very exciting, well for Eric and me anyway. We sang *Joyeux Anniversaire* and Happy Birthday – got to get the bilingual thing going early. Dad and Mum rang to wish him Many Happy Returns, and Mum also asked in her I-don't-want-to-interfere-but-I'm-going-to-anyway-voice whether I was going to encourage Ben to sleep on his back for another few months. Mum is a walking medical encyclopedia and is full of facts about how to rear infants as safely as possible. I reassured her whenever Ben feels like sleeping at night – maybe in the odd minute when he's not wanting to be rocked, sung to or driven around the block – we will make sure he's not on his tummy.

Ben and I went for a birthday walk in the sunny *jardin public* while Eric got on with preparations for his own BIG day. Not his birthday, but something far more important to Eric, which involves a great deal of physical exertion, stretch lycra and leg shaving. Yup, tomorrow is the start of his cycle racing season.

Cycling is a vital part of French culture. If asked to describe a Frenchman most people will conjure up images of a beret, a string of onions and a black bicycle. Berets are on the way out and I've never seen anyone with a string of onions around their neck, but the bicycle (*le vélo*) is evermore popular – despite all the doping scandals. France is the country where one of the greatest cycling competitions takes place – Le Tour de France – and here bikes are not just seen as a way of getting around but rather as racing machines. *Au revoir* to the sombre World War One relic, *bonjour* to the ultra-light multi-coloured titanium numbers which flash though our countryside.

Eric was brought up with the Tour de France, and like all French kids loved it when the race went through his town. A carnival atmosphere surrounds the tour; the *'caravane'* of cars which precedes the cyclists throws sweets and presents to the crowds of spectators which line the roadside. Music plays, confetti flies and the brightly dressed cyclists add colour to the party – everyone has a good time, especially children, who all dream of becoming a winner one day. Cyclists are heroes here, which is why the drug scandal hurts the French so much. Heroes don't cheat – *c'est pas possible*. It's easier to assume that these athletes are a little superhuman – after all they can cycle 250kms a day through mountains in temperatures which range from freezing to 40°C, and enjoy it. They may not be superhuman but they're certainly a bit bonkers.

Even your ordinary amateur cycling champ could be seen as a bit weird, especially to English eyes. They have long conversations with fellow cyclists about how to shave their legs so as to show off their muscles to their best advantage. I say "fellow" cyclists because the sport is male dominated, and to be a "real" man on a bike you must have smooth legs. I was a little disconcerted when I met Eric to find that my legs were distinctly woolier than his.

Women do have their own cycling heroine, Janie Longo, who has won every cycling competition imaginable. Sadly, women's cycling is ignored by the media, and most French people (well, men) declare that it isn't terribly *"esthetique"*, although some admire the women's legs. I saw one proposition in a magazine which seriously suggested women's cycling be screened on the satellite porn channel where it might get some viewers. God, can this really be the country which produced Simone de Beauvoir???? To say the French male is a bit sexist is like saying that the Klux Klux Klan is a tad colour prejudiced.

Once again the *vélo* thing has taken over our household. Every year Eric says he is too busy/old/tired/overworked to begin another racing season, but come spring I find him oiling his gears and polishing up his wheels. The clinching sign is when he gets out the news cuttings of races he's won is the past. Well, he's done all that this year, and he's signed up for his first race. He says he's bound to do better this year – now he's got another fan to cheer him on. Even if the aforesaid is only one month old.

Home. Sunday, 20th April.

As predicted, a Big Day.

The race was in the Médoc, through some of the most famous and expensive vineyards in the world. The circuit was flat so the organisers had made it extra long so it would be bit harder – we are talking triple figures here. I would have gone for a car and hotel stopover for that kind of distance.

The competitors can't have been put off by the length of the race, as 140 men turned up and at the starting line (but not so much at the finish, if I'm honest) they were all smiling. Tons of spectators were there too – it's odd how the French population is split on Sunday mornings. On the one hand there are the teetotal non-smoking cyclists (they are against

32

drink and smoking, even if the pros munch, inhale and inject some of the most dangerous drugs imaginable) who are up at the crack of dawn to race accompanied by huge family fan clubs to support them. On the other hand there are those who prefer to indulge in France's gastronomic (and alcoholic) delights, who emerge bleary-eyed at midday.

I was giving Ben a quick beginner's course in clapping when the starting signal was given. The *péloton* shot off, and we ambled at a gentler pace to find a shady spot on the circuit where we could watch Papa. The loop was only a few kilometres long, so Eric was going to pass us dozens of times. I had Strict Instructions to give him bottles of water whenever he went by.

It sounded easy enough. Unfortunately, there is nothing that looks so much like a cyclist as another cyclist; with heads covered with helmets, eyes by dark glasses and bodies by virtually identical coloured lycra it is Jolly Difficult to recognise anyone. Eric didn't seem to appreciate this, and yelled at me after the third time I tried to give a bottle to a competitor. It wasn't my fault, they did look similar, and besides I got distracted... a baby hedgehog emerged from the vines and wandered onto the road. It was determined not to be nocturnal, and it was suicidal to boot. For its own safety and for the sake of the race – just think of the effects of those spikes on the cyclists' tyres – I launched my Rescue Mission.

Hedgehogs are VERY spiky, and as I was gloveless I had to sit it on one of Ben's nappies in order to carry it away from the road. Twice, in fact, as it kept coming back for more. I began to suspect it was some kind of spiny missile, a losing cyclist's secret weapon.

After that I spread out a rug on the grass, and got Ben out of his pram so that he could kick his legs in the sun. He had a little feed and then dozed off, and I attempted to read in short bursts. Every time my book got exciting I had to leap up and try and give Eric his water.

After nearly three hours it was all over. Eric finished in the top twenty, and was very pleased with himself. I was also quite content – after all I had not only managed to give a few microlitres of water to Eric, I had also saved a small and spiky life.

More cycling next weekend. *Vive le vélo* and Long Live Hedgehogs.

Bassin d'Arcachon. Monday, 21st April.

Spur of the moment visit to Mum and Dad's. Ben got up so early this morning that we had four hours ahead of us before Eric had to go to work. At 7.30ish I rang Mum and Dad, who suggested Ben and I popped over for a couple of days. Eric is working so hard at the moment that we hardly see him in the week, and I am feeling a bit lonesome. Eric drove us over and was back to start work at nine.

I think one of the nicest things about a baby is sharing them. It is lovely to have someone else admire your little one, and also to have someone to hold junior for a few minutes while you brush your teeth or go to the loo. Babies really like to be carried ALL the time, and it sometimes seems like Mother Nature messed up when she forgot to give us a kangaroo pouch. Ben has to make do with sitting on my back in a carrier.

In the afternoon we went to the west side of the peninsula which protects the Bassin from the rough Atlantic. This is the Wild Side – great green waves smash against the purest white sand, scattering shells and driftwood up to the tideline. The horizon is vast and empty, these beaches stretch from the tip of Portugal to Brittany, and at this time of year are deserted. Ben bobbed along in the baby carrier on my back, taking in the space and beauty of it all. He was utterly silent; maybe he was mesmerised by the shifting sea and sands, or possibly he was feeling a mite seasick. In any case he soon got used to the motion, and must have found it soothing because within half an hour he was snoring.

Now we are back in Mum and Dad's house, and Ben is tucked up for the night – or till the next feed. Mum has cooked rice and salad, and Dad has charcoal grilled chops. One of these days we'll have to tell him that charcoal grilling does not mean turning your food into black lumps of carbon. Not that I'm complaining – it is so comforting to be taken care of that I wouldn't say a word.

I hope Eric is OK all by himself. It's only until tomorrow, but taking care of Ben and supporting Eric when the going is tough at work leaves very little time left for me. Twenty four hours of being looked after is sheer luxury.

Home. Tuesday, 22nd April.

Quiet day at the Bassin. We went to Arès beach on the inland bay, and it was perfectly still. The tide came gently in over the warm sand, and we sat on the stone jetty and dabbled our feet in the water. Ben had his first paddle – we dipped him in up to his knees. It's still a bit cool for swimming, but I'm sure he'll be sporting about like a baby dolphin before long.

We picnicked at lunchtime beside Arès' Weird Monument: the carved stone next to the beach which has a plaque on it inviting aliens to use the seafront as a landing site. Maybe they are preparing for the first wave of extra-terrestrial tourists. Its a bit mysterious. France is a surprisingly strange country sometimes.

Anyway, back in Bordeaux now. Ben is in bed and I'm getting ready for Eric to come home. I have made a special dinner – candles and everything. This is going to be Romantic.

Home. Wednesday, 23rd April.

Romantic *mon oeil*. Dinner was splendid, but the *suite logique* was not so hot. Ben, you see, has an inbuilt sex alarm. The slightest tremor of desire makes him wake up with a piercing shriek – he sounds just like the rape alarm I had at university. I'm not sure what kind of sensors he has, but Eric reckons he can smell my milk. Whenever my knees go wobbly milk comes spurting out of my bra like twin geysers.

Last night Ben let out his first howl when we had just got to dessert. We calmed him down and settled him back to sleep, and then we retreated on tiptoe to our room. Eric put a draught excluder under the door to try and stop and milk vapour or pheromones of any other kind reaching Ben's tiny nostrils. Still, it didn't stop the milk problem. I ended up putting my old waterproof and Eric's mac over the bed with two bathtowels on top of them. Eric took one look and declared that it took away the *je ne sais quoi*. Oh well. It **was** nice to be together again, and we can wait a bit for the rest to sort itself out. I mean it's not as though we don't have good books we can read at bedtime. Although maybe it's Bad News that Eric is reading a slim volume, whereas mine is 1250 pages long.

Home. Thursda, 24th April.

Off to the fruit and veg market in the Old Quarter with Ben this morning. Eric left early as he is working as many hours as possible to increase his sales for this month. He was so stressed out this morning that the entire flat seemed charged with negative vibes, so it was a relief to go out with Ben into the sunny morning to shop for apples.

I love markets. The people with baskets and the colours of the stalls and the smell of the fresh produce. There is something almost earthily reassuring about choosing your fruit and putting it into a paper bag while you chat with the market trader about where it was grown and when it was picked. And having it weighed on old scales with weights that look so honest and friendly.

After much deliberation I chose gleaming red apples and asked the lady on the stall which orchard these beauties came from. She gave me a wink, put her finger to her lips and whispered "South Africa."

Home. Fri, 25th April.

Eric rang me at midday today sounding much more jolly – he's sold another two machines, which means that this month he's made more than his target sales figure. He was so much more optimistic about his job that I couldn't believe it when just an hour later he came home looking like a thundercloud.

The boss had called him into his office and congratulated him on his sales, but then went on to say that as he'd gone over his predicted figure the company had decided to double it for next month to encourage him to sell even more. Talk about encouragement – he's exhausted with all the hours he's put in this month, and **doubling** his sales is going to be impossible. It's hardly encouraging, it's enough to make him give up. Happily Eric is a fighter, and he has decided to fight back on his terms. This afternoon he's off to a Mysterious *rendez-vous* which he said could sort things out. I'm not sure if he's thinking of a change of direction or planning to murder his boss.

7pm. Hooray! Good news at last. Eric has been off to some government department and has found out that as he has worked for more than ten years he's eligible for a study grant. He is bubbling over with enthusiasm and excitement and looking forward to studying something he's really interested in, something that is creative and fun. He has an old dream of designing parks and gardens, and has brought home a huge bundle of booklets about training courses to become a *paysagiste*. Tonight he is reading through them with a huge grin on his face, and is radiating *le bonheur.*

HE CAN LEAVE HIS JOB!!!!!!!!

Home. Saturday, 26th April.

It's amazing what a bit of good news can do for a family. The stress has melted away, and there is a new sunny enthusiasm in the air. Eric can't stop grinning; he said he even felt the result of his New Positive Direction during his cycle race this morning. Miracle of miracles, he finished in the top ten. Ben also seems more secure – last night he slept continuously for seven hours. That's the kind of miracle I needed.

Eric is going to skive off work on Monday so he can do some research into different study programs. On a grant we will be poorer, but I have proof that money (esp. earned on commission) doesn't buy happiness.

As for this weekend, Eric has said that tomorrow we're doing Something Different. He said we will need a picnic and that we will be gone all day. I'm not sure what he has in mind, but he's carried a long thin bundle out to the car. I'm dying to know, but Eric isn't giving me any clues. When pressed he just smiles and says, *"la patience est mère de toutes les vertus."*

Bedtime: Ha! If anyone is less patient than my good self it's Eric. He cracked at four o'clock, after half a dozen hours of secret-keeping. This is quite a record actually, usually we only manage to keep secrets for an hour at most. We are the kind of people who exchange Christmas presents in the car on the way back from the store where we bought them. In November.

Well, what he has planned for tomorrow is, surprisingly, fishing. He feels the *"calme et tranquillité"* and *"retour à la nature"* are just what we need. I'm not so sure about that. My fishing forays in England always seemed to stir up feelings rather than induce calm; we had cataclysmic rows of World War 3 (or at the very least, Trivial Pursuit) proportions, in which ancient relationships were painfully and bloodily severed – along with our fingers, on those beastly nylon lines and barbed hooks. And we never caught anything. Maybe the *mauvaise ambiance* was due to the Large Quantities of British weather flowing down the inside of our anoraks and drastically reducing the fishing stock in the lake. Maybe in France things might be better.

In any case the preparation for tomorrow's fishing trip has already revealed that Eric and I have somewhat differing ideas about Technique. We popped out to Carrefour before tea to procure some new hooks for our beaten-up gear. This was where the arguing began. Eric opined that we should get small hooks, so as to be able to reel in fish of all sizes. I maintained that I was only interested in Gargantuan specimens (yes, size DOES matter) so I wanted gigantic hooks. Eric stood fingering the minnow tackle and I the steel shark cable until we reached a compromise. We bought lousy medium hooks, and as is the way with compromises, we were both left feeling irritable and dissatisfied.

Next, the great bait debate.

"Maggots," I said, perhaps a touch bossily. Eric looked appalled and slightly queasy. He said we were going to fish for carp, and that no self-respecting French carp would eat such a thing. French fish are gourmets and must be caught with Camembert, and not just any old Camembert. (We found out later that the favourite bait in the country here is sweet-corn. The fish love it, and it also gives them gas, so if you can't catch the blighters you can always locate them by the bubbles.) Eric found a cheese to his liking while I bought our picnic for tomorrow.

Now everything's ready. All we'll have to do tomorrow is reel them in.

Home. Sunday, 27th April.

A memorable day with a lesson to be learned. Never go fishing with someone you love.

The day began well enough. We pootled along in Virginie to the woods where Eric raced on his bike yesterday morning. He'd glimpsed a lake through the trees which he thought might be a likely spot for fishing.

Ben slept in his car seat, and I read Eric his brochures about study courses as he drove. It seems he can do a sort of Open University course, studying at home with the odd week-long session with his lecturers. The courses sound interesting, and Eric's mood is becoming steadily more buoyant. We were so busy chatting about the future that the trip to the lake flew by.

We parked Virginie in the shade of an oak tree, and set off with Ben, the fishing gear and the picnic. Eric hacked a path *à la* Biggles through the undergrowth of the ancient forest. It took half an hour of tough trekking to reach (and in Eric's case to fall into) the deep, cool lake. These forests are so impenetrable that it is not surprising that people used to hide here during the war.

Eric was just getting over his impromptu swim when we got a second shock. We'd been warned that these woods are full of the corpses of chicken thieves, dispatched and dumped by villagers, but we were alarmed – to say the least – to see stiff, naked bodies strewn on the shore line amidst the willows. One hand poked eerily out of the water in true Arthurian style.

Upon closer examination by Eric (I was bravely guarding our rear behind a tree with Ben) these turned out to be plastic mannequins. I still though this was pretty freaky, but Eric came to find us with a Huge grin. *"Des GROS poissons,"* he said, his voice wibbly wobbly with excitement.

I followed him down to the bank where he'd ventured to take a look at the mannequins. We crouched low and gazed at the depths. I have read stuff about carp of monstrous proportions gliding among knotty water lily roots, but I'd never actually seen them as big as labradors. They slipped between sun and shade, slurping around, massively, just under the surface. I began to regret not buying the steel cable and shark hooks.

We had to decide where to fish. Eric was for a relatively clear stretch of bank, but I though there was too much chance of us being seen. He looked a little tight-lipped when I suggested we hide in the ferns and creepers, and after a few cross words I picked up my rod and Ben and headed for Tarzan country.

The problem with going off in a huff is that you have to go through with it or look silly. I had some misgivings as I strode forth amidst the brambles and the adders, but Ben was safely strapped onto my back, and besides my pride would not let me turn back. After all that woman in Crocodile Dundee got through the Australian bush (bigger, more poisonous) in a long skirt and a little white bra, so there'd be no messing with my Doc Marten's and jungle shorts. I plucked up my courage and found myself whistling The Dam Busters March as I stomped.

When I finally arrived at my perfect spot, somewhat battered and bleeding, I gave Ben a long feed and popped him back in my baby-carrier. Then I decided to show off to Eric with an impressive cast. I flicked my rod back whippily, and forward again... only to snag it on a tree. My tackle was left hanging aloft, and the Camembert was swiftly demolished by a cheeky woodland bird. Feeling a mite discouraged I quickly knotted on a new hook before Eric saw what had happened.

This time I cast my line very gently into the water, and slowly began to work it. Teeth gritted, I waited for the mighty bite, scrutinising every surface ripple. My one worry was whether I should have strapped myself to a tree to avoid being pulled into the water.

Ha! There it was! An impossible weight on my line. I tugged and tugged on my Moby Dick, but there was no shifting him. He did seem an oddly motionless kind of fish, and, leaning forward to spy him, I suddenly had to face facts. My monster was a water lily pad.

I jerked my rod back crossly, ripping off my second and final hook. I could see Eric sitting serenely on the other bank, his line dangling lazily in the water. His smile was disgustingly smug. There is nothing worse about when fishing badly than seeing someone else (especially a loved one) fishing well, so I thought I'd fake it. With a cheery wave I held my rod in postion, so that Eric would think that my line was snugly in the water. I sat down to wait – and wait – for if there's one thing that makes you good at fishing it's patience.

Happily, as afore-mentioned, Eric is no more patient than myself. Just half an hour later he stood up, rubbed his back and put his rod away. I got to my feet, looking as reluctant as possible to leave. I struggled through the undergrowth again to Eric, and asked him sweetly what he'd caught. *"Rien,"* he muttered grumpily, putting it all down to tricky light conditons and, possibly, the smell of his new deodorant. I complained about my reel, which "kept jamming at vital moments, making a good catch quite impossible." Strangely he seemed quite uninterested, and walked off moodily, uttering unprintable oaths, in the direction of our car.

We got back to Virginie and were unpacking the picnic in aggressive silence when Eric scowl suddenly cracked into a smile. "You know what," he laughed, "I have to admit I've been a complete idiot. I've been pretending to fish all morning because I lost my tackle in the first five minutes and didn't want to look stupid in front of you."

I decided to come clean too. We'd fallen for each other's subterfuge hook, line and sinker, so now morally all we could do was make up and enjoy our picnic.

As we polished off the last of the Camembert with a big glass of rouge we swore we'd never go fishing again.

At least, not for a long time.

Home. Monday, 28th April.

This morning dawned sunnily and noisily. Superman upstairs has recently installed chickens on his balcony, and at five o'clock his cockerel began crowing. I actually prefer a "cock-a-doodle-doo" to the electronic shriek of our alarm clock, but then I wouldn't set my alarm clock for five. Besides, this cockerel can't even crow properly – he sounds like a bugle crossed with a fog horn. Maybe it's his revenge for being woken up by Ben once too often.

Eric rang work at nine to say he was ill, as he had plans to visit two administrative departments to check on when he can start his course. Both places were right next to Bordeaux's central library, so I said Ben and I would have a look around while he was busy.

I am a confirmed book-worm (or a *"rat de bibliothèque"*) as they say here, and that is not just because Ben is currently playing havoc with our sex life. I have always loved reading, but I do remember at university how several of my French Literature lecturers would make snide remarks about how women with young children stop reading or doing anything intellectual, as though their brains functioned, at best, in neutral, but usually in reverse. I have found that since Ben has been born I've been almost constantly in top gear, as though having tiny spaces between Ben's naps and feeds actually helps to get me focused. As soon as he's asleep it's like the stop watch is set, and all neurones firing I use my time to write or paint or get things done. It's exhausting but I could hardly say I'm stagnating. So there.

It was great to get to the library. It is a gleaming, glassy multi-storeyed building, next to the ice-rink where France's pop stars (remember Johnny Halliday?) often appear in concert. The popularity of the library's modern architecture has recently suffered somewhat, as some of the plate glass windows detached themselves and fell several storeys onto the pavement below. No one was hurt, but there is now a protective scaffolding porch to shield pedestians from falling glass. (Undeterred, the city planners are still happily building all-glass structures, including the new court house. Here the glass is not just a physical but a logical problem. Transparency is a noble ideal, but some trials are confidential, and witnesses and suspects don't necessarily want to see each other.) Anyway, back to the library porch; it's a temporary thing, made of bits of wood, corrugated iron and flapping plastic. Smokers, who are banned from smoking in the library, huddle under it and try to feel reassured, although at any one time at least half of them are peering nervously upwards. They squeeze together like penguins, no one wants to be pushed outside, just in case.

Ben and I made our way in without incident. Once inside I treated myself to a cup of coffee, and then we set off to explore. It's a *"médiathèque"* as opposed to a *"bibliothèque,* so it has a lot to offer. There are books, of course, in French and other languages. There are European newspapers and magazines, and a huge compact disk collection. There are booths where you can watch films about Bordeaux's past, nature in Aquitaine and many other topics, and videos and talking books you can borrow. Kids are also well provided for, there are loads of books (including an English section) and CD-roms and tapes. There is also a cushioned reading room – a bit like a padded cell – with lots of cloth books for babies to chew. They can get their first real taste of literature, and their parents can flop on the floor cushions and have a well-earned rest. Ben liked peering out at everything, and I had a happy browse. I came out with Amélie Nothombe's new book, and – somewhat inexplicably – a book about goat husbandry. I can't even remember selecting that, so I must concede that if my brain is usually focused, it does have the odd lapse.

We met up with Eric for lunch. He had found out that he can enroll for a landscaping course which begins in July, and that he'll definitely be able to have a grant, albeit a small one. What's more, as he has paid holiday due in July, he'll be able to pack his job in at the beginning of June. Maybe that way his boss will work out that doubling your sales figure is not an incentive to work harder.

Home. Tuesday, 29th April.

C'est fait. Eric has resigned – signed on the dotted line and everything – and has told his boss why, in no uncertain terms. Sadly Monsieur Grand Chef doesn't care a jot if he's been putting so much pressure on his sales team that they've all been bordering on having nervous breakdowns. He made it quite clear that if his current team have burnt out there are three million unemployed people who can replace them. *Charmant.*

Eric is relieved to have said his piece. One of the things he hates about sales is dishonesty, and he was pleased to tell his boss what he really thinks of him and the company. He is going to have to work until the end of June, which could be sticky. Still, good things are ahead and that should keep him going.

Home. Wednesday, 30th April.

Ben has played with his rattle for the first time today. It is blue and in the shape of a telephone, and he has been shaking it on and off all day. His first mobile! I know everyone says that babies grow up fast, but it really is true. He is learning and changing every minute of every day... and he also manages to slot in extra lessons at night.

MAI

Home. Thursday, 1st May.

May! I love May! I always look forward to May in Bordeaux. It's usually warm and sunny and the trees and flowers in the city parks and the surrounding countryside are at their Most Splendid. In summer the sun burns the vegetation to shades of dusty beige and brown, but in May it seems to make the woods, meadows and hedgerows bright with glowing colour.

Even in the city centre it's obvious May is here. On every street corner there are people selling *muguet*. This is not the kind of sinister substance you can usually find for sale if you hang about on a street corner in any city for long enough, but sweet smelling, innocent bunches of lily-of-the-valley. In France it is traditionally offered on the first of May to bring good luck. We bought a big bunch for our neighbour; our flowers were mixed with *églantiers* – wild roses – because in the 18th century a *gentilhomme* called Fabre d'Eglantier declared Mayday to be a public holiday. When Ben and I got home with our bouquet we found our neighbour had also bought one for us. *Tant mieux*! We could use the luck to help us with our Big Changes.

Eric is on holiday today, and is thrilled to bits that his last working month is May. Employers can't stand this month; their employees have only eighteen working days. There are days off for this, that and the other throughout the month. Obviously it's not much fun when you're on commission, but we have a little saved up from last month to help see us through. At the moment I'm just delighted that Ben and I will be seeing more of Eric.

Home. Friday, 2nd May.

Another day off, yippee!

Home. Saturday, 3rd May.

Oops, the *muguet* didn't bring any luck as far as the weather is concerned. At midday yesterday a dark cloud passed in front of the sun, and it's still there. The rain is falling hard. The English would say it's raining cats and dogs, the French that it's raining ropes or, more popularly, that it's raining *comme une vache qui pisse*. The temperature has plummeted and I have put my shorts away somewhere in the bottom of my wardrobe and have rooted out our box of winter clothes. Eric looked glumly at me as he picked mothballs out of his pockets, and announced that today's /spring's /this year's weather were doomed.

We flicked on the morning news on TV, where ironically it was talking about global warming. Eric got crosser and crosser "if it's really happening, then why am I bloody freezing?" Well, the program said that it *is* true, and that at the moment it's getting warmer everywhere in the world. Er, except where it's getting colder. Well, I can't say I understood it all.

I had a good excuse for not concentrating on the science content of the program, and that was because I was working hard on improving Eric's mood. I can just about cope with feeling gloomy myself, but once Eric starts getting depressed I have to cheer up and cheer *him* up too, or else head for a cliff. In an attempt to make him see the brighter side of things I told him about how Brits have to deal with much grottier weather – snow, sleet, hail and hurricanes, and that's just in summer. "But what do you all do when it rains?" he asked. I thought fond thoughts of some of my favourite pubs, but as I'm now a Responsible Parent I thought I'd better suggest something else. "We go for Long Walks," I answered glibly.

I must have persuaded him, because half an hour later we were in Virginie and heading for the Dune de Pyla near Arcachon. It's Europe's biggest sand dune, and despite the wind and rain we though we'd climb it. It's not exactly Everest, but it **is** Le Long Walk *par excellence*.

When we got to Pyla we struggled to open Virginie's doors against the wind, and then spent some long time flapping about with waterproofs in the car park. It took a long time to get started, but finally we were off, up the steep flight of wooden steps towards the summit. Eric strode on ahead with Ben in his arms, and I tagged on behind with the oxygen bottles. Just kidding, it's not that high, but with the wind whipping the sand around I found breathing quite hard work.

My physical exhaustion was soon made worse by Extreme Mental Anguish. A group of people coming down the steps giggled as they went by. Then a runner sprinted up past me, and when he glanced back over his shoulder to say *bonjour* he burst out laughing. When it happened for the third time I found out why. My waterproof had been on top of the laundry basket in our flat, and when I put it on in the car park I'd failed to notice a pair of lacy knickers which had got stuck to the velcro fastening. Sir Edmund Hillary wasn't faced with that kind of stress. Red-faced I stuffed my underwear into my pocket and headed for the top.

Once I finally caught up with Eric and Ben (at three steps from the summit!) my Embarrassing Moment was forgotten as I gazed out at the Splendid View. We could see out right over the Bassin D'Arcachon, all swirling currents and dark reflected clouds. Big yachts were sailing back and forth at the mouth of the bay, their sails stretched to tight pregnant arcs by the gale force winds. Beyond that there was the open Atlantic, white with foam as far as we could see. It was magnificent. It was wild. It was cold. It was time for Hot Chocolate.

I wanted to leave a little flag, just to prove that we'd been there. We didn't have one, so we turned around and started our descent, arguing on and off about who had been first off the staircase at the summit. We had to stop bickering and run for it as the rain started cascading down once more. Ben was tucked hastily under my waterproof and we sprang down the steps like, er, chamois.

Soaked and tired we made it to the bar at the foot of the dune and ordered a Little Something. It was gorgeously warm inside, and we shed our layers one by one as our body temperatures gradually rose. Ben nestled under my jumper and had a feed, and Eric and I sipped chocolate and munched our way through a pile of *crèpes* that were swimming in Grand Marnier – the kind of *crèpes* that are good for the soul.

When we got home we were both feeling happier. Especially as we'd heard the weather forecast on the car radio. The mercury is rising!

Now, where did I put my shorts?

Home. Sunday, 4th May.

Philippe rang this morning. He's a friend from the LPO -- the *Ligue pour la Protection des Oiseaux* – like the RSPB. Eric and I joined the society three years ago, as we are keen on observing and protecting all forms of wildlife, including birds. Philippe was an Established Member, and was very patient with us while we learned the difference between male and female kestrels, counted migrating cranes (the feathery sort) and tracked owls through the woods. He even let us do some of the trickier stuff, like installing nesting platforms for storks and putting leg rings on the chicks when they were born. This morning he sounded *very* put out when he rang. He said that if he sounded bad he looked even worse, as he has a chipped tooth and a black eye.

I asked what had happened to him. Had he been attacked by one of the larger birds of prey (a condor at the very least)? Nope, he said he was sure that his attacker had had two legs, two arms and two fists. I was still a bit in the dark, but then he told me when he'd been attacked – on Mayday – and where – the *Point de Graves* – the penny finally dropped. Everyone in Bordeaux knows what can happen there to bird lovers at the beginning of May.

The *Point de Graves* is on the tip of the Gironde estuary, just North of Bordeaux. It is a wonderful place for observing migrating birds – dozens of varieties, rare and beautiful, fly overhead on their long journey. Sadly, for many of them, their migration ends here. French hunters continue to defy EEC legislation and blast away at the birds from this unique vantage point. These guys dress up like Rambo – army camouflage, cartridge belts and BIG guns – and then they go for it, bang, bang, bang. It all seems so pointless and cruel; I mean these machos don't even feel bad about shooting robins. As children they probably cheered when Bambi's mother died. They claim they have the right to hunt as the tradition of hunting animals is so ancient – although oddly enough they don't seem so keen on conserving other aspects of their prehistoric heritage; no one campaigns to preserve the right to make fire with lumps of flint, dwell in caves or indulge in a spot of trepanning. Hunters only represent 3% of the French population, but unfortunately they have managed to project a 'Back to Nature' image that gets their political party lots of votes. Well,

I suppose they do like nature in a way. With peas and carrots.

Every year on Mayday at the *point de Graves* there are clashes between the *verts* and the *chasseurs*. Brigitte Bardot often turns up to encourage the *verts* (as Philippe said, she always has two black eyes) but he hadn't even got a glimpse of her. He was caught up in a fight after just one hour of protesting, and he spent the rest of the day lying in bed with an ice-pack on his face.

We commiserated, and after the phone call Eric and I started chatting about how marvellous it would be to create our own mini nature reserve, a *chasse interdite* zone. We could have a wildlife garden, with birds and butterflies, foxes and hedgehogs. We could grow vegetables and Eric could practise his landscaping. "And," I yelled excitedly, burrowing under our bed in search of my library book, and happily brandishing it at Eric, "we could keep goats!"

Tonight we are both full of plans. A full-scale reserve is *mission impossible,* but there is actually nothing to stop us renting a place in the country with a garden rather than a basement flat in Bordeaux. Dog will be able to discover her sheep-dog origins! I will be able to wander around my vegetable patch in a long dress and straw hat while Ben picks flowers, learns what cows look like and grows as strong and healthy as the Milky Bar Kid. Although on second thoughts I'm not sure we'll be able to grow Milky Bars in the vegetable garden. Maybe he'll have to be a Green Giant instead.

Home. Monday, 5th May.

The move is still on! More than ever, in fact, as Eric and I rang a few friends today to find out the price of country accommodation, and it might end up costing us a good deal less than the flat. We love Bordeaux – the pavement cafés, the theatre, the shops and the restaurants, but financially we won't really be able to have a social life on a grant, and with a small baby I'm sure it will be easier living out of town. I keep thinking about how well Ben sleeps whenever we cross the river and go into the trees. The idea of a Good Night's sleep is irresistible.

I have been flicking through the goat book – talk about fate taking a hand, there I was just thinking I was being dippy getting that book out of the library, when all the time it was Destiny revealing herself. Well, I do *hope* I'm not going mad. Anyway, goats do sound quite interesting. Not only are they endearing creatures, but they will also be able to provide us with milk, cream, butter, yoghurt and cheese. I will be able to skip the entire milk produce aisle in the supermarket and save money for more wholesome things such as M&Ms etc...

The goat book has a chapter on other useful animals for the smallholder. Eric, however, has said no (so far) to alpacas *and* llamas, which I think is a bit small-minded of him. I'll have to see what else I can come up with.

Home. Tuesday, 6th May.

Ostriches?????????

Home. Wednesday, 7th May.

I did the accounts this morning. Eric's grant will be about 5000 francs a month, and rent will probably use up half of that. That leaves us 2500 francs to live on, run the car, buy nappies etc...etc... Am a little worried about how many animals we will be able to support – maybe one very small anorexic hamster.

Rang village halls all the rest of morning to find out if they have any cards up on their notice boards advertising houses to let. Twelve negative replies, and then on my thirteenth attempt I got somewhere. The secretary said she might know of a farmhouse which was vacant, and that she would ring back this afternoon. Could this be lucky thirteen? The village is tiny and in the most gorgeous area of countryside. A farm there would be idyllic. God, I hope it isn't a corrugated iron shack or a concrete bunker left over from the war. The suspense is killing me.

4pm. She rang back!!!!!!!! She couldn't talk this morning as she isn't allowed to do private business at work. She has a small farmhouse for rent, and it is empty as the previous tenants moved out last month to buy their own place. I was dying to know more, but thought I should let her do most of the talking. We got on well on the phone, which is important. Being a tenant is not a Happy Position to be in in France – house owners are so afraid that tenants will default on rent that they want pay slips which go back years, employer's references, guarantees signed by parents, bank statements and, possibly, blood.

Well, I stayed off the subject of us living on a grant, and said Eric was going to commute to Bordeaux every day. Without a little lying you never get anywhere. We chatted for about ten minutes, but she was curiously cagey about the farm. I asked lots of questions, but she said that the best way to get the feel of the place was to come over on Friday morning and have a look. Tomorrow is yet ANOTHER holiday, *Armistice* (VE day) and she is off visiting her family, but Friday is also a day off. French government departments usually declare the day linking a public holiday to the weekend to be a *pont,* literally a bridge to the weekend. Eric is also off on Friday so we'll be able to go together and take our time.

Eric got home all happy as we're in for a long weekend, and he was very excited when I told him all about the house. He's a bit worried it might be a wild goose chase because I mentioned she reluctant to talk about the place. Oh well, there's no point worrying, we'll know soon enough.

Home. Thursday, 8th May. Armistice.

Peaceful day at home together. It was wonderful for Eric to have a chance to play with little Ben. It is so sad that he hardly sees him in the day, and that when he does get home from work in the evening Ben is often crying with colic. Today he saw him smiling and snuggly and cute and well, just GORGEOUS! It is going to be so much better when Eric starts his course and can be at home. At the moment he thinks Ben has him down as the Stranger with the Attaché Case. I reassured him and said that soon Ben will be calling him Papa the Farmer.

Home. Friday, 9th May.

9am. Just about to leave. Lovely to have Eric with me – hooray for *le pont!*

9.15am. VE day aftermath: Quick chat with other half about war. He thinks he won it all by himself, or France did anyway. Talk about gratitude. Mentioned Allies, but he just went on about De Gaulle. The cheek of it.

Bedtime. *Une grande journée.* I'd better begin at the beginning, although I'm so excited that it's tricky to remember the exact chronological order of today's events. Here goes.

We couldn't get off the subject of the war, and argued in the car more or less all the way to the village about whether England had done more or less than America, and then changed tack and started to quarrel about whether Steve McQueen could act or not. The argument lasted for thirty five kilometres, over the graceful arched bridge out of Bordeaux, along the fast route towards the west and through the sleepy lanes that weave through the dappled forests towards the North. As we neared the village the fire of our argument died, and we both drank in the splendid scenery, only uttering the odd "could" or "couldn't" for form's sake.

The lady from the town hall was waiting for us on the square. She gave us a friendly wave and said for us to follow her. She set off at breakneck speed, out of the village and down towards the river. She suddenly took a tight turn, and Eric swung the steering wheel round as hard as he could in order to follow her and avoid a tree. Mobiles and rattles bounced from one side of the car to the other, and Ben opened his eyes for a brief second before falling back into his slumber. I was panicked – we were already close to the river – was she actually going to plunge into it? This woman may have had the general appearance of a middle-aged *fonctionnaire*, but she had the soul of a Mad Bad French driver. I'm sure Formula One fuel pumped through her veins.

It was soon apparent that she was driving along the old tow path which flanks the river. We followed as best we could, Eric peering through her dust trail and trying to keep her in his sights, and myself gazing out the side, getting the odd glimpse of bright river through the willows and the alders.

It only took five minutes to get there; the length of your average roller coaster ride. I think we spent at least half the time off the ground. Virginie bounced so high off every rut and pot hole on the rough lane that she flew most of the way. When we eventually landed I didn't bother to check on her suspension, I was too busy just feeling glad we were still alive. We were dusting ourselves down and I was getting Ben settled in the baby carrier before I really took a look around me. I fell in love on the spot.

The house was perfection. A long, low stone farm, with soft blue shutters, an ancient iron-studded front door and hollyhocks growing against the butter-coloured walls. It was facing south, looking towards the sunshine and the river at the bottom of the garden.

Inside it had been converted, but I'm not sure what into. A long line of four biggish rooms, all leading into one another, with a stone sink at one end of the house, and a huge fireplace at the other. The bathroom is in a space at the end of the barn which runs all the way along the back of the house, and you get to it from the "kitchen". It isn't luxury, but at least the shower works. Anyway, the honey coloured floor boards and the view over the water had already won our hearts.

After we had explored inside we went out again to see the garden and the land that came with it. That was really the best part. Oooops, Benjamin has just woken up. This will have to be a cliff-hanger ending. More anon...

Home (but not for much longer), Sat, 10th May.

....ah, back again. Ben is soundly asleep tonight, so maybe I'll be able to finish! He slept really badly last night, as I think he dozed too much during the day. He seemed to find roaring around the countryside in our little car positively soothing.

Well, there we were just stepping out of the farmhouse. Next we looked at the cow barn on the north side. The landlady explained that traditional farms always have a barn facing north to protect the house from the cold. Not only does it mean that cows rather than the farmer get the brunt of the winter weather, but they also give off heat which warms that side of the house. A great idea, but I'm not sure if it will work if we just keep a hamster in the barn. In any case, 'cow barn' seemed an inappropriate term to describe this huge building. The foot thick stone walls, gigantic oak beams and the sheer scale and majesty of it made it feel more like a cathedral than a barn. It even had a kind of font: a stone trough which was constantly replenished with trickling spring water.

I asked the landlady about the spring and she explained that the whole house was supplied with its water rather than the mains. It was not only pure but also locally renowned for its good taste and healing properties. Plus it's great for the skin; imagine bathing in Evian! We climbed the steep limestone hill behind the house to see where it bubbled out of the hillside. The water actually comes from the Charente Maritime, the county next door, before gushing out of the earth in Aquitaine. We stood and watched the water and also took in the view; the south-facing slope, covered in wild flowers and springy grass, the terracotta roof of the farm, its red, ochre and rich brown tiles baking anew in the sunshine, and finally the river gliding by. Beyond that we could see the valley and its meadows full of cows and far, far away in the distance the church spire in

Saint Emilion.

The landlady brought us back to practical matters, pointing out the limits of the land. Twenty acres of wood and pasture – heaven! Then she looked a little uneasy and said we should have *une petite explication*. At last we were going to get to the bottom of why she had sounded a little strange about the place on the phone! It seems that in winter, if it is exceptionally wet, the road in front of the house floods. The house itself has never flooded as it is part way up the hill, but if the road is under water the only way in or out is on foot via the hill and the little lane along the

ridge at the top. She said she'd lived in the house for twenty years and had lived through floods many times (with small children!) and as the house always stayed safe and dry it wasn't too much of a problem. She did concede that it was somewhat inconvenient, but then she wasn't charging much rent. Less than our flat in Bordeaux and less than I paid for a grotty room in London when I was a student. 2500 francs a month and it could be ours.

Eric and I had a walk around by ourselves, and then we sat under the lime tree in the front garden while I fed Ben and we made plans. The flooding wouldn't be too bad as neither of us will have a 9 to 5 job to get to, and if we fill the freezer before the winter and get a good stock of firewood we should be just fine. And the longest the flooding has ever lasted is only a couple of weeks, which isn't exactly the end of the world. And the farm itself is magical. Eric will be able to study here, and put some of the things he learns into practice. We have the spring to water the future vegetable garden, and enough land to keep animals. It was just what we were looking for.

The landlady was so worried we'd say "no" that she hardly asked us any questions about our income, and we got on so well that I think she trusts us anyway. One minute we were chatting about the wildlife in the area, and the next we were actually signing our contract.

Tonight it all seems a bit of a dream, and we keep having to pinch ourselves. This is *really* happening. We are moving on the 6th June!

Home. Sunday, 11th May.

Had sketch books out all day, drawing plans of things we can build, and of where we are going to put everything in the new house. Made endless lists of:

1) things to pack

2) things to throw away

3) things we aren't-sure-whether-to-bring-with-us-or-not

4) animals we can keep (including giraffes now, due to ceiling height in the barn)

5) crops we can grow (nb: veggie garden has now become "crops")

6) fruit trees to plant. Only really agreed on bananas – also very good for weaning babies.

7) things to fix/paint/replace in the farmhouse

8) the most URGENT things to do

9) things we must ECONOMISE on

10) outgoings (a long list, that one)

11) sources of income (grant, family allowance, money from sale of surplus bananas)

Knackered now as all this list-making is mentally exhausting. We're trying to have an early night as Eric has a tough day tomorrow. It is the start of the big May exhibition, and he is manning the stand for his company all week. Ben and myself are going to go with him – hooray! Can't wait, lots to see and freebies to sample. Yummy things to taste, too. I'm going to get to sleep ASAP, I just hope Ben knows what an early night means.

Home. Monday, 12th May.

He doesn't. Looking on the bright side, at least he's helped us along with our planning. He didn't sleep at all between 2am and 4am, so Eric and I chatted about fencing and firewood. It was a useful discussion that

I'm sure neither of us would have missed for anything – except, possibly, a good night's sleep.

We also had time to write a letter to the agency which owns our flat to say we are moving, and put it in the post before breakfast. There shouldn't be any problem with giving such short notice as flats in the centre of town are easy to rent out, but we wanted to get the letter off as early as possible. As Ben was up at five that wasn't too hard.

After breakfast we set off for the exhibition – *La grande foire*. It was certainly very *grande*: the exhibition centre in Bordeaux is a kilometre long – and that is just the main hall. There are other buildings and there is also a gigantic open-air exhibition. What's on show? Just about everything. The idea of the May fair is to be a kind of *vitrine*, a shop-window, for every business, club, farm, or association in the south-west of France – more than 2500 exhibitors in all. There are settees and space-rockets, caravans and carpets, wine producers and windows, prize pigs and planes. You can sign up to join the army, buy a living-room suite or even a herd of cows. I was under strict orders to do none of the above.

We parked (for free!) next to the main hall, and got Ben into his pram. We were going to do so many kilometres that I wasn't sure if my back would survive if I put him in his carrier. I wonder if kangaroos get lumbago? Anyway, I was very agreeably surprised when the ticket-seller explained that *la foire* was free for foreign visitors. France is wonderful sometimes.

Eric had a few minutes to spare before he had to go to his stand, and we decided to go and look at the one thing that was really dominating the skyline – a humungous roller-coaster over 30 metres high. It looked positively ghastly. There were young things just coming off it when we got there. They were looking very pale but were chattering enthusiastically about how it felt to go loop the loop at 100 km/hour. Eric got all excited, but I discouraged him; after all this is the man whose stomach is so dodgy on any form of transport that it has earned him the nickname *Monsieur Vomit*. (Mind you, his motion sickness didn't put him off joining the Navy, but he paid for it dearly. He was sick every day for four years, but then, as he has often explained to me, he just didn't think of that when he signed up – *on ne peut pas penser à tout, tu sais!)* In any case, today he said he was just pleased to see something at a fair that looked like a fair, rather than PVC gates and agricultural equipment. I merely suggested that if he were looking for a fairground *ambiance* he'd probably be better off settling for a toffee apple – not a bad idea I thought, but Eric's pride was hurt and he walked off to his stand.

We had so many things to look at that it was hard to know where to start. Ben took one peep out of his pram and went to sleep, so really it was up to me to decide which hall to visit. It was chilly so I thought I'd leave the open-air part for later and go into the main hall.

First I inspected the aeronautical stand, one of Bordeaux's most important industries, and was pretty impressed. One rep. asked me if I wanted to sit in the cockpit of a fighter plane, but there didn't seem to be enough room in there for me and the pram, so I declined. After that I browsed around *planète jeunes,* until I felt too old and depressed. It was a mix of careers advisors, Sega games, skateboards and baseball, and made me feel about a hundred and ten. Everyone here was walking on Nike Air except for me.

After that I set off for the home expo part, where almost immediately I was set upon by a salesman. He was one of many who were trying to sell leather settees. These guys were a breed apart; they were obviously trying to look as sexy as possible – and failing miserably. They were wearing strangely cut shiny suits, croco shoes and positively indecent amounts of hair gel and *eau de cologne.* I couldn't decide if they looked more like dealers or pimps, but it was hard to think about it clearly as one of them had me firmly by the arm and was leading me (and pram, *mon dieu!*) over to his horrible sofa. I mean did he want me to buy it or sleep with him? In the end I did what a girl had to do – I ran away. I sped through the whole section, relieved to leave the salesmen, the cloying odour of perfume and the lumps of dead cow behind me.

I walked all they way along the main hall until I got to Eric's stand. He was making a sale, so I carried on looking around. After a while I'd had enough of recycled air, and thought I'd see what was going on outside. The warm blast really hit me as we stepped outdoors – the morning was ripening into a sunny afternoon, and May sun can be HOT! Happily we were in the food section, and it wasn't hard to find a cool drink. There were mini restaurants everywhere, where people were sipping cocktails and sampling Bordeaux' culinary delights. I nibbled samples of cured ham and tasted wild lavender honey. Quite revitalised I set off to visit some more of the outdoor stands, like the swimming pool sales area... all that cool turquoise water on such a warm day was tempting. Mind you, despite the heat I also looked at the traditional woodstoves. The farm could be cold in winter.

I had a sandwich with Eric for lunch, and the day passed quite merrily. I had the odd sit down to feed Ben, but otherwise walked pretty well all day. I must have walked at least fifteen kilometres. My feet hurt so much tonight that I've decided not to accompany Eric tomorrow... it'll all still be there on Wednesday and I'll go back with him for another look. Next time I'll wear better shoes. Maybe I should get some Nikes.

Home. Tuesday, 13th May.

Stayed at home today. Ben had a very active time – lying on a rug on the floor, chirruping at his toys and kicking his legs. Mind you, if I spent the day doing that no one would say *I'd* been active. Being a baby must be bliss; every time you eat you get praised, every kilo you put on is a victory, and if you settle down for a long nap in the day you aren't shaken awake and accused of being slothful, *au contraire*. Adult life is so hard in comparison.

At 10-ish the agent rang to say that they don't mind us moving out on the sixth, as they already have three couples interested. But the flat has to be spotless. It was a good thing that Ben was keeping himself happily occupied, as the place does fall somewhat short of the *agent's* requirements.

I did a bit of housework and then had a busy time taking down the shelves we'd put up in our bedroom and packing their contents into unwieldy piles. I had nothing to put stuff into, so I popped out to pick up half a dozen boxes at the *épicérie*. Oh, and I also collected Ben's prescription for his first vaccine at the pharmacy – his routine visit is in a few days. Anyway, the boxes were a bit on the small side, but enough to take a lot of the paperbacks. The problem was the big, dark holes left in the white wall once I'd got rid of the screws and rawl plugs; we weren't supposed to have put anything permanent in the walls whatsoever. I was a bit desperate for a solution, but by the time Eric got home I'd cracked it. I chewed bits of white paper into soft balls, and then rolled them in Tippex. Then I poked them into the holes with a matchstick. *Parfait!*

Eric came home in a good mood as he'd sold several machines at the fair. It was a change to see him coming home from work with a big smile. He came straight into the bedroom to give me a hug – and fell over my pile of boxes. His smile faltered somewhat. Never mind – he was Most

Impressed with my efforts. He said my wall was perfect, but that we shouldn't try and fiddle about with billions of tiny boxes. Tomorrow we'll go with him to the fair again, and we'll pick up a couple of giant-sized ones that photocopiers come packed in. I should be able to put all the rest of our books into them – every box packed seems like another step towards the farm...

Home. Wednesday, 14th May.

Back to the *foire* to have a more thorough look – and to find a bigger box for our books. It's amazing how different it seemed, its sheer size and diversity mean you never visit the same fair twice.

This time I started off at the International Hall, and watched little Ben's nostrils twitch as we drank in the aroma of rich dark coffee beans from Africa and incense from all over the world. There was everything there from children's wear from Madagascar to musicians from Peru. We had a whale of a time. We were also given a present; a Tunisian potter made a clay ashtray for Ben, perhaps a tad inappropriately as he is not even two months old. It was *very* generous, but perhaps a *cadeau empoisonné* – a dripping clay object is not the easiest thing to carry around a crowded show.

Despite the difficulties of manoeuvring a wet ashtray, a pram and a small baby around the hall, I had a great time ...and then it got even better. Eric had made a big sale, and as a 'reward' got an hour off to spend with us. We headed straight for the acres and acres of the exhibition which were devoted to farm animals.

After the exotic odours of the previous stands it was oddly reassuring to smell hay. It is a warm, homey kind of smell; it reminds me both of summer fields and of Christmas creches in the heart of winter. Something fresh and new and at the same time something which is very ancient. Mingling with it was the smell of every kind of animal you can find in the South West of France – a local Noah's ark.

Perhaps the cattle were the most impressive. Soft, curvy cows – the top models of their breed gazed at us coyly through their thick eyelashes. Then there were the bulls – mighty beasts of chunky muscle and enormous horns and gigantic... er, well, I won't spell it out but it got the groups of school kids giggling. Crowding around these stars were the animal equivalent of stylists and make-up artists, clipping fur, washing hooves and brushing aside stray wisps of hay. The owners were also on hand, checking every animal and making sure they were comfortable and had plenty to eat. These guys were often tiny, made to look even smaller by the size of their livestock. Still, they strutted around their stands, chests puffed out and glowing with pride. They gave lashings of attention to their animals but also took the time to chat to other farmers – the *foire* is one of the most important *rendez-vous* of the farming year.

We admired all the breeds, and then moved on to check out the pigs and then the poultry. The day-old chicks, were my favourite – a definite must for our farm. After that we found a small pen full of angora goats. They were so cute – improbably woolly and gentle. We couldn't resist climbing into their enclosure to chat with the farmer and stroke them. All too quickly Eric's hour was up and he had to rush back to his stand, picking bits of straw off his suit and stamping his feet to knock off the manure.

The day passed by most agreeably, and tonight we are both planning our farmyard. The *foire* has given us so many ideas, we just can't wait to move and get started.

More than 350,000 people visit the fair, and although they buy anything and everything I'm sure we brought home something that no one else did: we have the biggest cardboard box on the planet, let alone in the South West of France. I'm sure I'll be able to pack the entire flat into it.

Home. Thursday, 15th May.

I spent half of today taking down the rest of our shelves and disguising the holes in the wall. I must say I am now such a dab hand at this that I think I could quite easily move onto plastic surgery, and make a small fortune repairing the faces of the rich and famous. Anyway, absolutely *all* of our books and bibelots fitted into the Monster Box. I was thrilled with my packing... until Eric came home. Looking on the bright side, at least he didn't fall over half a dozen boxes like last time. In fact he didn't fall at all. The problem was that I'd put the box in the hall all ready to go, and I'd placed it a little too close to the front door. When Eric got home (all jolly from a good day of sales) he threw the door open triumphantly; only to have it rebound against the box and crash back in his face. His nose bore the brunt of it, and his nostrils immediately began gushing blood, all over his suit and white shirt.

Unfortunately, slim and fit as Eric is, he couldn't get through a six inch gap between the door and the box. As I frantically tried to shift my Enormous Parcel I could hear him muttering something (through the blood) about bleeding to death outside his own flat. In the end I gave up on trying to move the box and just started unpacking it. It was two thirds empty by the time I could move it, and I was knee deep in candlesticks, novels and the Peter and Janes I'd put aside for when Ben starts reading. Eric staggered in, slipping about on the books while I howled in pain as I got a crystal duck (one of those unwanted presents one is never allowed to throw away) jammed between my toes. Eric, pale of face but bloody of clothes, staggered past me to the bathroom as I hopped about in agony.

Tonight we are reconciled. Eric said *of course* anyone could make the mistake I made. He also said maybe I should give up any thoughts of a career in furniture removals. *"Bien-sûr, chéri,"* I said smoothly, and talked to him about my alternative idea of becoming a plastic surgeon. *"En plus"* I added, "you can be my first patient."

Home. Friday, 16th May.

Phew, Eric's nose was salvageable with a kiss and a smear of Lacto Calamine – I didn't even have to use Tippex. I was worried he was going to have two black eyes, but he's got off lightly. Thank heavens... I'm not sure black eyes would have gone down well at a trade fair.

Eric is the only wounded member of the family, but it was Ben and myself who had to go to the doctor's today. *Rien de grave* – just Ben's two month check and his first vaccination.

I had got quite organised about the visit this time. Before we set off I made sure I'd got his health carnet, my cheque book, a spare nappy and the vaccine itself. I was feeling very pleased with myself, and was half way out of the door before I realised I'd forgotten Benjamin.

The visit went fine. Ben didn't even cry when he had his vaccine! We chatted about how he's sleeping (or not), and I sympathised with the doctor when she said that her little one is still waking up every two and a half hours. It wasn't really what I needed to hear, but never mind. I thought I'd lighten things up and pull her leg a bit, so I told her I'd found the solution to infantile insomnia: buy a bottle of ether from the pharmacy and sprinkle the baby' bottom sheet with it. She went quite pale, and though I reassured her I was only joking I saw her scribble something down in her notes. Help! I hope she hasn't noted us down as a Problem Family. Eeek. (On second thoughts, maybe she was just jotting down my remedy for later use.)

As we left the surgery she said that the vaccine may have a few side effects. Ben may be out of sorts this evening and could have a disturbed night. Well, that'll make a change.

Bassin d'Arcachon. Saturday, 17th May.

Eric is working at the exhibition all weekend, so I have come over to Mum and Dad's for a seaside mini-break with Ben. Actually I feel quite refreshed already; Ben slept miraculously well, a full six hours of non-stop high-quality slumber! If that's the result of the vaccine then I'm going to have him vaccinated on a daily basis from now on.

Told Mum and Dad all about the farm, and drew plans out for them. They are very cautious about how much money we should put into it, and I failed to reassure when I explained that as we don't *have* any money to invest there's no need to worry.

Ended up chatting about keeping goats. Mum and Dad can't really get me on that one, because they are wild about them. In fact, when Dad was working all hours as a junior doctor in a hospital, and Mum struggling on her own to look after four young children, what did they come up with to improve family life? A Swiss au-pair? Nope, a Swiss Toggenburg – the sweetest kind of goat imaginable. She was one of the family and went with us everywhere – from the Cumbrian hills to Devonshire beaches. I'm not sure if the people in our village thought we were eccentric or just stark raving mad. Perhaps it was fortunate for us that some of them never even realised we *had* a goat; we once heard one of the villagers talking about "that funny dog the Franklins have – the one with the hooves." So, although Mum and Dad muttered something about the expense of vet's bills they still had an excited glitter in their eyes. They have even asked if they can look after Ben *and* the goats if ever Eric and I want to go away for the weekend.

Pootled along the beach together looking for Interesting Things on the tide line. Mum wanted to bring home a mahogany tree trunk that had drifted thousands of miles from exotic climes. It *was* beautiful, but did weigh a couple of tons. Dad refused, but then got all grumpy when Mum wouldn't let him bring back a trawling net that had been washed up in its entirety – including barnacles, crabs and Large Quantities of rotting fish. Dad wanted to do a restoration job and then use it to fish from his dinghy. Mum (cruelly) pointed out that the net was substantially heavier than Dad's craft, and made him leave it behind. In the end they brought home a selection of sea-scoured sun-bleached planks to make new book-shelves, and looked very content with their find. Ben came home with his first suntan; I'd put sun cream on him to protect him from the UV Nasties, and without even the hint of redness his skin has turned a light golden colour. This babe could star in *Baywatch*.

Home. Sunday, 18th May.

Instead of going to the beach we struck out through the woods today. It's not hard to find a nice trail to walk along – in this area the forestry commission has built over two hundred kilometres of cycle tracks in the coastal pinewoods. Inland it is just as easy to discover cycle paths. The regional council is busy building tracks along abandoned railway lines, linking up villages and providing safe and interesting routes to explore, deep in the countryside and far from traffic. You can even cycle from Bordeaux to the surfing beaches – although I can say from bitter experi-ence that it's a bad idea to attempt this with a surfboard on your back when it's windy.

We strolled along a cycle path that was once a *piste de résiniers*, one of the trails resin collectors would use when they went into the pinewoods to tap resin from the trees. These cycle paths are my favourite; they are deliciously perfumed with the smell of resin and dry pine needles. Even on a hot day the light is never too harsh, but takes on the soft red, violet and mauve colours of the bark of the trees. When you venture along these gently tinted trails it is difficult to understand why the Impressionists were considered barmy when they insisted shadows don't have to be painted in tones of grey and black – it just seems so obvious that they can be purple.

Well, we were pottering along the trail, Mum way out in front push-ing Ben in the pram and Dad and I sauntering along behind when two cyclists raced past us, chatting away in German. As they went by Mum and Ben they veered sharply to one side to avoid the pram, and we heard one of them shout out something. They had disappeared by the time we caught up with Mum, and she was looking puzzled and a little upset. "I just don't understand it," she said, frowning, "that man just yelled *psychopath* at me."

We carried on with our walk, having various hypotheses about what on earth he can have meant. Half an hour later we were enlightened: The cyclists came back the other way, and bellowed the same thing at all of us. All I can say is that it's amazing (with the right intonation and a German accent) how alike *psychopath* and *cycle path* can sound.

These cyclists obviously thought that as pram-pushing pedestrians we were *off piste* on a cycle path, but I can't see that we were doing too much harm. And being shouted at was enough to make all of us feel, well, a little *piste off*...

Home. Monday, 19th May.

Two months old today!!!!!!! He has changed so much already. It is so cute to see him peeking out of the pram, and smiling at people when he catches their eye. In fact, I think I might sell our pram (where he can only really lie on his back) and get him one where he can see out a bit. I'm sure he'd love it. I'll have to see about putting an ad in the paper.

Eric is back at work instead of working at the exhibition. It was very gruelling, but he has earned a lot more than usual. We have such a lot to pay out in the next month that I'm keeping my fingers crossed for our finances. We have to pay our deposit on the farm – two months of rent – as well as paying bills for the flat. There are tons of things to buy for the house, and sometimes the sums involved seem a bit alarming. Still, I remember something from 'O' Level Maths about two negatives making a positive, so if we write cheques on our overdrawn account maybe the laws of mathematics will bounce us back into the black. You never know.

Home. Tuesday, 20th May.

Ben had a grumpy day today. He had to be fed, rocked, given soothing baths, pushed about in the pram, burped, changed, fed, rocked etc...etc...all day. I love him to bits, but – somewhere between his sixty-fourth feed and forty-sixth bath – I seriously thought I was going to go bananas.

By the time Eric got home in the evening he'd settled. "Ahhhh!" said adoring father, "you can see he's getting bigger. He is turning into such a calm, sweet little boy."

Well, I howled inwardly, but I must say he *does* look like the cutest baby on earth tonight. Maybe I won't go bananas after all.

Home. Wednesday, 21st May.

Another difficult day. Ben was so unsettled that I decided to go to the pharmacy and pick up his new vaccine... it made him sleep so well last week that I hoped just seeing the box would send him off.

French pharmacies are really worth visiting. They aren't hard to find – they are so popular in France that there is one about every hundred metres in town, and even the tiniest village has at least one. France is Europe's biggest consumer of medicines, and when the demand is that high you need suppliers; consequently there are pharmacies galore. It isn't just the number of pharmacies which is astonishing, but what you can find inside. Our local one is no exception...

The entrance is lit up with an eerie green glow, which comes from the neon cross over the door. The green cross is the pharmacist's symbol – which reminds me, I really must explain this to my Dad one day. He's colour blind and therefore (logically) has it down as being a red cross. Anyway, counter-balancing the ultra-modern neon are the traditional jars lined up in the window, labelled *lavandre, camomile, digitale...* If the cross looks like something from a SciFi film then these jars are straight out of a Victorian apothecary's shop.

This ancient/modern thing can be observed everywhere inside. There are space-age diet powders (straight from Nasa) next to herbal remedies to calm your stomach which have been used since the Middle Ages. You can buy newly invented chewing gum to protect your teeth, or opt for the tooth cleaning powders that people used when Balzac still had his milk teeth. You can pick up a brand new drug on prescription, or choose homeopathy. It's the French Medical Paradox. My sister in England was surprised at how interventionist childbirth is here, and it *is* hard to explain that although the French love epidurals for a Mum-to-be they are also willing to recommend *tisane* as effective pain relief for someone with cancer. Baffling.

One thing for which there were dozens of cures, both ancient and modern, were *jambes lourdes*, or heavy legs. Syrups, capsules, tablets, injections, creams, infusions and support tights all promised immediate relief. It was all very strange – I mean what on earth are heavy legs???? There must be an awful lot of them about or else there wouldn't be so many remedies. I'll have to keep a look out and see if I can spot any.

Picked up the vaccine and also stuck a card on the till advertising our pram. If the sight of the vaccine doesn't calm Ben down, perhaps a new pram will do the trick.

Home. Thursday, 22nd, May. Ascension.

ANOTHER day off!!! Today is a holiday, and once more there is a *pont* (Friday) to the weekend. Ben was happy all day – I think he really likes seeing his Daddy. Eric was also pleased to be home. I think I'm the only one who isn't relaxed; it *is* nice to be together, but I'm beginning to freak about our finances. Eric is on commission only, so if he doesn't sell anything we will all starve.

Eric refuses to get worried. He said Ben won't starve because he's breast-fed, and that we'll soon be drinking goat's milk and guzzling honey (latest project) from our beehives. The farm is beginning to sound like the Promised Land.

Home. Friday, 23rd May.

Piddling down with rain today. Actually it's been raining solidly since last night, and the morning papers are full of horrific photographs of car accidents that the poor weather conditions are said to have caused. *Sud Ouest* seems to have pictures of mangled metal on every page. Gruesome.

Although the weather was blamed, I was alarmed to see how many of the crashes involved alcohol. Drink driving is tragically common in France; young and old from every sector of society drink and drive with few signs of a guilty conscience. More often than not drinking wine is not even regarded as consuming alcohol. One wine-grower I know swears blind that a well-balanced Bordeaux claret cannot make you drunk. I hope that the message that alcohol and driving do not mix will eventually be accepted, but in the meantime people will keep on dying.

We stayed in all day, avoiding the rain and the roads. There wasn't much point in wandering about town as the shops are closed. Anyway, it was a good thing we were *chez-nous*, as a lady rang to ask about buying the pram. She's coming round tomorrow morning. Hooray!

Home. Saturday, 24th May.

Very Strange Lady came today. Most women in Bordeaux are very *chic,* but she was wearing a giant-sized *Chicago Bulls* tee-shirt, flowery leggings, orange sandals, a pink leather effect jacket, and, to crown it all, what appeared to be a bright yellow wig. For once I felt really well-dressed in comparison.

Well, I showed her the pram, and how to take the carrycot on and off the base. I kept smiling even when the sliding mechanism guillotined my fingers (I've never really figured out how it works) and managed to keep up my repartee while discreetly staunching the flow of blood with my hanky.

"Very clever design," I explained, "It's German, you see. Clever lot, the Germans." (Quick pause to discreetly check the blood wasn't actually coming from an artery). "I mean Einstein was German, wasn't he?"

"*Quoi?*" said my would-be buyer, "Did he make prams and all?"

Tonight my index finger is very sore. I can't face going to Casualty, as I'm sure it'll still be full of road accident victims and I'll have to wait for hours and hours. It'll feel like weeks. By the time I get my finger stitched it will be time for Ben's feed, if he isn't actually old enough to cook his own tea. I'll go and see Dad tomorrow – it is useful having a doctor Dad who can do running repairs.

Anyway, I mustn't moan too much. There is one piece of good news... she bought the pram.

Home. Sunday, 25th May.

Off to the coast for a spot of darning. The last time Dad stitched me up (literally, I hasten to add) I was only ten. I remember lying on the kitchen table – stomach churning – while he boiled up the needles. During the actual stitching I didn't feel a thing, in fact Dad looked like he was suffering more than me. Mum was his assistant, helping him to put in the local and at the same time singing to me to calm me down.

Fifteen years on and the scenario was much the same. This time I was allowed to sit up and watch, although I wish I hadn't. It made me feel horribly queasy. Dad looked as bad as me, and Mum, instead of looking after us, just messed about with my son. Kids! There was I suffering, and it was Ben who was getting her rendition of *Muffin man* and *You are my sunshine*. (On second thoughts, maybe it was just as well.)

I only needed two stitches, which means my finger is in no imminent danger of falling off. Dad said I should avoid getting it wet – no long soaks. God, I can't even remember the last time I had a long hot bath, without Ben needing changing or feeding in the middle of it. And two half baths, with a chilly twenty minute period in the middle, just don't make a whole.

Eric didn't seem to get the same message as I did. "Don't worry," he reassured Dad, "she won't have to get it wet at all. I'll wash tonight – Louise can dry."

Home. Monday, 26th May.

Moving day is getting closer and closer, and despite my promise to Eric to stop putting things into boxes I had another go at packing. Our flat is tiny, but it is amazing how much junk we've managed to fit into it. We are going to have to get rid of some of our stuff, or else I can't see how we're going to move it all in one day – especially as we can't afford to hire a removal van. We have friends coming (Véronique and Stephan) who are going to put stuff in their car, and the rest is going to have to fit in Virginie. *Mon dieu.*

Chucked out a huge pile of Eric's cycling magazines (well, I've put them in a clean bin bag, Eric can make the clinching decision – one false move on my part could mean divorce) and I also sifted through a ridiculously enormous pile of administrative bumf. Do we really have to keep bank statements from four years ago? Or my first pay cheques? Or ancient bills from *Electricité de France?* I'm not sure, so I put everything I had doubts about in another clean bin bag to sort later.

Sorted clothes out next. I threw out the really worn stuff (another bin bag) and put aside reasonable things for *Secours Catholique* – a charity a bit like Oxfam but whose name does give it that French touch. I packed our sheets and blankets in yet more bags, as I'm sure that if we keep our parcels soft we will be able to squeeze more of them into the cars.

Eric came home to find a glistening black mountain of bin bags in our main room. He looked a tad alarmed but was quite pleased when I showed him how much stuff has been packed away. He won't, however, give way about the cycling mags – he says "if they go, I go." Hrrumph.

Ben seemed quite moved by the huge pile of bags – or at least his bowels were. He filled his nappy and the inside of his pyjama suit. Eric was holding him, so he was the man in the hot seat to do the change. He is brilliant at it – in two minutes had him in a clean nappy and sleep suit. He handed him to me with a smile... which quickly faded when he realised that as I had my hands full he was going to have to deal with the used nappy and the pile of evil looking baby-wipes. The bathroom bin was horribly full already, so he went into the kitchen and I heard him rooting around under the sink. He emerged twenty seconds later empty-handed and swearing under his breath.

We'd run out of bin bags.

Home. Tuesday, 27 May.

Went out shopping for bags, labels and masking tape. Incidentally, I'm sure the latter is only ever used by people moving house. Anyone who has ever tried it for painting knows it's useless. It either utterly fails to stick, so paint just creeps underneath and stains what you were trying to protect, or else sticks so hard that when you finally manage to rip it off it takes off several layers of paint. If you've never tried it take my advice: only ever use masking tape for making parcels.

Packed many more bags, including our shoes. I found my one and only pair of heels – the ones I wore for our wedding. I thought I'd try them on for old time's sake, and got a terrible shock – I mean it's one thing not being able to fit back into your wedding dress, but not managing to get into your shoes is quite unheard of.

I tried and tried, but there was no fitting my feet back into my dainty slippers. I have no idea what's happened – whether pregnancy has increased my shoe size or what – but apparently Cinderella has turned into an Ugly Sister. It's enough to make any girl despair.

I was still upset when Eric got home. I told him tearfully what was wrong, and he tried (unsuccessfully) to help me get my shoes on with a shoe horn and plenty of brute force. He also suggested using Vaseline, but I thought that was just getting obscene. In the end we gave up.

"*C'est pas grave!*" said my Prince Charming, " Ben still needs his 11pm feed, so you wouldn't have been able to go to the ball anyway."

Home. Wednesday, 28th May.

I've had enough of packing, so Ben and I accompanied Eric today to

Saint Emilion. He had to deliver and install a photocopier he'd sold at the *foire* to one of the most famous *châteaux*, and I thought that Ben and I could amble around the village while he worked.

It is a stunning place – a medieval village built on a rocky island surrounded by a sea of green vines. It is very close to Bordeaux, but has its own magnificent wine reputation. There are about a thousand *châteaux* here, but it is a little disappointing if you're hoping to see turrets. It's the quality of the vineyards which make a *château*, not the architecture of the buildings.

It wouldn't do justice to Saint Emilion to call it "quaint." There is something more than that here, something ancient and noble. It has a maze of higgledy-piggledy cobbled streets which run up and down its steep slopes, and two *lavoirs* where people once washed their clothes with fresh spring water. There is the fabulous monolithic church on the main square, and the cool, calm cloisters of the monastery. Under the village there are kilometres of catacombs – the ancient quarries which supplied the stone for the village. Now these caves have found their true vocation – as cellars for some of the world's finest wines. Wherever you are in the village there might be wine just beneath your feet, gradually maturing at a constant 12°C.

I carried Ben up the winding steps of the *Tour du Roy*, the King's Tower, and from the top we looked out over the red roofs where tiles are set at every angle, rippling down the straight slopes and swirling around the tops of other towers. Cats gaze haughtily from every crevice, blinking at the tourists and washing their paws in pools of sunlight. Beyond the roofs is the Dordogne valley, green fading to blue fading to sky.

Ben slumbered as I had a drink in the *bistrot* on the square. It was so bright I closed my eyes as I sipped my *citron pressé*, soaking up the sun and trying to absorb some of the inherent grandeur in the air, which permeates every stone in the village. It is a very special place.

It was peaceful today, which is more than can be said of the place in summer. Around one million tourists besiege the village. Serious wine buyers (they're the ones in suits, often Japanese) stride purposefully between the 99 wine shops. German tourists taste wine in every shop and buy very little. The Brits wander around looking baffled, and constantly appear to be looking for a Supermarket – of which there are none in the village.

Eric and I had an inside view of the wine industry here, as we both worked in a wine boutique during our first summer together. Our boss gave us strict instructions about how to sell wine, "What counts here is **selling**, not wine. Tell the customers any old thing but SELL THE STUFF!"

Five simple rules:

1. Always taste the wine with the customer and look intimidating.

2. Always hold the glass by its base (tickle its foot, not its tummy).

3. Hold the glass up to the light and utter thoughtful "aaaghs".

4. Stick your nose into the glass as far as you can, and always add at least two flavours to the ones your customer finds. Any old thing will do here; banana, ash, granny's knitting... you name it, a wine taster can find it.

5. Be nice to Japanese clients.

It was a terrible job, as the competition is so tough. I was feeling very despondent one day when Eric came in from his lunch break with a giant-sized Rum and Raisin ice-cream for me. A few minutes later, just as I was savouring it, the boss arrived. I hastily looked for a place to conceal it, and poked the point of the cone in one of the rubber bungs used for keeping the wine fresh and shoved the whole lot under the counter. When the boss left an hour later my glorious *glace* was just a yucky mess. I wiped off the bung as best I could and popped it back in the bottle.

Later on in the afternoon a group came in to taste wine (Japanese! Japanese!) and I poured them each a glass. I did everything according to the five simple rules (especially the last one) and there was much earnest discussion about what the flavour made them think of. After some time they came up with a unanimous decision; the dominant *parfum* was rum. Trying hard not to laugh I got on with preparing their order – they went away with six cases of the stuff.

Anyway, today we were here to relax. I sipped and eavesdropped on other people's conversations – my favourite *passe-temps*. A couple of English tourists were asking the senior waiter what Saint Emilion was like during the war – they wanted to know whether the villagers hid resistance workers or Jewish families in enormous labyrinth of tunnels and caves under our feet. The waiter looked uncomfortable, which is how most French people look when you ask them about the war. *Oui! Oui!* their families were all in the Resistance, but when you ask who did what and when, there it is again, that nervous tic in the eyelid and a gallic shrug. I'll always remember Eric producing a *froid* when he asked about his own family's role. What he deduced was that they organised a thriving section of the black market. It may not be *Secret Army* stuff, but it means he has salesmanship in his genes, and that this bodes well for our future income.

Well, this waiter had obviously been asked the same question many times before by tourists (er, except maybe the German ones) and trotted out his reply, "You know, the war was over, Germany had won and we had to get on with our business: selling wine. At least the Germans liked wine – not like those American troops who came after. They drank poison; Coca Cola!" Although he was very cheery about it, I still found it difficult to deal with. It *is* hard to imagine how one would react in a similar situation. Could carrying on with every day life, i.e. trading, really be seen as collaborating? Is surviving a crime? Of course not, but being rude about your liberators is a bit much. *Merde alors!*

Ooops, boys are back, *à plus!*

Home. Thursday, 29th May.

Back to yesterday, then! After my eavesdropping session in the *Bistrot* Eric came back unexpectedly and picked us up. I have no idea how he guessed that I would be in the bar having a drink rather than doing something cultural – it's a mystery to me. Anyway, he had said to the *château* owner that we were with him, and as he is a really nice chap he said we could come and have a look around his cellars.

It was a wonderful visit. Although the outside of the *château* looked modern and uninteresting, the inside was amazing. Computer controlled steel vats keep the wine at an ideal temperature at the surface level, but once you go underground you step back a few hundred years. We went along narrow tunnels hewn into the rock, and it felt as if we'd walked into the set of an *Indiana Jones* film. The catacombs were cut into the limestone in the Middle Ages, and wind under a monks' cemetery. Skulls stick through the roof and bones were piled high on every ledge. I looked carefully at the ground in front of us to make sure there were no swords about to spring through the floor, and sneaked a glance behind us to check for tunnel-sized boulders – the kind that bowl down passages like giant meatballs, crushing everything in their path. Everything seemed calm. After a few feet of passage the surface of the wall changed from rough rock to the glinting, smooth face of the round ends of bottles – the edge of a fifty thousand bottle stack of wine. This was just one year's harvest, now slumbering in the dark. *"Eh bien,"* chuckled the owner, stroking the glassy wall, "this is what *I* call Saint Emilion wallpaper."

The air was damp and cool, and smelt of vanilla and liquorice, which bodes well for the wine. As we explored we chatted about wine-making, and I asked if there were any *châteaux* left where grapes are crushed by people trampling on them with their bare feet. Even in the dark I could see how shocked he was. Stuttering slightly, he replied that in the past people used their feet to make wine, but now they use their heads. I had this mad image of people doing headstands in a vat of grapes before I realised what he meant. Oh dear.

He let me taste some of his delicious wine at the end of the visit, and I did pluck up the courage to ask him one last (and hopefully less idiotic) question – what was needed to make truly great wine? He laughed and said that one was easy; you need "old vines, poor soil and rich men." His vines were first planted by the Romans, the soil here is rock, and he *is* rich – not just financially, but rich with real love, knowledge and respect of his product. Maybe his recipe for wine is perfect; his wine *was* spectacular... even little Ben looked all excited when I tried some, I'm sure he wanted a taste. I suppose he really ought to wait a year or two.

Eric finished installing the photocopier and we were off. We thanked the owner for his visit, and he smiled and said *"de rien,"* – he was used to showing his *château* to people. The rich and famous have been here, and Chirac and Mittérand are both inscribed in his visitor's book. And now Ben's name is in there as well.

Home. Friday, 30th May.

Mad day at home, packing and unpacking things. WE ARE MOVING NEXT SATURDAY! ARGHH!!!! Eric leaves work next Friday!!!!!! It's all happening, yet we're stuck in an awful week of limbo. I have packed practically everything that is packable, so now all I can do is wait.

In the afternoon a couple came round to see the flat. They said it looked in good nick, so my Tippex balls in the wall were an obvious success. They seemed to find it quite small, but that may have been due to the fact that about half the flat is filled with boxes and bin bags. They had a peek into our back yard, but Dog was doing her impression of a sabre-toothed tiger, so they stayed on the safe side of the French windows. In spite of everything they were keen, and went off to the agents to sign. They are going to move in on Sunday. It all seems very imminent...

Mooched around trying to put things into boxes and then taking them out again. We can't really pack all our saucepans just yet, and we do need our bath towels, I suppose. I gave up and rang Véronique. I haven't seen her since she popped into the *maternité* to see Ben, as her little boy (who is 18 months old) got a bad dose of chicken pox just after, which she thought she would spare us. She has promised to come around tomorrow to help me make lists of last-minute things to do before they help us move next weekend. She said if we can't pack any more stuff tomorrow she will just admire Ben and make me cups of hot chocolate. Thank God for friends!

Last Saturday in Bordeaux centre ville. 31st May.

Stephan and Véro came – *génial!* Stephan and Eric went out for the day – they appear to have spent the morning wandering around Hifi shops, and the afternoon in a bike shop. Véro and myself shook our heads in bewilderment when they enthused about what a blissful time they'd had.

As promised, Véro admired Ben. He is the most gorgeous baby on the planet, after all. Her little Théo (cutest *toddler* on the planet) was more interested in all the boxes than in Ben. In fact, when we popped into the kitchen for a cup of tea he unpacked one of my larger parcels and post-ed the contents down the loo. Life is such fun when you are 18 months old.

We made lists about what we need to do this week, and planned Moving Day. One of the things I have to do pronto is replace the glass Superneighbour broke in the French windows when he rescued me, or else we'll lose a chunk of our deposit. There are lots of other little things to be done, but we've worked out a plan of action. As for Moving Day itself, we have a foolproof plan. We will all drive over to the farm with as much stuff as possible, and then Eric and Stephan will go back to Bordeaux to load up once more while Véro and I deal with the first load. We will keep the littl'uns with us, so we'll have to make sure we have all the necessary stuff for them in the first car load. (Nappies for the kids, the kettle, tea and a plentiful supply of Jaffa cakes for us. That should just about fill up Virginie.)

We all ate together this evening. Well, as together as you can be when you have small children. Ben needed feeding, bathing, changing, dressing and popping to bed (all of which happened during the starters and main course which Stephan and Eric had cooked) and Théo had all of the above – plus story time which is a recent addition to the evening routine. We couldn't sit down together until the meal was over and done, and then it seemed a bit pointless to sit around a pile of dirty dishes. We ended up having a *digestif* (this is the after-meal equivalent of the *apéritif,* it's alcoholic and has nothing whatsoever to do with biscuits) and then wandered into the kitchen to do the washing up. Is this the shape of dinner parties to come????

JUIN

Home. Sunday, 1st June.

Yummy sunny day, made sunnier by the fact that this is the last time Eric has to get ready for work on Monday morning! No more Sunday evening depression! On Monday morning next week he'll probably be out of doors at dawn, digging the garden or building a dry stone wall or some such. No more evil boss! No more office! No more suit and tie! (No more income...)

Home. Monday, 2nd June.

Eric set off to work early, determined to make as much money as possible in his last week at work. I had Ben all ready for action at 9 o'clock – dressed and fed and in the baby carrier – and we went out to buy a new pane of glass for the French windows. The local hardware store isn't far, but it was still quite a challenge to carry a baby and a large sheet of glass home. I must be Wonderwoman.

The lady in the shop had explained very carefully how to fit the pane, so after Ben's morning snack I set about it. She'd said that it was very important to make sure the frame was clear of any bits of glass, then fit the pane and smooth the putty all around the edges. Easy enough. I had no problems at all until the last part, when I was slicking the putty into the join – and making a *very* professional job of it, I might add. Sadly, I can't have done the first step properly, because a razor sharp piece of glass sliced into the top of my finger. The same one as I hurt last week. Oh God.

It was bad. On my personal scale of badness – at number one you have paper-cut wounds, and at ten chainsaw injuries – this scored a definite five. I left a note for Eric (he said later that the bloodstains on it were pretty scary, he thought I'd either been murdered or that it was a suicide note) then I bundled Ben into the car and drove to Mum and Dad's. Mum shook her head with disbelief when I showed her what I'd done. Dad just went off and got his stitching gear. He took out the stitches he'd put in last week and put in another two at the top of my finger.

Now I'm back home, all mended. I have a stern warning to be good from now on – any more cuts and he'll use his medical knowledge to skin me alive.

Home. Tuesday, 3rd June.

I was flicking through the paper today (taking great care not to cut my finger tips on the edge of the pages, *bien sûr)* when I found an ad for a pushchair – the exact same one that I've been saving up for. The ad also mentioned *articles diverses pour bébé.* It sounded interesting, so I thought I'd give it a whirl.

I was a somewhat thrown when the lady who picked up the phone spoke in a voice that made me think she was about a hundred.

Was this a *maman?*

"*Bonjour!*" I said brightly, and asked what exactly was for sale.

Many *ehs* and *comments* and *quois* later I managed to get across the idea that I wanted a list of what was for sale. It was hard going – this was a crackly line to the heart of rural France. Madame was hard of hearing and didn't even know that there was an ad in the paper, and her husband, who had placed the ad for his daughter, didn't have his dentures in and didn't want to come to the phone.

There was a great deal of relaying of messages and Marital Dispute before I got an answer.

"*Bon, des vêtements pour bébé, une poussette et une charrue.*" I understood but only on a linguistic level; they were selling baby clothes, a pushchair and a ... plough.

"A plough?" I echoed faintly. "What exactly are you calling a plough?" – thinking it might be some natty piece of baby equipment I hadn't yet discovered.

"In the olden days," she said, "oxen used to pull..." *Mon Dieu!* I thought – she really *is* talking about a plough. I thought I should get her off the subject, so I asked whether the pushchair would fit into the boot of a car.

"Well," she replied, "I can't see any problem with fitting the pushchair into a car boot, but you'll need a trailer for the plough..."

I rang off after that. Rural France is a Strange and Scary place – and we're moving there.

Home. Wednesday, 4th June.

Rang the owner of the house today to see if we can bring over any of our stuff before Saturday. Our main problem is the washing machine. It will take a separate trip to take it over, and as time will be tight on Moving Day it would be as well to do it before.

The owner said *pas de problème*, we could come around tomorrow. As Eric wanted to take it over straight after work, we thought we'd load it tonight. It wasn't fun.

We measured it and measured Virginie's boot and doors. It didn't take a genius to see that there was no way it would fit in. Happily I had a brilliant idea (that *did* require genius) and suggested we lower it in through the soft top. Eric looked appalled, but it really was the only solution. And as I was the brains behind the idea I thought Eric could be the muscle.

Eric copped out of doing it alone, and called up to Superneighbour, who was on his balcony. He didn't actually fly, but he bounded down the staircase three steps at a time – obviously he'd just had a fresh dose of kryptonite. In no time at all they lifted the machine out to the car, but then they stalled. It wasn't going to be easy – this machine is Seriously Heavy.

I retreated indoors with Ben, and as I fed him I watched them through the window. Superneighbour was on the other side of the car, and was hidden by the machine's extraordinarily bulky bulk. I could see Eric though – swearing and sweating as he tried to get the impossibly heavy machine through the small sunroof. I'll never forget his look of panic and severe pain. For just a moment I had the feeling this is what I looked like when I was giving birth.

Now all is well. The washing machine is in Virginie, and she weighs about twice as much as before. Superneighbour, having drunk lots of tea and eaten a dozen chocolate biscuits, has retired upstairs, and Eric is nursing his torn muscles in a hot bath. He has to recover ASAP – I mean tomorrow he's got to lift it *out* of the car...

Home. Thursday, 5th June.

We set off to our new home when Eric got home from work. Ben sat in his car seat in the front, Eric drove and I perched on the wheel arch, squashed between the washing machine and the wall of the car. It was agony, but nothing was going to stop me from enjoying myself. The countryside was utter heaven – the grass so sweet and long that hay-making will start any day, and the grape vines in flower. We went the scenic way to the farm, and just the names of the villages we passed through got me sold on the idea that this was a weird and wonderful place to live. Imagine living in a place called *Chant de Merle* "Blackbird's song", *90 Journaux* "90 newspapers" or even *Guette s'il pleut,* which means "Take a peek and see if it's raining." Our hamlet is called *La Grave.* It doesn't sound cheerful in English, but in French it means gravel, which the river has scattered along its banks. We will be just a stone's throw from another hamlet named *Bonnet.*

Our landlady was waiting in the garden with her two sons and daughter. They'd all come over to help clean the house before we moved in. We went inside to admire the work. Eric said it was very kind of them, but that he actually enjoys doing housework. He spent four years in the Navy washing down decks, so washing the kitchen floor is a cinch is comparison. "I like doing housework much more than my wife does." He said.

This is considered quite a revolutionary concept in rural France, and everyone stared at me. There were terrible vibes, and I'm sure they have me down as 100% sluttish. I tried to change the subject – we were standing in the kitchen, and in a flash of inspiration I asked what they were taking with them and what they were leaving. *"Le réfrigerateur, par exemple,"* I said, vaguely gesturing at a big white metal machine in the corner of the kitchen. They all looked at each other, and my landlady (looking at me as though I was either mentally subnormal or from another planet entirely) informed me that what I'd taken to be a fridge was, in fact, a top-loading washing machine.

It was an uncomfortable moment – not made remotely better by Eric's attempt to rescue me. (Actually, it wasn't so much an attempt to help me

78

so much as wanting to show we'd keep her house spick and span.) "Er" he said, " I clean the kitchen at home every day, but my wife, well, she's a dab hand at cleaning windows."

It was all very embarrassing, but we didn't dwell on it for long. Eric pointed out that we had to get our washing machine out of the car, and asked whether her sons and daughter (all fully grown and sturdy looking, I might add) would help us.

Things got better after that. Eric and his team hauled the machine out as I held Ben and chatted to our landlady, who told me to call her Marie -Thérèse. I noticed the giant-sized cross around her neck (almost as big as the original version, so I could hardly fail to notice it) and struck up a conversation about Pentecost, which is this weekend. She looked thrilled to find someone who knew a little bit about it (C of E infant school level, anyway) and by the time the washing machine was installed she'd declared herself to be a *grenouille de bénitier,* or Font Frog. This is what you call keen churchgoers in France. In my enthusiasm to get away from any subject whatsoever relating to housework I chatted away eagerly with her, and I have a horrible sinking feeling I might have given her the impression I'll join the church choir. Oh dear.

When we said *au revoir* she squeezed my hand and gave me a mean-ingful look. *Mon dieu* – I felt such a rat. The ride home, however, jerked me out of my *crise de conscience;* Eric was all smiles because he leaves work tomorrow, little Ben was cooing in his car seat, and Virginie bowled happily along the lanes, glad to be rid of her terrible burden. Life is too wonderful to feel bad for long.

Last day in Bordeaux. Friday, 6th June.

Nearly there! We are actually doing this thing! Eric came home from work tonight and took off his suit for the last time. Tomorrow our lives are going to change.

It is going to be so different having Eric around, and seeing him doing something he really wants to do. Even tonight he's got one of his new textbooks out and has started studying. Of course the thing that will be another major change will be to share Ben more. Not that I haven't enjoyed having him all to myself. I had been warned that the first three months of a baby's life are tough, and they certainly were. I think Spock's phrase from *Star Trek* sums it up – "It's Life, Jim, but not as we know it." It's a strange time, a piquant mix of joy, despair, bursts of energy, chronic tiredness and oddly stained washing.

Maybe in the new house I will shortly give up my membership of the Lonely Parents' Night Club; that international society of adults who freeze away the moonlit hours on the landing, wondering whether to hang on for another five minutes before going to bed (briefly) or wait until Junior rises again. New parents are a Pale Nocturnal Species akin to ghosts... the time I stumbled into Eric at 3am in the corridor, when he was off to the loo and I was coming back from breastfeeding Ben (with my white tee-shirt still over my head) I nearly gave him a heart attack. I lacked only a clanking chain. Still, in the new house I'm sure Ben will sleep properly, drunk from the country air and all that.

These last three months have been hard, but I suppose it's a difficult period for any couple to get through. We've had nights when it seemed it was the end of Us and the end of the world. Sometimes (somewhat, unfairly, perhaps) I claimed I wasn't thinking of becoming a divorcée but a widow. Now things are settling... our couple has become a family.

My friends have cheered me up by saying that the first eighteen years of child rearing are the hardest. Others have added that having kids is a very hit and miss affair – sometimes you hit them and sometimes you miss them. I'm looking forward to giving Ben a Perfect Childhood, out in the fresh air with cheeks ruddy like sweet red apples. And telling the time on dandelion clocks, his fingers all purpley from blackberrying.

Oh dear, maybe this is becoming a little fanciful.

Time for bed.

Home. Home on the Range (and totally knackered). Saturday, 7th June.

Chez-nous at last. Moving Day is now a thing of the past – thank God.

Véro, Stephan and Théo arrived at eight o'clock, which was wonderful as we had an awful lot to move. Our few sticks of furniture suddenly seemed like a mighty forest. Stephan is a physicist, and said we should have a scientific approach to furniture removals. Each vehicle would take about two cubic metres of stuff, so we should try to count up the total number of cubic metres and divide it by the number of vehicles so as to calculate how many trips it was going to take. I can tell you one thing – it is *hard* to imagine one's possessions in cubes. I tried to visualise how big a cube my aquarium, boots and coat-stand would take, while Eric worried about whether he wanted his much-loved racing bicycle to share a cubic metre with anything at all.

Stephan was still doing his sums while Véro and I loaded up *Virginie*. Apparently Ben, Théo, Dog, the kettle, Jaffa cakes and a collapsible carrycot take up two cubic metres of space. A bit more than that, in fact, as the top of the carrycot was poking out of the sunroof. It was a good thing it wasn't raining.

We were off before Stephan had finished calculating, leaving Eric rushing around and carrying things out to the other car. He was having a hard time keeping the television, the remote control and his sanity together.

Véro was amazed when she saw the farm. She wandered around the house and through the garden, and within minutes had installed Théo on a swing under the lime tree. They both had blissful smiles on their faces, as though they'd just found paradise.

I put the kettle on, and took the back seat out of Virginie and put it out on the grass. We sat down and had our first cup of tea in our new home, while Ben slept in his carrycot, Théo swung and Dog bounced happily through the grass, scattering the crickets and the butterflies.

The arrival of *les hommes* was a little unwelcome, as we had to get up and start work. They dumped everything on the lawn and went back to Bordeaux, and we started carrying the boxes one by one into the house. Ben woke up half an hour later, and by the time I'd fed him and changed his nappy they were back with another two loads, as they'd taken both cars. We were a little overwhelmed, as Ben was fretful and Théo wanting lunch. While we ate our sandwiches more stuff arrived, and we felt even more lost. We worked hard until four o'clock ferrying boxes inside, but just as we sat down for a breather our new neighbour arrived.

She is quite a character. She is a roofer, tall and tough with shoulders as wide as a barn door. We were amazed to find someone who dared defy sexist tradition, and curious to find out more we accepted her offer to pop round to her house for a drink.

'Pop round' was not really the right term, as although she's our nearest neighbour she lives about nearly a kilometre away, next to the landing stage on the river. Her cottage was sparsely furnished but welcoming, and as we sat around her scrubbed wooden kitchen table with our little boys on our knees it felt positively homely. She (oops, I should really say at this point that she introduced herself as Cathérine) gave us a tumbler glass each, and Véro and I looked at each other with astonishment as she all but filled them up with whisky. We weren't sure how to refuse, especially as she banged her fist on the table and said *"buvez, mesdames!"*

We didn't drink much, but it was enough to stop me following her conversation about how she came to be a roofer. She also got out all her hunting trophies and showed us her gun, and by the time we eventually got away Ben and Théo were asleep in our arms, anaesthetised by the whisky fumes.

It was late afternoon when we staggered back to the farm – Théo squealing with delight as the ride on his Mummy's shoulders was so wobbly. Stephan and Eric had just arrived, and were a little nonplussed to find so much stuff still in the garden. Still, Eric swung me into his arms and gave me a kiss to welcome me to our new home. He put me down a bit abruptly though. "I thought you two were going to be drinking tea this afternoon – how come you smell of whisky?"

I tried to stand up for us, but my legs failed me. Véro was already lying down on the grass, and I joined her. Eric and Stephan said we should be ashamed of ourselves, and accused us of being drunk in charge of two boys and at least twenty cubic metres of cardboard boxes. We lay there in disgrace while our boys slept and our husbands carried the most essential of our things into the house. The furniture was set to spend the night under the tree.

Véro, Stephan and Théo left in the early evening, and Eric and I grabbed a bite to eat (which fortunately absorbed the rest of the whisky that had been sloshing about uncomfortably in my stomach) then we set up our bed and Ben's cot in the main bedroom. We turned in early; we both need to get our energy levels up for a day of unpacking tomorrow. Eric fell into an exhausted sleep straight away, but I'm lying awake, in this strange and wonderful room, writing my diary by the light of the dozen candles I found on the kitchen shelf. I can hear the unfamiliar sound of the river, and now it's really dark our upstairs neighbours have woken up – it seems that there are barn owls in the hayloft over our heads. They are hissing away up there – maybe they have chicks? Tomorrow we'll have to sneak a peek through the *oeil de boeuf* in the end wall of the loft and see. But then, as they say, tomorrow is another day. Right now all I can do is sleeeeeeep...

Home, Ferme de la Grave. Sunday, 8th June.

The start of our first day here was just *merveilleux*. I'd fed Ben and brought him into our bed at some ungodly hour of morn, but then we fell sound asleep again. Without the noise of Bordeaux' rush hour, the dustmen or the cracked crowing of Superneighbour's cockerel (the poor creature's larynx obviously couldn't cope with traffic fumes) we slept until 8.30am – our longest lie-in for months.

We didn't realise it was so late, as it was so quiet and dark that it felt like the dead of night. The old wooden shutters may look battered but they keep out even the tiniest chink of light. When we did open them the daylight came as a shock, so bright and warm already. The greenery looked almost fluorescent and the river alight with golden sunshine. It was irresistible.

Still in our pyjamas we raced out into the garden. The remains of the morning mist was rising, and it felt like we were in a dream. It was too beautiful to go back indoors, and we were glad that we hadn't brought in the furniture yesterday. We put Ben in his bouncy chair next to us, and dragged our table and chairs out from under the tree and into the sun. Cornflakes al fresco are wonderful! Better still, when I accidentally knocked my coffee off the table we didn't even have to reach for the floor cloth. You don't have to mop a lawn.

During breakfast we noticed that there was a good deal of splashing going on in the river. Squinting at the shining surface we could see dozens of fish jumping. I think we may have to go back on our promise not to go fishing again, especially as some of these guys are big. They are obviously some kind of a freshwater variety of tuna. Or whales.

Today we had other things on the agenda, but as it turned out we didn't do that much work. We carried our furniture inside and each piece found its new home – it was strange how everything fitted where we wanted it to, as though the house had been expecting us – but we didn't slog all day long. At lunchtime we'd already started pottering around the garden and the barn, and by two o'clock we'd packed up work entirely. The boxes could wait – we had exploring to do.

We began by walking up the hill behind the house. At the top there is our very own wood, which is starting to take over the entire hillside. Hawthorn and wild roses grow in thick woody clumps, and saplings are springing up everywhere. There are paths all over the hill, made by deer and rabbits and other furry friends. It was quite hard to get into the little wood, and we had to cut a path through the brambles that surrounded it. It was like the garden around the palace in *Sleeping Beauty,* but once we were into the wood the ground was clear, as there wasn't enough light for brambles and creepers. Our eyes took a while to become accustomed to the gloom, but soon we could make out the different sorts of trees and see the forest floor. And it soon became clear that we were not alone.

Eric found our woodland dwellers first. He was walking along holding Ben in the baby sling, and looking more at Ben's dear face than at the ground, when he put his foot down a huge hole, more than a foot across. (Well, more than Eric's foot and half a leg, anyway.) He extracted it and we looked at each other with wide eyes. Had we found another Lascaux? I said I was sure this had been dug by an animal, but what could be so big? They have bears in the Pyrenees, but not here. We took a good look around and found many more tunnels and banks of sand over three feet high which had been dug out of them. We also found shallow holes filled with animal dung, but we weren't sure what kind of animal was responsible. It was only when we made our last find – piles of used straw bedding – that we finally agreed on what we were looking at: a gigantic badger set.

We're going to keep our discovery a secret, as badger culling is approved of both on a national and on a local level here. We don't want the beastly hunters to get ours. The reason given for all this killing is that badgers eat crops, especially corn. In England the argument behind limiting badger populations is that they spread tuberculosis to dairy cattle, but France is a little idiosyncratic about this disease. For example, it was a Frenchman, Louis Pasteur, who invented the brilliant pasteurisation processes which means milk can be free of germs, yet the average French person still sees *lait cru,* literally raw milk, as the healthy option. Cheese made with *lait cru* is a delicacy. Anyway, Eric says that he thinks badger culling in France has precious little scientific evidence to justify it. I'm sure he's right, and that the bottom line is that many macho Frenchmen love blood sports... and the hunting lobby is powerful. We are going to keep quiet about our badgers, and just enjoy their company.

We had a picnic tea under the apple tree halfway up the hill, and then we went back down to the house. We were covered in thorns, burrs, grass seeds, dust, dirt and a thick layer of fatigue, and we decided it was bath time.

Our bathroom is tiny, and not like something you'd find in *Ideal Home*. The walls are an ugly gas-station shiny blue and the sink is hanging on by a couple of rusty screws and a thick strand of cobweb. The toilet is cold and iron-stained (well, I *hope* it's iron) and it has a horrid cracked bakelite surround that has already pinched my bum twice today. But the bath – the bath is *magnifique!* It is huge, a claw-footed *piscine*, and we filled it right up with spring water which spouted out of the antique taps. Eric and I sat at each end, with Ben between us. He took his first strokes in its white enamelled depths, wriggling through the water from one end to the other. This wasn't just bath time, this was a Life Experience.

Now he's tucked up in his cot, and Eric and I are lying awake listening to the owls. Eric says he has half a mind to walk up the hill to the woods, and watch for the badgers in the moonlight. But then there are other things to do after dark... Ben is sleeping *very* soundly, after all. And neither Eric nor I have unpacked the books we've been reading at bedtime. Hmmm, I think I'll put my diary down.

Home. Monday, 9th June.

Delicious lie-in again, made better by the feeling that other people were going to work. Ha!

Eric sat down to do some studying in the morning, while I got on with unpacking. We are so happy with the few things we have unpacked that the dozens of boxes piled up in the end room seem a bit like an unwanted and cumbersome burden at the moment. Still, we will have to deal with them all sooner or later, and I made a good start by unpacking all the kitchen stuff.

I lay Ben down on a floor cushion while I dragged the boxes into the kitchen, and his bright eyes watched my every move as I worked. I screwed hooks into the shelf above the sink, and hung up all our mugs. Then I hung all our steel saucepans from the wooden curtain rail. We don't have any curtains, after all, and Ben loved watching the pans shining in the morning sun. They were better than any mobile – a little knock with the broom handle to set them swinging and his little face flowered into a smile. We have one very tall and thin cupboard (a supermodel among kitchen furniture) and I was packing plates and bowls into it and thinking how roomy it looked inside when I worked out why. Our

cupboard didn't have a scrap of food in it – I guess it really *does* have a lot in common with a supermodel.

I went outside to tell Eric I was going shopping. He was sitting under the tree studying at the kitchen table, which we still haven't brought indoors. Dog was lying at his feet, stretched out in the sun and looking a picture of happiness. Eric shoved aside his books (it is hard concentrating when you are studying at home) and said he wanted to come with me. We left Dog to guard the house and were off.

We drove to the village – Eric was all excited about seeing people working while he's free. Strangely, there were lots of people about, playing *pétanque* on the tiny square and chatting in the sun. The two village shops were closed. We were baffled and Eric was Positively Annoyed – he'd come to gloat and had been done out of it. And we couldn't buy any lunch. We drove all the way to the nearest town, Libourne, before we found a shop that was open. Only then did it dawn on us why there were so many people in the streets – there was a sign on the supermarket door saying it was open for *Pentecôte*. A tad disorientated by the move we'd completely forgotten it was Pentecost – another day off in France. The entire country was on holiday!

We bought a few things – cheese, ham, olives, bread and a bottle of red wine. Going round the supermarket here was not the same as shopping in Bordeaux. In the city people keep themselves to themselves, but here people kept stopping to look at Ben. Unfortunately, it wasn't to admire him but to tell me I should have put a warm hat on his head, to cover his ears. Never mind the sunny weather, a cold draught from somewhere or other could harm him. It's an old wives' tale in France that cold air gives babies ear infections, and plenty of people (not just old wives!) came up to tell me so. Eric shrugged it off but I got more and more irritated, and it was a relief to finish the shopping and head for home. The bread smelt so delicious in the car that it took every scrap of our willpower not to guzzle it all on the spot. For once we succeeded, and when we got back we ate outside. Ben lay in the warm sun next to us – oblivious to the threat of dangerous draughts – gazing at the leaves with a contented smile on his face. Eric said he was just enjoying being outside, but maybe he was thinking about a career in botany. We'll see.

After lunch I cleared the table (well, chucked the paper plates away and put the remaining crumb of cheese into the cupboard – at least 100 calories, that cupboard is going to double in size) and got on with finishing the kitchen. Ben was being angelic, still grinning at the saucepans, so I set about rigging up a kitchen worktop. Marie-Thérèse had left the kitchen empty except for an old stove which I swear starred in an episode of *Upstairs, Downstairs.* We really needed some work surfaces, so I put two trestles against the wall and placed planks – our bookshelves from the flat – across them. Once I'd put a cheerful table cloth on top it looked great. I unpacked the rest of our glasses and lined them up along the back of it, and with the addition of a big vase of daisies from the garden it looked Splendid. Laura Ashley, pah! I'm just as good.

I called Eric in to have a look. He was having another study period in the garden. Actually, he was studying lying down on the grass with his eyes closed, but said this was just a concentration exercise. He came into the kitchen and said *bravo, ma chérie!* He went over for a closer look, and tested the work surface for strength. He banged his hand down on it, and it stood firm. I don't know why he did the next thing, but he shook it from side to side. Instantly the end trestle capsized, and before we could do anything about it the glasses and the vase had smashed on the floor. The tiles were covered in fragments of glass and a lake of water from the vase, but amidst the chaos Ben lay on his cushion in the corner, his smile ever wider. I may be no great shakes at home decoration, but I'm the Very Best in home entertainment.

Well, enough of that game. I'm in need of fun and fresh air. Tomorrow we are going to stay out on the river bank in the sun. That crumb of cheese is going to be put to good use. We're going fishing.

Home. Tuesday, 10th June.

We breakfasted under our tree once again, and as we munched we discussed fishing strategies. We're both experts, of course, and it's quite hard for experts to agree. Ben sat it his bouncy chair looking from one of us to the other, as though trying to make up his mind who was right. We agreed that we'd fish on the same bit of bank, so that we could share looking after Ben and show off to each other as we landed our catch.

Our first step was preparation – neither of us could remember which box we'd packed the fishing rods in. This was also somewhat complicated by the fact that of the remaining thirty or so boxes eight are labelled 'books' and the other thirty-two 'various.' We opened quite a few at random, and found the Christmas decorations, Eric's trainers and the photograph albums, but nothing resembling a fishing rod.

We were in a bit of a quandary, but decided we'd pop along to the village shop and see what they had. Eric assured me that the cheapest bamboo rods are cheap, the price of a kilo of fish, and providing we fished well with them they would pay for themselves. He finally convinced me by saying that a couple more rods would always come in useful. We could have fishing parties with friends, and our Dads would both be delighted to have a go. And Ben could learn to fish with one of the new rods. (I thought this was a little premature, but he'd already won me round anyway...)

We drove to the village, which was empty today except for a couple of old ladies carrying their shopping. Some people are at work in Bordeaux, but most are back in the fields working on their farms. On the way to the village we'd seen farmers busy inspecting the vines and the corn, and others cleaning their grass cutters, getting ready to gather in the hay. We were the only two young people out shopping, and we felt suddenly guilty about having free time. Eric promised he'd do twice as much studying tonight to make up for it.

The village store was a weird shop, dark and dusty and a bit like Aladdin's cave. It was full of cobwebs, not in the least bit like any of the shops we'd seen in Bordeaux. There were things piled high on every shelf, and on top of the piles there were cats. It was hard to see what was actually for sale, but as far as we could tell they seemed to specialise in brass horseshoes, engine oil, spades, bizarrely assorted vegetables and peculiar children's toys – such as hard plastic dolls with strange complexions, leftovers from the fifties. Hanging from the ceiling there were fish traps, rat traps, mole traps, fly traps and, I think, man traps. But I couldn't see a fishing rod anywhere.

Eric rang the brass bell on the counter, and a man emerged from out the back. He was tiny and wrinkled, and on his head (which Eric said later, rather unkindly, looked as though it'd been shrunk by cannibals) he had the largest beret I'd ever seen. He was carrying a huge tom cat, and struggling under its weight he heaved himself up onto the stool behind the counter, set his cat down on the counter itself, and began to talk quietly into one of its furry ears.

He seemed to be so deep in conversation that we didn't want to interrupt, but Eric cleared his throat and asked politely whether he had a fishing rod for sale. He looked up at us and glared, as though we'd made some terrible *faux pas*. With a dark scowl he pointed us in the direction of the toys.

He was so objectionable that we almost told him to keep his fishing rods and go and boil his head, but he looked like he'd already done that. Instead we went to the back of the shop and sorted through the toys. There were only two rods, a bamboo one about three feet long with a cowboy and Indian painted on the handle, and the other bright pink plastic, decorated with a topless mermaid and with a reel shaped like a killer whale. I thought I might be able to use the bamboo one, and Eric had immediately fallen for the voluptuous mermaid. It was a bit embarrassing purchasing such items, so we thought we'd pretend we were buying them for Ben. I'm not sure he was taken in by our *"c'est pour le petit"*, but he wrapped them up in brown paper and took a few francs for them without saying a word. Eric whispered in my ear that he was glad he wasn't there to sell him a photocopier.

It was only as we were going out the door that he finally said something. He got off his stool, shuffled towards us and pointed at Ben with one gnarled finger. *"Madame,"* he croaked, his voice rusty from disuse, "you ought to buy that baby a warm hat."

When we got home we tackled (no pun intended) the bait problem. We only had one small piece of cheese, so Eric thought he'd dig a few worms. And dig he did, because the worms appeared to have gone into hiding. Eric scraped under logs, lifted up flagstones and dug holes all over the lawn. He said if chickens – which aren't reputed to be terribly bright – can find worms then he wasn't going to fail. He began to dig a hole which got so deep that I wasn't sure whether he was digging or mining. And still no worms.

I didn't want him to spend all day in a hole in the ground, so I suggested we go back to the village store to see if he had any maggots for sale. Many general village shops in France do sell bait and I thought it was worth a try. I'd definitely seen some in the racks of vegetables, but I wasn't sure whether these were for sale. I stayed in the car with Ben while Eric went inside to investigate, and he emerged a few minutes later with a white tub of maggots. The shop-keeper hadn't been any nicer, but at least he'd found what he wanted.

On the way back I twisted round to put the tub on the floor, as I wasn't really enjoying having a stinking mass of maggots on my lap. I was just lowering them over the back of the seat when the car hit a rut – the tub bounced out of my hand and split open when it hit the floor. Instantly the car was filled with a terrible stench, and there were maggots wriggling all the place.

Eric screeched to a halt, and we spent a very nasty few minutes scrabbling around in the back trying to retrieve as many maggots as possible. Ben, as is always the case when we have a disaster, was obviously thoroughly enjoying himself. I'm sure he thought we were having a great time.

Once home we called Dog and went off to the river – at last. We baited our hook with a smidgen of cheese and with a maggot or two – which seemed to be a delicacy for the local fish. We were astonished when we had our first bite, and even more so when our trusty mermaid and Wild West rods began reeling in the fish.

Soon we had so many that we had to stop. We don't have a freezer and it would be pointless to catch more than we could eat. I sat in the garden while Ben had his sleep and Eric built a barbecue with stones from the river. I must have dozed off with Ben, because when we both woke up the garden was filled with the mouth-watering smell of fish grilling over the fire. Minutes later we had one of the most delicious meals in my entire life: fresh fish, home-caught and home-cooked.

I could get used to this.

Home. Wednesday, 11th June.

No need to go fishing today. Eric went to explore the village library this morning, as he thinks it might be easier to study if he's away from distractions – such as myself, hrumph. I went off for a walk with Ben to see the badger set, and when I got back I saw someone had closed our kitchen shutters.

I wasn't sure what I expected to find, but when I folded them back there was a bloodstained package behind them. In the back of my mind I began to panic – this was scary stuff. Struggling to be Grown-up and Sensible I opened up the newspaper surrounding it, and was horrified to discover fur. Upon closer inspection, all was revealed. There was a very dead bunny on my window sill.

I wasn't sure what to make of this. It was only when I found a piece of paper pinned to the rabbit that I understood what this was all about. It was short and sweet, simply saying: *"Bon appetit, Cathérine."*

I brought the rabbit into the kitchen and waited for Eric to get home. I haven't the faintest idea how to skin a rabbit, let alone transform it into something you would enjoy eating. I was a vegetarian throughout my teenage years, and this kind of thing goes a little against the grain. Eric, on the other hand, was brought up in the country, and knows about Such Things.

Eric came up trumps, and when he came home he not only skinned and gutted Buggs, but also turned him into rabbit stew. He told me to stay away during the preparations, as he didn't find my gagging particularly helpful.

Tonight we have dined handsomely. If I put the animal out of my mind I found myself eating with gusto. Eric couldn't understand why I was worried about eating a 'real' rabbit. He argued that it had been reared outside in Cathérine's rabbit pen, eating nothing but fresh grass and vegetables. He said it wasn't like the kind of farming you see on TV, where animals live in cramped surroundings and are fed antibiotics, steroids and proteins of dubious origin so that they put on a maximum amount of weight before dying a miserable death.

It may have been an ordinary rabbit stew for Eric, but for me it was food for thought.

We had a walk along the river afterwards, as dusk fell. Although it was late an elderly couple and a younger man were out in their meadow, gathering in the hay. The light was soft and warm, and swallows were skimming over the surface of the field. They were feasting – scooping up the insects that rose in clouds whenever another hay bale was tossed with the fork onto the trailer.

It was hard work, and we saw the two men stop to have a drink. They had both taken their tee-shirts off, but their suntans made it look as though they were both still wearing white ones. The old woman, who was driving the battered tractor (surely an antique?) gave us a friendly wave. As we turned back towards home the men picked up their hay forks again, and work started anew. We heard the woman's voice asking which gear to use, and the old man's reply, which seemed to come from another age (before the rat-race was even thought of) warmed our hearts. He looked around, taking in the beauty of the evening, the rosy sky and the hay bales still to be gathered, before calling out *"lente."*

Home. Thursday, 12th June.

Our spring water has stopped running! I was washing up at lunchtime when the water from the kitchen tap slowed to a trickle, and then stopped all together. It had also stopped running into the trough in the barn. We were philosophical, and decided not to grumble but to go out and buy some mineral water to drink, and some more paper cups and plates.

Eric phoned Marie-Thérèse tonight, but she was oddly evasive on the phone. She said to wait a couple of days and it should get back to normal.

No bath tonight!

Home. Friday, 13th June.

Friday the thirteenth, but nothing particularly dreadful happened. In France it is seen as a day of luck, which may be good or bad, but we didn't have any good luck either. Our water hasn't started flowing again. The worst of it is that we're sure the spring hasn't dried up – on the hillside it is bubbling over the top of the cistern. It's maddening to have so much water and not be able to have any in the house. I'm sick of trying to wash with a mingy wetwipe instead of cavorting in the bath! I'm tired of eating picnic food as we can't cook! And if this goes on for much longer we're going to be in Serious Danger of being smothered by the biggest pile of dirty washing known to humankind.

Home. Saturday, 14th June.

STILL NO WATER!

Home. Sunday, 15th June.

Eric was trying to shave with baby oil this morning when his patience over the water situation finally ran out. He told me to man (or woman, or whatever) the taps in the house whilst he went to inspect the pipework on the hillside.

I turned on all the taps while he went up the hill. I thought his inspection was going to be Highly Technical, but I'm not sure that kicking a pipe with all your might and swearing at it is what a real technician would do. I couldn't hear much as the spring outlet is some way from the house, but did make out the French equivalent of "sod you, you bastard, I want a bath!"

Seconds later he was leaping down the hill, waving his arms above his head in victory and yelling with delight. He'd heard a gurgling noise in the pipe, and then had seen the water start to flow into the house pipe again.

We went into the kitchen, where nothing was coming out of the tap, and saw the same thing in the bathroom. Then we went into the stable, where we thought we could hear a faint hissing from the big pipe which fills it. Eric (really getting into this technical thing) gave it an almighty whack, whereupon one dead and well rotted mole shot out. It must have decomposed just enough to fit through the pipe, and now it was out the water could go through again.

We went inside the house and found water pouring into the sink and bath – hooray! Still, it is UTTERLY GROSS to think our main water supply had a dead animal in it. I mean I'm only just getting used to eating animals again – I'm certainly not keen on drinking them. Ugh.

Eric has rigged up a kind of filter with some wire mesh, so I hope it won't happen again. We have left our taps running all day to clean them out, but it's going to be a while before I will be able to contemplate drinking the water. It was Wonderful to have a bath, though. I just wasn't so sure how I felt about brushing my teeth...

Home. Monday, 16th June.

I rang Marie-Thérèse this morning to tell her the water problem had sorted itself out. I didn't want to explain things further – I'd really like her to pay for us to be connected to the mains, but as we've only been here five minutes I don't want to put pressure on her. Especially as I didn't turn up for choir rehearsal.

Maybe I should say at this point that I am in NO way against choirs. I sang in the choir at school (the Klangers Choir) and liked it, and when I came to France to teach English in the *lycée* (as part of my university degree) I joined the local choir to meet people. There was a generation gap – a ravine, actually – but I had fun and also met one of my dearest friends, Danièle. She was a student, and we immediately got on like a house on fire. I remember going back to her house one evening after choir practice to have dinner with her. Choir didn't finish until 11pm, and by the time we'd drunk our *apéritif,* dined, chatted and drunk a bit more (and a bit more and a bit more) it was four o'clock in the morning. I stumbled back to the boarding school where the foreign language *assistants* were housed, and tried to let myself in discreetly. Unfortunately, I couldn't get my key to work, and I was fiddling around with it when the caretaker came out. As I stood there swaying in the dark, surrounded by a halo of alcohol fumes, he asked me what on earth I was up to. "Oh," I said brilliantly, "I've just got back from choir practice..."

Anyway, I didn't say anything about the choir to Marie-Thérèse, but I asked her advice about which GP is best in the area – Ben is due for his second vaccine. (When you think what we've got in our water you can see why this kid needs vaccinations.) She suggested a doctor in the next village, and gave me his number. I rang up just after to make an appointment for this afternoon.

I wasn't sure what to expect when I took Ben (and his papers and vaccine!) along to the surgery. It didn't have the starched look of the doctor's in Bordeaux, but was a rambling stone house smothered in roses. Inside the waiting room was empty – unheard of in town! – and there were tons of toys for Ben. We were having a great time with the different sorts of rattles when the doctor called us in.

He was absolutely *adorable.* He looked something like Mr Badger and was really kind and friendly. He took the time to talk to me about our move, where we were living and what our plans were, as well as chatting at length about Ben. He examined him carefully and did his vaccination gently, and didn't suggest I buy a woolly hat for his ears. Phew.

Now I have found a lovely doctor for Ben I feel we are settled here. One more step though – all our health papers are registered at our old address, so I will have to re-register everything! This is going to be hard work; dealing with the *L'Administration Française* takes strength, and just thinking about it makes me think I could do with a stiff drink. Sadly, the only drink we have in the house is our spring water, which isn't so much a stiff drink as a drink with stiffs in it...

Home. Tuesday, 17th June.

We spent the day in our outbuilding, sweeping and washing the floor. Somehow that kind of work is much more fun than housework. As Eric remarked, the house now looks like a pigsty, but the pigsty is gleaming.

It is an extraordinary building. Apart from the dark beams and the stone, which already make it quite stunning, there are carved oak stalls for cows. Each one has an oval opening in the wood for the cows to pass their head through to reach the manger on the other side. We want to keep some goats in one end of the barn, and set aside the other end for chickens. The manger will be perfect for them to lay their eggs in. I can't wait to see it full of animals, to have our own milk and to find eggs in the hay every morning.

This evening we had a joint effort at tidying the house, which was quite successful. We have no excuse for not doing the washing now as the water is on again, so tonight we are going to have a jolly time sorting our dirty laundry and doing at least two loads. Sounds like fun.

Home. Wednesday, 18th June.

It was a Good Thing we cleaned up. Mum and Dad came over today, and although they would never, ever be put off by our household chaos I do think they might have found a pile of unwashed underwear on the kitchen table a bit unappetising. Last night we did some of the washing and I cleaned the table – it's now so clean you could eat your breakfast off it.

Mum and Dad loved the farm. They were a trifle unnerved about how we'll keep it warm in winter, but any objections they might have had were cast aside when they began exploring outside. They love barns, streams and untamed gardens full of brambles and wildflowers. Within minutes they were planning where to hang a swing for Ben and which tree to build his first tree-house in. He is only three months old tomorrow, but I suppose you can never start thinking about these things too early.

In the afternoon we showed them the badger set, and they were quite amazed by it. Every time we go up there more has been dug out of the holes, and the great banks of freshly turned sand make it look like a sizeable building site. There were paw prints were all over the place – there must be a large family living here. Some of them were tiny paws, so there must be babies. We feel very privileged to have them so close.

We had tea, and once Ben was tucked up we sat out in the garden and chatted. The evenings are long and warm, and sipping drinks and watching the sky turn from blue to burnt orange over the river seemed to be one of the best ways imaginable to spend the evening.

Mum and Dad left when it was dark, but have promised to come back soon with working overalls and gardening tools – that's what I like to hear. Eric's parents have also rung tonight to see if they can come and visit us, to meet little Ben and to help us with the house. We have so many volunteers that I'm sure we'll have our veggie garden dug and our animals installed before the month is out...

Home. Thursday, 19th June.
Ben's 3-month birthday!

Three months! – I could have sworn someone told me they usually sleep through the night at this age. Never mind, I have tried to cheer Eric up by saying that every time we have to get up we have a good chance of seeing one of our nocturnal neighbours. Eric just said something unprintable, but there you are. He'll thank me when he comes face to face with a badger.

Eric accompanied us to help with the supermarket shop this morning. We have decided we'll just do one big shop a week, but I'm not sure if we'll stick to this plan. As we can't go to the cinema because of Ben (and we haven't got any money anyway) going shopping is our Outing. Seeing what's on special, what fruit is in season and what's-new in breakfast cereal is our primary source of entertainment. Oh dear.

We got back home to find a cardboard box on the doorstep. It was tied up with string and looked like a perfectly ordinary parcel – except that it was moving. There was an explanatory note on the top of the box, which still left us rather in the dark. It said: *"Pour les vipères. Bienvenue! Votre voisin, Monsieur Beau."*

Eric said he thought Monsieur Beau must be the old man in the tiny cottage downstream from us, as the only other neighbour is Cathérine.

But what could be in the box? And what was this about adders?

The box rustled even more as we undid the string, and there were scrabbling sounds inside. At least this parcel wasn't dead. Ben shrieked with excitement, and Eric, caught up with his enthusiasm, ripped the top right off. We all peered inside, and Eric and I looked at each other with delight.

Inside were two little chickens. They were terrified, huddled together into a tight ball of feathers. I'm not sure what they were supposed to do to the adders, but they were certainly very cute.

We took our new lodgers (Scramble and Omelette) into the barn so they will get used to us before we let them loose in the garden. They have the trough of spring water to drink, and I left them a handful of corn-flakes to peck. They were looking quite content when we went to thank Monsieur Beau.

He is a nice old chap. At first we were nervous, as he has a Rottweiler that looked as though it might just eat us. Once he'd stopped it leaping at Virginie's tyres we were able to say *bonjour* and introduce ourselves. I thanked him for the chickens, and asked him what he meant about the adders.

He suggested we go inside to talk about it. We sat down at a huge table (covered with a table cloth showing hunting scenes of animals dying bloody deaths) and he got three glasses out. He wanted us to have a whisky – and there was I thinking the French drink *pastis* and cognac – but we wisely refused. "*Non, merci*" is never, ever taken at face value here. We had to back it up by saying we are both on antibiotics and can't combine them with alcohol. And we both have serious liver complaints.

He didn't look too convinced, but he poured us each a glass of juice, and a generous drink for himself. Then he explained about the chickens; everyone in the country should have at least two, as they peck about in the grass and discourage adders from coming into the garden. If they actually come across a snake they polish it off in lightning speed, more efficiently than Rikki Tikki Tavi. I'm not sure our two would look for a fight with a big snake, but we were wanting to have chickens anyway, and Scramble and Omelette are a nice housewarming present.

Monsieur Beau said he'd bought himself a few more chickens, as most of his had disappeared. I couldn't help wondering whether they'd van-ished down some snake's gullet. He said he thought that a fox was the culprit, but that you can "never trust a snake." Local folklore has snakes mixed up with superstition and witchcraft, and I'd already heard a tale or two about snakes in the village. In the *boulangerie* I'd eavesdropped on a story about snakes which bite their own tails to become wheel-shaped, and which then roll at incredible speeds for mind-boggling distances before sinking their toxic fangs in their intended victim. In the Post Office I'd heard another tale about snakes using their fangs to milk cows at sunset, before sliding off into the dusk, their blood warmed by the milk.

Real life, he said, can be as scary as superstition. Four years ago a giant python escaped and moved into the forest nearby. It was so big that the villagers said it wouldn't bother eating anything smaller than a deer. Monsieur Beau was worried about the sheep he rears. Mothers in town were frightened for their children. There was a general sigh of relief when it was recaptured in the autumn, having spent the entire summer basking in the countryside in the hot French sun. When it was caught it had lost more than a dozen kilos, which makes you realise how big it must have been.

Or of course, everyone concerned may have been lying their heads off, but we didn't think it tactful to say so.

Now we are in bed, and I suppose we should feel much safer now we have Scramble and Omelette to protect us. I might even have an egg for breakfast.

Home. Friday, 20th June.

Let the chickens out today – but they just huddled together under the raspberry bush. I gave them some more cornflakes, but they refused to come out. In the end I went to the village and got some more cereal. A handful of Cocopops did the trick – in a trice they were out and pecking about in the grass. I always knew a detailed knowledge of breakfast cereals would come in useful one day.

Home. Saturday, 21st June.

Jean-Pierre came over on his ancient, rattling moped this morning. It was nice to see him, but I was busy trying to unpack. Eric's parents are coming next weekend, and the sitting room where they are going to sleep is still packed full of boxes. I didn't have much time, so I pointed him in Eric's direction.

He pottered into the garden to find him. He was trying to learn his chemistry – part of the soil-science component of his course. Jean-Pierre sat on a tree stump and lit up a *Gitane* while Eric grappled with his atoms. Suddenly Jean-Pierre grinned, and broke wind voluminously.

Eric told him to restrain himself, as he was trying to concentrate. Jean-Pierre just laughed even harder, "I may not know what an atom is," he gasping with laughter, " but I can certainly define the rectum!"

Home. Sunday, 22nd June.

Scramble and Omelette are behaving oddly. Instead of scratching about in the garden they are hell-bent on coming into the house. It's a bit disconcerting really – I'm beginning to worry about what they're so afraid of outside. I had to retrieve Omelette twice from the pile of shoes inside the front door, and battle for the best part of an hour to dislodge Scramble from behind the stove. It's getting ridiculous.

Home. Monday, 23rd June.

No progress with the chickens. They are still spending most of their time in the kitchen. Eric thinks maybe they are after the odd crumb we drop, but as we eat outside it seems unlikely. It's all Very Unnerving.

Eric laughed at me when I voiced my worries about a Giant Serpent in the garden. It's not my fault – I just have a healthy respect of reptiles. Snake, crocodile, komodo dragon, Jack Nicholson (not strictly a reptile, but he looks like one)... you name it, I respect it. Anyway, Eric is just as much of a sissy. It's just that he's afraid of something else – mice. Even Mickey Mouse brings him out in goosepimples. So he can hardly laugh at me.

One good thing about having the chickens inside – less far to go to collect the eggs. This time they both laid for the first time since they arrived here – in the kitchen sink!

Home. Tuesday 24th June.

The chicken mystery has been revealed. I was just putting the washing on the line this afternoon when I saw Dog creeping round behind Scramble and Omelette, who had just ventured down the front steps. Suddenly she dropped down low, and belly scraping along the grass she

99

worked her way towards them. When she was a hair's breadth away she leapt up with a triumphant woof, sending the chickens squawking back into the house. Scramble scrambled and Omelette, er, omeletted.

Dog has become a sheepdog! Well, a chicken dog, anyway.

Now I have tied her to the tree, and the chickens are having a dust bath in the flower bed. Dog looks Most Frustrated, but quite pleased with herself, as though she's just dying to say, "Look, see, you *can* teach an old dog new tricks." The chickens are looking totally relaxed, so I suppose I can forget all about a Big Snake Menace. Eric teased me and said that we can all rest easy in our beds now. Hrumph.

Home. Wednesday, 25th June.

The joke, I think, is on Eric.

We went to bed early last night, and some time around midnight Ben woke up. I fed him and was just settling down again when a moth dive-bombed me. There are always so many of them in summer that I didn't think much of it, but a few minutes later I felt another one in my hair. I lifted up my hand to brush it away, but as I touched it I realised this wasn't a moth. It was a mouse.

I'm not particularly worried about mice, but Eric is pathologically afraid of them. There is a difference between seeing one in the garden (or even in the breadbin) and having one in your hair. As I sat up and shook my head it wriggled out and fell on my pillow, and then shot down between the sheets. I thought (very calmly) about how to react, and shook Eric awake.

He opened one I blearily, but when I whispered '*souris*' and pointed under the blankets he was out of bed like a rocket. He leapt up onto our chest of drawers, and looked so pale that I thought he was in imminent danger of having a heart attack.

"Er, more a vole than a mouse, *chéri*," I said, trying to take some of the drama out of the situation. Eric wasn't coming down though, and told me that if this was a joke – revenge for the snake – he would kill me.

I stripped the bed, and as the creature fell on the floor he saw I wasn't joking. He took a flying leap from the chest of drawers out through the bedroom door. He slammed the door, shutting me in, and said he'd leave me to deal with it.

I spent an hour hunting for it, but it had vanished. I even lifted Ben out of his cot, but it wasn't there either. In the end I went to find Eric.

He was in the kitchen, dragging in the table from the garden. He explained that he was going to sleep for the rest of the night on it, out of reach of any possible rodent. I told him this wasn't a good idea, as (a) the mouse was no longer in the bedroom so he could come back to bed and (b) the kitchen table is only four feet by three. He wasn't going to be moved, so I used my last card. "Eric," I murmured, "I just saw something move by the stove." Within seconds he'd raced back to the bedroom, shut the door and got into bed. I joined him, and some time later we managed to go back to sleep.

When Ben woke me at six Eric was already up and dressed. He was determined to go out and buy a mouse trap, and we know a good shop for buying traps... He couldn't go to the village store until it opened at nine, but he started his all-out assault attempt on the mouse before then – spending three hours wandering about the house carrying a broom handle. He didn't catch a thing, but when he got his trap later on in the morning he caught our mouse within an hour.

I disposed of it, and just out of curiosity I set it again – and caught another one. It's now bedtime, and we've caught five. I hope that's our lot, or else we're in for more Nocturnal Antics. Maybe we should just give up on the mousetraps and buy a bigger kitchen table...

Home. Thursday, 26th June.

Last day before Eric's parents arrive. I have spent all day getting ready, as I want them to like the farm. My mother-in-law is a little Intimidating on the housework front, as she seems to spring-clean all year round. Floors are vacuumed and washed, bathrooms are sparkling and surfaces are free of dust. I have flogged all day, but I know I won't be up to her standard.

To be fair, Eric has helped me physically and morally. He has done a good share of the cleaning, and has encouraged me by saying his parents love me, and they'll love Ben, so there won't be a problem. He has reassured me a bit, and I can't wait to show Ben off anyway. He's so adorable he's bound to be a big hit.

JUILLET

Home. Wednesday, 2nd July.

Back to normal. Eric's parents have left, and the dust (which has been vigorously attacked by Lucienne's duster over the last few days) is just beginning to settle.

We have had a good time together. They both thought Ben was delightful, and he spent much of his time being passed from lap to lap. Lucienne offered to baby-sit for a couple of hours while Eric and I had a walk by ourselves. It turned out we were getting more than free-time; when we got back she had somehow coaxed Ben to have a nap, and had washed all the floors and windows. She'd even managed to light a fire in the kitchen stove, and as the oven had reached a high enough temperature she was busy making a pie. I felt a bit bad that she'd worked so hard while we were frolicking, but Eric said I should gratefully accept her help. He wanted her to stay for longer – until Ben was about twelve, I think.

Eric's dad, Gilbert, also helped us a lot. He is a good gardener, and he and Eric spent hours digging a vegetable patch. Looking like characters out of Pagnol they dug grooves all around it, and channelled water from the spring into them. We have irrigation!

We all went to the market together in Libourne on Sunday morning to buy seedlings. The market takes place on the square, which you can walk around under cover when it's raining or too hot, as the houses are built out over the pavement. There are arches linking every house, and on the ground level of each one there is a shop – the square is really a kind of medieval shopping centre, a 13th century shopping mall...

Lucienne and Gilbert were pleased to find themselves back in Libourne, as they both grew up in the area. Gilbert's work took them out of the county, but now that he's retired I wouldn't be surprised if they moved back some day. Watching Lucienne chat to cousins who have a stall selling wine, and seeing how happy Gilbert was to discuss with an old school friend what sort of lettuce to plant, I'm sure the move will be sooner rather than later.

It was really hot by the time we loaded up Virginie's boot with the first lot of plants we'd bought. Parsley, sage, rosemary and thyme (that sounds familiar), twenty or so lettuces, currant bushes, rhubarb, cabbages, chives and various other green things that have lost their labels and are too small to identify. They could be potatoes or triffids, at seedling stage they all look the same to me.

After we'd bought the plants Lucienne said we had one more thing to get. We followed her through the crowd to a stall selling live chickens, rabbits, guinea fowl and geese. The stall-holder gave her a wave and got a box out from the back of the stall. Somehow she'd nipped off while we were buying the plants, and had bought us two goslings. Through the ventilation holes in the box we could see their greeny yellow heads and shiny eyes.

Now they are safely installed, and seem to get on well with the chickens. They all enjoyed eating many of our new plants, so Eric and his Dad have made a fence around the veggie patch with palette wood. We would have used chicken wire, but our money is running low and we just can't afford it. Never mind, we'll be harvesting our own vegetables soon.

Although it was a bit difficult all living together in a small house (the rooms all lead in to one another, so one person getting up in the night disturbs everyone) we all had fun. Ben has two more fans, and they are coming back to visit in the autumn. Next time they come Gilbert wants to help us a plant an orchard, and he and Eric have plans to make fencing for goats. Our farm is going to become a real farm again.

Home. Thursday, 3rd July.

We visited the cows in the next field for the first and last time this afternoon. Eric had been studying hard, and was in need of a break so he came with us. The cows' meadow is between the road and the river, and looked like a nice place for a walk. We had brought crusts of bread for them, and I was sure that this was going to be the beginning of a beautiful friendship. I should have known better.

I had taken a liking to them as I'd never seen cows which like bathing. I love animals which are a little *extraordinaires.* Now the summer is really here and getting hotter day by day, they seem to spend more and more of their time in the river. As the sun climbs in the sky they wade in slowly, turning the water to gold as the wildflower pollen floats off their legs. The more adventurous ones go in up to their stomachs, wallowing about like hippopotami and snuffling at the dragonflies with their big wet noses.

These cows, like the hippos they were imitating, had Jeckyll and Hyde personalities.. They are a gentle looking, creamy-coloured local variety called *Blondes d'Aquitaine,* and when we were our side of the fence they looked as though butter wouldn't melt in their mouths. Once we were on the other side, strolling towards them with our crusts, their behaviour changed. Suddenly, some of them began snorting in a Most Alarming Fashion, and although Eric tried to reassure me by saying cows are shy, retiring animals, I was not persuaded.

Eric carried on walking towards them, but I was carrying Ben and set off back to the fence. I didn't want to have to have to make a run for it with Ben in my arms. Eric accused me of cowardice, and said I was being ridiculous as there was no bull in the herd. He was looking back over his shoulder at me, so he didn't see one of the larger cows lower her horns and charge. He must have seen me go pale though, because without even stopping to look round he started running.

I have never, ever seen Eric run so fast, but even at his top speed he only just made it over the fence before a dozen cows got there in one dusty stampede. He collapsed, whimpering, onto the ground, while the cows circled round and round, pawing the torn-up grass with their sharp hooves. They looked more like something out of a bullring than the cows you see in a Dairylea advert.

We walked back to the house in silence, Eric still shaking his head in disbelief. I'm not sure he appreciated my humming *Carmen,* but I couldn't resist it.

We have decided we won't visit them any more – and I don't think Eric will ever trust a *blonde* again.

Home. Friday, 4th July.

Got a phone call from my Uncle and Aunt in America. It's Independence Day and they're on holiday. My Uncle has recently become an American citizen – he really is doing the Independence thing. I wonder if he could be tried for treason if he ever goes back to the UK.

He asked me something about Lafayette, but I was a bit stuck to give an opinion. I mean I thought Lafayette was a shop. History is so complicated. I don't know anything about any American war except Star Wars, but I have done my homework there and seen all the episodes. French history is even harder. I was hoping it was just going to be a question of learning the kings and queens, just like the history I learnt in England, but as they had the Revolution my learning stopped in 1789.

Every other historical person since has had their name pinched to christen a square, bridge or street. Everywhere in France you can find a *Place Gambetta* (sounds like a prawn) or a Rue Charles de Gaulle. The problem is is that whenever someone Big and Famous dies these things are re-christened, thus the Pont so-and-so becomes the *Pont Mittérand*. It's hopelessly confusing, and one of the reasons I get so lost in town.

I suppose I have to face up to it; I'm not great shakes at history, but I'm not exactly brilliant at geography, either.

Home. Saturday, 5th July.

Eric was in the vegetable patch this morning, sticking bits of litmus paper in the soil (he's really taking his chemistry seriously) when the postman arrived. He is a really friendly, but thinks I'm very rude as I laughed when he introduced himself when we moved in. It wasn't my fault, I just thought he was joking when he said his name was Postman Pat.

Anyway, Patrice (I can just about face him without giggling if I use his unabbreviated name) had a great pile of gardening catalogues for Eric, and also brought in a letter for me.

I thought it might be from my sister Anna in England, but as he handed it over I saw *Yves Rocher* had found me. Old Yves is better at tracing people than the FBI. I've only just moved in and here he is already, trying to get me to buy make-up, shampoo which smells like boiled sweets and tea bags that are supposed to dissolve my fat and make me as beautiful as the models in the catalogue. Eric always asks me which box he

105

has to tick to get a woman like that through the post.

Actually, the ticking-the-box thing is very complicated, worse than the multiple choice exams I did at school. It's a sort of multi-discipline order form, where you have to tick things, stick labels hither and thither and scratch boxes. If you make a mistake you could miss out on your free digital watch or cuddly toy, so you have to pay attention – the stakes are high.

Being a sad case and having nothing better to do I set about completing the form. Their sun-creams are good value, and there was a small bottle of aftershave which I fancied for Eric. He usually smells of horse manure these days – but then it's probably worth it, the garden is coming on a treat. Still, a little *eau de cologne* would make a welcome change...

Well, I'm ashamed to admit I gave up on ordering. There were so many bits of paper it got too confusing. Anyway, Eric came in from the garden and I didn't want to spoil his aftershave surprise. Maybe I should just swallow my pride and ring Lucienne for her advice: No one knows more about Yves Rocher stuff than Lucienne, not even Yves Rocher himself.

Home. Sunday, 6th July.

Still not sorted out what to order. By the time I get everything ticked, scratched and stuck I think I'll really need their anti-wrinkle cream.

Home. Monday, 7th July.

Gave up and rang Lucienne. She told me to chuck the catalogue, and gave me her own résumé of their best products. She also told me to order by phone, as it saves on all the arts and crafts stuff you have to do to the order form. Now I've not only got my order sorted out, I've got her Christmas present as well. You can't plan these things too early...

I mentioned to Eric how efficient I'd been, but he was very sarcastic. He told me that taking three days to understand a simple catalogue was probably a record. To defend myself I reminded him about when he ordered cycling-shorts from a sportswear catalogue. He was a bit slap-dash about copying down the references, but wouldn't let me interfere. I can still remember his face when he opened his parcel a few days later. Instead of finding cycling shorts inside he found a pink aerobics bra.

Anyway, he didn't thank me for remembering his mistake. He mumbled something rude and stomped off into the garden. I've half a mind to cancel my order for the aftershave.

Now, how do I do that?

Home. Tuesday, 8th July: Wedding Anniversary.

We've been so caught up with getting the house straight and the garden underway that we almost forgot our anniversary. We're still counting our years in single figures, but what the heck, such things should be celebrated.

Our families had remembered our anniversary, and Postman Pat brought us stacks of cards this morning. We also got a nice cheque to buy ourselves A Little Something, so we drove off to Libourne to look around the shops.

We had a couple of hours to choose, and we set off in different directions. Ben and I went to Eric's favourite cycling shop, where I found a flash pair of racing wheels. They were second-hand but still looked new, and Didier, the manager of the shop, assured me they were every cyclist's dream. With wheels like that Eric would be winning races in no time. Well, I was sure they were just the thing for him, so I bought them. Didier did a brilliant job of gift wrapping them for me – he even tied a bow around the parcel with handlebar ribbon.

We met up at lunchtime, and Eric's face lit up as he saw me coming down the street towards him. It's hard to disguise the shape of bicycle wheels with wrapping paper. He gave me a big hug and took a package out of his pocket. I just *adore* presents, and just as quick as I'd said *"merci, chéri"* I'd ripped off the paper. Eric had bought me perfume – I just hope *he* doesn't think *I* smell of horse poo.

Eric explained that it was a new fragrance, which is supposed to smell like the sea. I took it out of its packaging and splashed it on liberally on the way home in the car, just to show Eric how much I appreciated it. I saw Eric's nose twitch, and then as I kissed him to say thank-you he recoiled in horror. He went pale and told me I didn't so much smell of the sea as something *out* of the sea, like a mackerel that had been dead for a very long time. Seconds later he unrolling the sunroof with one hand, and pinching his nose with the other. God only knows who was driving.

107

As a little aside, Eric could be accused, well, of having a rather idiosyncratic driving technique. It's not that he drives fast, no, more like he just has a problem with staying on the road. He always seems to have an excuse though. The time he put Virginie in a ditch, for instance was due to a *petite erreur d'inattention*. Another time (and there are many to choose from, let's face it) he banged into the car in front in a traffic jam because he was looking at a girl on the pavement. *"Mais mon amour,"* he said sweetly, "I wasn't looking at her because she was beautiful. I was looking at her because she was ugly."

Still, it would be unfair to think of such things on our anniversary...

I had a bath to get rid of the smell this afternoon, and another one before we went to bed tonight. I think it's gone now, but in any case Eric doesn't seem to have noticed my presence in the bedroom tonight. He is sitting up in bed with his new wheels, spinning them around between his thumbs. Great.

Maybe our anniversary hasn't been the best, but our Wedding Day itself was perfection. And as Eric is still twiddling with his spokes I may as well write about it. (Ben is also looking restless, I hope these cycling vibes aren't getting him already. Two cyclists in the family is going to cost me a fortune in wheels.)

The run-up to the wedding was pretty stressful. First, there was my in-laws' reaction. Gilbert spoke to me on the telephone, and he wasn't terribly encouraging, "Christ!" he gasped, "what the bloody hell do you want to marry him for?"

Happily our families were soon won around, but our next step was to battle through the French administration. We were living just outside Bordeaux (it was before Eric's job was transferred to the centre of town) and we had to go to our local *mairie* to ask for our 'Getting Married' dossier to complete. It was a weighty thing, and required us to produce every kind of document imaginable. Our birth certificates even had to be accompanied by a document to prove we were still alive. I pointed out that this was somewhat illogical as dead people don't usually get hitched, but the administrator in the *mairie* wouldn't have it. We also had to have a full medical, where we were strongly advised to have both an AIDS and a syphilis test. *"Pourquoi?"* I asked, getting a bit stroppy. *"Eh bien,"* said the administrator "because there's a blank space on page 23 of your dossier which has to be ticked or crossed – you can't leave it blank. Everyone finds it strange the first time." And there we were only planning to get married once.

Come to think of it, the dossier was a bit like a giant version of Yves Rocher's form... I wonder which one influenced the other???! And if we'd have been more careful about completing all the boxes in our marriage dossier, might we have won the digital watch and cuddly toy???

Anyway, we were so worn out by the preparation for the legal marriage ceremony in the *mairie* that neither of us could face arranging the religious ceremony in the church – especially as in a fit of *pique* I'd written Eric and myself down as 'druids' on the marriage form. One ceremony seemed quite enough, so we chose to just get married in the town hall.

Our wedding day eventually dawned, and it was bright and clear. My family, the Brits, arrived in suits and looked very smart. Eric's family also were dressed up, but they had obviously taken a look at the blue sky and dressed for a hot day. Although they weren't really united by their dress styles, they were by their *bonhomie,* and the ceremony in the *mairie* was a cheerful event. I even got my own back as Wicked Administrator struggled to read out my parents' birth certificates. The mayor also made things jolly, by kissing me on both cheeks and giving us a medal to "celebrate our love." (As Gilbert still says, whoever took Eric on deserved a medal.)

When all was signed and sealed we drove back to our house, everyone tooting their horns in the French fashion. We had a giant slap-up homemade lunch in the garden, but as the temperature was over a hundred no one was very hungry. We were left with over a hundred chicken legs in the freezer, which we ate for a month afterwards. Gradually the remaining suits were changed for shorts, and as I sat and smoked the cigar destined for the groom everyone played frisbee with the paper plates. The Brits, needless to say, played badminton...

In the scorching heat of the afternoon we gave up and all drove to a nearby lake to cool off. The bride, bridesmaid (Danièle) and other girlfriends stripped down to barest essentials and plunged, while the men abandoned their shorts and leapt in from the diving board. In the late afternoon Eric and I managed to sneak away together – I'm sure we're the first couple ever to leave their wedding on a pedalo.

It was a wonderful (if unconventional) day, and just thinking about it makes me feel all lovey-dovey. I may just prise Eric away from his wheels, especially as little Ben has dropped off to sleep.

Oh no. Eric's asleep as well.

Home. Wednesday, 9th July.

Eric sat and watched the *Tour de France* all afternoon, sitting in the dark with the shutters closed. The *Tour* lasts for three weeks, and it is hard to get any French person who likes cycling to leave the TV set for even five minutes. When I think about it, it's a miracle that we managed to get married in July. I suspect Eric consulted the diary of the races before he picked a date, so as not to miss one of the Pyrenean stages of the race. How Romantic.

I suppose at least this year Eric can baby-sit for Ben, who has a sleep after lunch. I spent my afternoon putting up some perches for the chickens in the barn, and it *was* nice to swing a hammer about without being encumbered by a baby-sling.

I thought Eric would come and join me when the race was over, but later on he appeared wearing all his cycling things. He passed Ben to me, who had just woken up and was wanting a feed, and told me he was off for a ride. He was meeting up with our Postman (Patrice is also a keen cyclist) and the two of them were going cycling, to chat about the day's race and, I think, to imagine they were the latest cycling champions.

I fed Ben and showed him my handiwork in the barn, although he looked more interested in the geese and the chickens than in my carpentry. Then we went indoors where it was much cooler than in the garden, and I let him play on a blanket on the floor while I rang Véro. Stéphan loves cycling too, and she had spent the afternoon by herself with Théo. We were in full moan when I heard a familiar noise like a lawn-mower outside, and Jean-Pierre arrived on his moped.

I said goodbye to Véro and poured Jean-Pierre a cool drink. I was surprised to see that he was also dressed up like a cyclist, and asked him if he'd taken up the sport. *"Pas du tout,"* he said, cheerfully, but explained that with his moped he could pretend he was doing the *Tour de France*. He'd even shaved his legs.

I was chatting to him about cycling, but I couldn't help but notice that he kept wriggling on his stool. I took at discreet look at the ground to see if any ants had come in from the garden, but I couldn't see any on the floor or on the legs of the stool. Watching him jiggle more and more I just had to ask what was the matter.

He went red, and leaping up and pacing around the room (scratching himself wildly all the while) he explained that his whole body was itching like mad. At first he thought he'd caught fleas from his landlady's dog, Bébe Béatrice, but now he thought it was due to this 'cycling thing.'

"What 'cycling thing?'" I asked, intrigued.

"Well," he replied, "This shaving. It seemed odd to stop at the top of my legs as the rest of me is hairy, so I carried on." And on, it seemed, right up to his eyebrows. He'd shaved every square centimetre of his body, and all the round ones as well. Uncomfortable stuff.

I tried to sympathise, but I couldn't stop laughing. Eventually Jean-Pierre got sulky and left, heading off into the twilight on his racing moped. Poor Jean-Pierre. He may not get far with his cycling, but I think he deserves full marks for effort as far as *épilation* is concerned.

Home. Thursday, 10th July.

Despite the heat we did some work on the house today. Eric scrubbed the quarry tiles and oiled them, while I painted a corner in our room which is set aside for Ben. I painted giraffes and elephants on the wall above his cot – their proportions are a bit odd, but then they are in real life as well. They are standing under trees (of uncertain species) having a drink in a cool lake. I dipped Ben's feet in watercolour to do a little line of footprints leading down to the water, which we both loved doing. Once I'd rinsed his feet I drew him a couple of hyenas, which I'm feeling quietly confident about.

I'm Pretty Pleased with the result this evening – but I've got a crick in my neck from painting clouds and birds on the ceiling. I wonder how Michael Angelo coped?

Home. Friday, 11th July.

The temperature rocketed even higher today. It was boiling even at half nine in the morning, when we went to the village to do some shopping in the general store. (I wanted some sandpaper as I'm worried that my rather rough perches might give the chickens splinters in their feet.) It was so warm that I was sure that this time I wouldn't get any comments about a woolly hat for Ben. It's surely too hot to think about headgear.

I was out of luck. Monsieur Ronchon, it seems, will always have something to reproach me for. This time he fixed me with a beady glare, and wagging one finger at me said, "*Madame*, that baby needs a sunhat."

Home. Saturday, 12th July.

Another VERY big anniversary. Nothing to do with our wedding, no, this was something Far, Far bigger. This as the anniversary of the day when France won the World Cup.

Now, I used to be *Madame L'Indifférente* as far as football is concerned, and the run up to the World Cup didn't help. Seeing that irritating blue Footix character everywhere (the symbol of the competition) really got on my nerves, and hearing about nothing but football on the TV and radio got me down. The whole country was at a low ebb just before the competition started, and I wasn't convinced football was going to help us.

Then the games started, and although there were predictable problems with the fans, the Feel Good factor here began to rise. I found myself watching the matches, and getting excited. I wasn't the only one to strike up conversations with complete strangers about how the World Cup would end. After each match smiles grew broader and broader, and now the *Bleus* were playing brilliantly the conversation in every market and on every *terrace* was about how *good* the French were at something. Often the French seem to have a giant-sized *frite* on their shoulder about how Anglo-Saxon culture dominates France, but now *France* was dominating.

And then we won! We won! Zidane changed in my view from being a bit of a baldie to a Sex God – who can also play football. The whole team became National Heroes. Their mixed origins proved that a multicultural France is the key to success, which took the wind out of the National Front's sails. We won! We really won! We went wild! We partied at each other's houses, we beeped our horns all night, we blew trumpets on the *Champs Elysées*. It was wondrously, riotously noisy.

For days, weeks and months afterwards the country boomed. The World Cup was in everyone's minds, and some had even persuaded their pets to get involved. I saw one white dog that had been dyed red, white and blue.

Véro said (sighing over a postcard of Zidane) that she'd never been much of a fan, but now she'd put her name alongside mine on the 'converted' list. She said at last the French had shown they were fantastic at something.

The best in the world, actually.

Home. Sunday, 13th July.

Bastille Day tomorrow, a *fête nationale* in France to commemorate the French Revolution. There will be fireworks tonight in villages and towns all over the country, and Paris will be just amazing. It closely coincides with the World Cup victory which will be celebrated as well, and the partying will go on until the early hours.

As we have little Ben we can't stay out too late, but we will probably drive into town to see the fireworks later. It is odd having to wait so late for them, but we have to wait until it is really dark – until at least half past ten. In the UK, of course, the fireworks are on the fifth of November. As far as I remember it gets dark at about four o'clock in the afternoon – if the sun has actually bothered to rise at all – so the 'party' can start early and be slotted, hopefully, into a gap between the downpours. Everything is over by the time *Eastenders* begins.

I suppose the latter may be more convenient for kids, but I still know which one I prefer...

Home. Monday, 14th July. Bastille Day.

A day off for everyone today, but I began by doing some work. It was another scorcher so I put on my bikini – and my wellingtons because of the risk of snakes – when I headed for the garden to do some weeding. Eric refused to join me, saying that there was no way he was going to cut the hedge with the electric trimmer while wearing only a pair of swimming trunks. It made him worry about the chances of Ben ever having brothers and sisters. Inside it was a lot cooler, and he sat down to study. (He admitted later that he flicked on the TV, but as there were only repeats of *Charlie's Angels* and *Starsky and Hutch* he turned it off again. Most French people LOVE these series, but fortunately Eric isn't one of them. So he opened his books and studied – even soil science is more exciting than 'French' telly.)

After an hour he stuck his head out the window to say hullo to me, and said that I quite put him off his studying. He was planning to open one of his maths books, but the sight of me in my bikini gave him other ideas.

Not *those* kinds of ideas. He suggested we go swimming.

There are loads of lakes around here, but not all are good for bathing. There's the *lac bleu,* for instance – a bright blue colour due to mineral deposits in its clay bed – which is extremely deep and dangerous. We chose a lake we'd seen advertised in the village, which offered safe swimming, slides and swings for children (but maybe Ben is a bit small) and a clean, sandy beach.

It only took a few minutes to drive there, and we soon were aware that we weren't the only ones who'd had the idea. There were cars every-where, and there was a Bastille Day *pétanque* competition going on under the pine trees. The competitors were quite a funny sight: they were all elderly men, and most of them had had an *apéritif* too many, so much so that they were having to prop themselves up against the tree trunks. They were mostly wearing athletic shorts (the *pétanque* player being, by nature, a *sportif*) bob hats and nothing else. Some were polishing their cherished *boules* on their ample stomachs and eyeing up the next shot. We stood and watched them for a few minutes, and were surprised to see that despite their level of intoxication they were playing surprisingly well. But it was just too hot, and the idea of a swim too tempting, so we left them to it and strolled down to the beach.

I was delighted to see how nice it was. The sand really *was* golden, and there were lots of people sunning themselves. The owners of the lake had catered for English tourists – there was a badminton net. The French had taken it to be a washing line, and were drying their beach towels on it. I asked Eric why the French don't play badminton much, and he said that it's because they save their energy to win at other sports, like foot-ball. There's not much you can say to that.

As Ben has had two vaccinations we let him come in the water with us. The bathing area was *full* of kids, bobbing about gleefully in a curi-ous soup of inflatable boats, multicoloured beach balls, snorkels and masks and the odd sticking plaster. Ben *loved* it.

It was the hottest afternoon yet, so we spent most of it in the water. When *maman* and *papa* were too exhausted to bounce Ben around any longer we packed up our things and set off for home. Looking at my bright pink nose in the mirror tonight I vowed I'll go to the village store before we go swimming in the lake again.

I've got to buy a sun hat.

Home. Tuesday, 15 July.

Woke up today with Ben tucked between Eric and myself. I couldn't remember the early feed, but as my tee-shirt was still only half on I was sure it had happened. I lay there cuddling him, and he nestled his little hard head into the curve of my shoulder. A bright ray of sun was coming through the shutter, and was shining on his dark blond hair.

It's strange how such things can move you, but suddenly I was stroking his soft back with tears in my eyes. Lying there next to me he was the most beautiful thing I'd ever seen.

I felt so light with happiness, and at the same time so heavy with responsibility. He was just stirring and sniffling his nostrils, smelling the milk for his next feed, when Eric opened his eyes.

I kissed him hello, and tried to explain how having a baby is making me realise who I am, it's like I'm finally seeing the deepest part of myself.

"Yeah," said Eric wearily, eyeing my wonky tee-shirt and Ben who was nuzzling me, "it's like you've finally realised you're a mammal."

Home. Wednesday, 16th July.

Our house is a mouse-free zone at last – phew. I couldn't stand much more of Eric flinging open the kitchen cupboard at twenty minute intervals throughout the day (just to check there were none inside) and then leaping backwards across the kitchen floor because he thought he'd seen something moving. It made me want to put a rubber rat in the cornflakes packet. Anyway, we scattered breadcrumbs on the kitchen floor last night, and they're still there today, so either the mice have moved or else they're cutting down on their carbohydrates.

Eric, however, has still not given up the chase. He staked out the barn after lunch, hiding in the old oak manger with a catapult in hand. He hit two mice with pellets as they scurried along the beams, but mostly his afternoon was a long camouflage exercise. He explained that the mice needed to feel there was no one in the barn in order to come out and expose themselves to fire, so he covered himself up with hay and stayed absolutely still. Unfortunately he ended up falling asleep, and awoke in the late afternoon to find that the chickens had laid their eggs on him. And, far worse and much more Mysteriously, he discovered he had mouse droppings in his ear.

I spent my afternoon in the garden. Ben slept in his carrycot under the old apple tree while I weeded and watered. It was heavy work turning over the clay soil between the rows of plants, and it took me all afternoon to get to the end of the vegetable patch, where Eric has planted carrots. There was a surprise awaiting me; someone had already turned the soil over. It hadn't been well done, but it had definitely been dug.

I went into the barn, where Eric was dusting the hay off himself and rubbing the sleep out of his eyes, and asked him whether he'd been gardening in the morning. He shook his head, and followed me out into the garden. We both inspected the carrots again, baffled.

We are still discussing who or what has been digging, and Eric is sure it's some Nocturnal Creature. What we've decided to do is to get up after Ben's 5am feed, and look out of the shutters to see if we can spot the culprit.

The suspense is killing me!

Home. Thursday, 17th July.

Mystery solved.

As soon as Ben had had his last sip of milk this morning we tucked him up again, and then we quietly opened the shutters. We *were* planning to go outside, but neither of us quite fancied it. One's courage can feel a Touch Subdued when it's still dark and one is uncertain what might be Lurking in the garden. I'd had nightmares all night about a psychopathic gardener murdering us with his gardening fork, so I for one wasn't going to risk it.

We peered out the window, and almost instantly spotted our Visitor – and he wasn't human. He was swimming across the river from sandbank to sandbank, and we half expected to see Obelix in his wake, for our animal was a huge wild boar. He looked more like a waist-high buffalo than a pig – not at all pink and oblong but dark brown and furry, with massive muscular shoulders and a steeply sloping back. On closer inspection we came to the conclusion that he was quite endearing, with his trim little hooves, funny short tail and tiny tusks.

It's increasingly rare to see wild boar here, as they're relentlessly pursued by the *chasseurs français*. As is the way with any animal they feel like slaughtering, boar are cited as dangerous, and as being major crop destroyers. Mostly the poor things hide in the thickest forests to escape humans, and are so shy that although they are not nocturnal animals they only dare come out at night. These guys are not exactly spoiling for a fight.

If we're talking about *danger* here, then I should really point out that you're more likely to be shot by a hunter than trampled by a wild boar, especially if your walk in the woods is after lunch, and your average hunter has downed his *rouge*. I've heard somewhere that the police actually breathalise hunters now, but only a minute proportion are tested and hunting accidents are common.

I heard one story about a hunting accident from my uncle in America. (Hunters are much the same over there, only they drink Heineken instead of red wine.) Anyway, a hunter shot a hiker in the forest one winter, and came up with a brilliant excuse to get himself off: The woman he killed was wearing white gloves, and he thought they were a deer's pale behind. So we can all conclude that if we walk in the woods we do so at our own risk, and if we dress to look like the back end of a deer (any white, cream or beige clothing) we're dicing with death. And what an epitaph to have on your gravestone, *"here lies Thingumybob, sadly mistaken for Bambi's bottom."*

Well, back to our boar again... he came out of the river, and instead of going into the vegetable garden he went to the lime tree in front of the house. Dog, poor thing, was whimpering with fright, and fulfilled her rôle as a guard dog by whining and hiding behind the tree trunk. We weren't sure what the boar was planning to do next, and we watched in fascination, noses pressed to the window pane, as he polished off the kitchen scraps I'd put out for the birds.

He stayed for about fifteen minutes, nose rooting about in the grass, until the noise of the elderly farming couple (whom we saw gathering in the hay) disturbed him. They meant no harm – they were only moving their five milking cows from one meadow to another – but it was enough to frighten him, and in a flash he was gone.

Eric and I looked at each other afterwards, flushed with excitement. There is something wonderful about having a wild boar in your garden, even if you have to get up at 5am to see it.

We're going to put more scraps out for Boris (he was christened on the spot) and try and befriend him. As Eric said, all animals are welcome here.

Except mice, of course.

Home. Friday, 18th July.

Oh God oh God oh God oh God. I forgot my Granny's birthday. Mum rang me up this morning just to check I'd sent a card for *yesterday* (eek!) and I had that horrible sinking sensation when I realised I'd forgotten. She is so dear to me, and now I've messed up.

I had a Massive Guilt Trip this morning. I rang Gran to say Happy Birthday for yesterday, and told her a card is already on its way but that it must have been delayed in the French post. So now I've added lying to my other crimes...

The worst of it is that I *do* think about her so often, and now I've completely failed to show it. To try and make up for forgetting I've bought a card and stuck some pictures of Ben inside. Hopefully the sweetness of my son will make up for the wickedness of his mother...

I wonder if Gran will believe I sent the card before her birthday. Probably not – but she'll pretend to, because she always has Unshakeable Faith in me. Despite my failings she always trusts me. It's one of the reasons I love her so much.

Home. Saturday, 19th July.

Another birthday – Ben is four months old today. Now he can roll from side to side, chuckle and when we tickle him he squeaks and squeals like Flipper the dolphin. He seems to listen in on everything – there's no lying him down in a carrycot anymore – he wants to be propped up so he can see everything.

The first part of his birthday was not the best part for him. We went to the doctor's, where he had his third and final vaccination. I felt myself flinching when I saw the needle, but he didn't seem to feel it. Needles are never nice, but it *is* comforting to know that he is resistant now to five nasty diseases.

The doctor said that when he has his mumps, measles and rubella vaccination (when he's a year old) he'll be allowed to have a sweet from the jar on his desk, but as he's too young at the moment he gave one to me. Sucking a sherbet lemon felt good for my soul – I think I prefer *confiserie* to traditional, mainstream medicine.

After the doctor's I went home to pick up Eric, and we went to buy Ben's present – a third of a year is a date to remember, after all. Poor Ben has been without a pram since before we moved house, and we wanted to get him some wheels. We set off to Bordeaux, to get an ultra-light, easily foldable pushchair, the sort a baby can either sit up in, or lie back and sleep. (Well, the lying back and sleeping bit does sound a bit improbable, but then you never know.)

It was strange going back to the city. There is just no traffic noise whatsoever where we live, and Bordeaux now seemed unbelievably loud, roaring with engines. Even the smell of exhaust fumes was overpowering. Although I generally detest shopping malls, we headed for the giant Auchan complex, just to get away from the cars and to breathe filtered air. Once inside we didn't feel much better – I've got so used to wearing wellingtons that my feet hurt in shoes, and I couldn't concentrate on the shops as I was worried about whether I'd remembered to leave the door to the barn open. Scramble and Omelette wouldn't be able to lay inside if I'd forgotten.

We sat down so that I could feed Ben, and Eric and I had a cup of coffee. I talked to Eric about how weird I was feeling. He said he wasn't thinking about the chickens, but was angsting about whether his lettuces had enough water, as it was so hot. We both came to the conclusion that in less than two months we've become country bumpkins.

We thought we'd hurry up and buy the pushchair as quickly as possible, so that we could get home. It wasn't quite that easy – many of them seemed to have a zero too many on the price tag, and were only marginally less expensive than the price of a small family car. Then there were the sort that looked brilliant when they were unfolded, but when folded seem to triple in size, so that you would need a boot the size of a builder's van to accommodate them. Others wouldn't fold or unfold at all. We forced one of the ones that seemed designed to stay umbrella-shaped to open, and it *did* stay like that for a few seconds – until we put Ben in it. Then it folded up again all by itself.

It was a nightmare.

By five o'clock we'd had enough, so we chose the simplest kind which would fit into our car. Ben, by then, was fast asleep. It made me wonder why we were buying a pushchair at all – he'd dropped off lying on Eric's jacket in the supermarket trolley. He'd been ecstatically happy in it all afternoon, as though it was a mobile play-pen, and now it had turned into a cot. I'd half a mind to help Eric lower it in through Virginie's roof and take it home...

This evening we've been out to give the new pushchair a test-drive, and I must admit that the wheels on it are better than on a supermarket trolley. Ben sat back happily, gazing out but also playing with the toys I'd strung across it. We walked along the river all the way to the elderly couple's farm, and although it was getting dark they were out milking their mini-herd of cows. Huguette held each one in turn by a weedy looking piece of string around their horns – they can't really have been wanting to escape – while Henri sat on a three-legged stool and did the milking.

We walked across the field to see them, Ben's pushchair bouncing over the bumps, which he loved. Henri and Huguette were friendly, and proud to tell us how they still run a farm at their age. They are actually brother and sister, and have been together since forever. There are many rumours about them in the village, but as we crouched on our heels in the quiet evening and watched them milking their five cows, there was only a feeling of gentleness about them.

Henri told us that they have no running water or electricity at the farm, as they prefer to live *à l'ancienne*. They don't have any clocks either, as they live by the sun. (It is a bit odd that considering the sun dictates their work they always seem to be doing their milking etc. in the dark, but never mind.) Maybe it's part of this old-fashioned method of farming or just a facet of Huguette's nature, but she really loves her cows. She chatted to each one as her brother milked, addressing them seriously by their names and tucking wildflowers behind their ears to make them even more beautiful. She seemed to converse with them about what were the tastiest plants to eat, and whether such-and-such a flower would make their milk creamier.

I felt as though I was interrupting when I told her about the big dairy farm I lived next door to near Bristol, where the cows don't have a name, just a number. Huguette couldn't believe it – she asked me how they could come when you called them if they don't have a name. It was hard for her to conceive of a farm where cows are never called by name, and don't even have personalities any more. She asked whether physically they look the same, and I told her that most don't have horns, as horns are 'undesirable.' She really couldn't take that on board – how could you lead the cows to be milked if you couldn't put a piece of string around their horns..?

The mysteries of modern farming are unknown to her, but as I saw her slip her arms around her favourite cow's neck it struck me that Huguette knows an awful lot about love.

Home. Sunday, 20th July.

My sister Anna telephoned this morning. She has saved up enough air-miles to come and see us, and she's coming next weekend! She is so looking forward to seeing Ben; I've sent her loads of photos, but it's not as good as the Real Thing. Ben has made her an Auntie, and I have the feeling she's going to arrive with a suitcase full of presents for him.

Our little family has increased in size today. We went off to the market in Libourne this morning to buy some more chickens... Scramble and Omelette have been providing us with an egg each every day, but we really need a few more if I'm ever going to be able to cook flans, sponge cakes, soufflés and all the other eggy things I'd like to cook. 'Home grown' eggs just *look* so natural and healthy that I want to cook with them all the time – I can't classify eggs as cholesterol balls any more. Eric said he was also fantasizing about grilled drumsticks, so unless Scramble and Omelette were to become amputees we needed a few more chickens.

The market was busier than ever, but Ben's new pushchair is a splendid battering ram, and cleared the way through the crowd. We went straight to the poultry stall – it was easy to locate as a cockerel was crowing its head off. When

121

we got to the stand he was the first thing we saw. He was tied by the leg to the stall by a grubby piece of string, but he still look magnificent. He ruffled his beautiful russet, gold and emerald feathers, tipped his head back and let out a deafening *'cocorico'* (French chickens don't say 'cock-a-doodle-do'.) He was a prince among cockerels, and we had to have him.

The stall owner named his price, which was only 50 francs. Cockerels are much cheaper than laying hens, and most country folk don't bother to keep one any more. Most people worry about the noise annoying the neighbours, but our neighbours are far away. He is not only beautiful but he'll be handy – our alarm clock stopped working in the move, so it will be useful to have a cockerel to wake us up in the morning. This cockerel's crow is nothing like the asthmatic hiss of Superneighbour's cockerel in Bordeaux. The stall holder has promised us that it will be louder than a TGV's whistle – that's some alarm clock...

The stall owner bundled him unceremoniously into a cardboard box, and then helped us pick out three more laying chickens and a dozen month-old pullets, which are destined to feed us in the autumn, poor things.

We paid up and carted the boxes back to the car. The boxes were really heavy, and we were glad to unload them. The chickens squawked all the way home. but when we got back I found one of them had laid an egg in the car. Things are looking promising for my soufflés.

Scramble and Omelette were wary of the newcomers, and huddled together in the corner of the barn, clucking away as though they were gossiping about them. Eric rigged up some wire netting at one end of the barn to keep the pullets together, as he's nervous about them getting eaten outside – we'll keep them in for a week or two. The three new hens pecked about with delight in the mangers, until we let the cockerel out. In five seconds flat he'd herded all the chickens – including Scramble and Omelette – into a flock, and was marching them about the barn. Eric said it was good that he was keeping them together, as they'll be safer from foxes – but I couldn't help thinking he looked like a real bully. Any chicken that stepped out of line got a hard pecking.

Cockerel (now called Godzilla, inspired by the way he stamps about on those muscular, scaly legs) has made all the chickens sleep on the same perch tonight, while he has a perch all to himself. I'm a bit cross that the girls aren't rebelling, but they just tip their silly heads on one side and blink at him in dumb adoration. It's very frustrating.

Eric has just told me why the symbol of France is a cockerel. Apparently it's because the French can still crow, even when they have *de la merde* right up to their ankles.

Home. Monday, 21st July.

Godzilla started crowing at 4am, and woke us all up, including Ben. Is he mad?????????

Home. Tuesday, 22nd July.

That bloody cockerel. Up again at four, and then strutted around annoying the hens ALL DAY. He keeps them rounded up, but at regular intervals he picks one off, chases her behind the blackberry bushes and forces himself on her. Do they all mate like this???? It's perfectly horrible, not at all the kind of birds-and-the-bees barnyard romp I thought it would be. I mean here they are, free range and everything, and all Godzilla is into is battery.

Home. Wednesday, 23rd July.

Honestly, the poor hens can't go on like this – all their eggs will be scrambled. We've got to find a solution.

Home. Thursday, 24th July.

Well, I give up, I really do.

I went out this morning to put the washing on the line, when Godzilla came charging out from behind the barn, racing towards me. Maybe it was my floaty red skirt that did it, but whatever it was that cockerel went berserk. He squawked and stamped and rushed at me, talons first. I wasn't sure if he was planning to attack me or march me off behind the blackberries, but I ran for it.

Eric was watching from the window, and I haven't seen him look so jolly since the *Tour de France* ended. I slammed the door behind me and collapsed on the settee, and yelled at Eric to go outside and *faire quelque chose*. Still chuckling he went into the garden, and tried to chase Godzilla into the barn.

Godzilla, however, wasn't having it. He'd obviously summed Eric up as a rival, and it took Eric the best part of the morning to shut him away. Dog was of no help whatsoever – she's terrified of Godzilla and would have no part in the herding. She spent the morning hiding under the kitchen table, paws over her eyes. Eric finally bolted the door on Godzilla at lunchtime, and he came indoors and sat down, dazed, on a stool in the kitchen. He was exhausted from running up and down the garden, and he also had blood running down his legs from where Godzilla had pecked him. Never try to catch a cockerel when you're wearing shorts.

We ate outside, and it was good to be able to wheel Ben about in his new pushchair without worrying about whether a psychopathic chicken would attack us. I was feeling very cheery until I saw what the other five chickens were up to. I thought they'd be happily scratching about in the grass, each relieved to be able to go her own way. I was shocked to see that the were all hanging around the door of the barn, gazing at the lock. It wasn't fear they had in their eyes, it was naked longing.

"I've had it with them," I said to Eric, "Even if they can't judge character, I can."

Eric got the message.

Drumsticks are now on the menu.

Home. Friday, 25th July.

Anna's here!!

It's wonderful to see her again. She stepped off the plane with a holdall containing most of Mothercare for Benjamin, but she had nothing at all for herself. The luggage she'd put in the hold had got lost, and is rumoured to be somewhere in Brussels. Hopefully it'll be here tomorrow. In the meantime I'm lending her my clothes, which I'm not sure she's thrilled about. Since I've had Ben I've only really added a couple of pairs of tough trousers to my wardrobe (strong enough to repel brambles and cockerels) and a wardrobe composed of maternity wear and ex-army supplies can't be that tempting.

She may not be wild about my clothes, but she *is* wild about Ben. She cuddled him all afternoon and evening, and looked quite grumpy about handing him back for feeds. She said that she'd decided with her scrumptious boyfriend, Neil, to wait for a while before they have kids, but I'm sure that it won't be for long. Next time I visit them I'm sure their wardrobes will be full of babygear instead of skis and scuba equipment, and there'll be a cot where their multigym is. The only thing that makes me think she may not be ready yet is when she asked about childcare – do I think it's possible to find a creche which stays open all night?...

Home. Saturday, 26th July.

Had a lovely day with Anna, relaxing and catching up on her news. I feel so out of touch with England that it's nice to hear what's going on, even if I don't know half the people she tells me about. England suddenly feels like a soap opera that I used to watch every day but which I haven't seen for about five years, so even if I'm familiar with the themes I don't know any of the characters any more.

Anna is a chiropractor, and Eric and I were both treated to some free back-cracking. It made me feel much better, and made up for the downside of having a chiropractor sister, like the "sit up, you're slumping" and "don't stick your chin out, it makes you look like a vulture' comments. (That side of chiropractic is a right pain in the coccyx.)

Eric had to have his back fixed a second time, because when a taxi arrived with her lost luggage he put his back out getting it out of the boot. Having a chiropractic sister may have its uses after all...

She loved the farm, but was a little nervous about the self-sufficiency. She thought it would be wonderful to have our own fruit and veg, but she wasn't sure she could face meat unless it was wrapped in cellophane. I told her that the taste of free-range chickens just isn't the same, and that we'd prove it to her. (I turned our cockerel into *coq-au-vin* yesterday, and I was sure the flavour would win her over.)

She looked apprehensive, though, as we sat up to dinner. And we didn't exactly set her mind at rest. She sat there, nervously poking at the stew with her fork, and asked what the meat was. Eric and I, without thinking, both mumbled the same reply....

"It's Godzilla."

Home. Sunday, 27th July.

Anna has gone home. I'm feeling a bit blue tonight, but she's promised to come out again soon. She cried her eyes out when she kissed Ben goodbye, and he seemed sorry to see her go. (Well, he wouldn't let go of her right earring, anyway.)

She bought us a brilliant leaving present. We went back to Libourne market this morning, and she chose another cockerel for us. This one is a pale golden colour, and sat in his cage looking dreamily about him. He doesn't have any Godzilla's bright colours and stroppy nature – but I think he has the soul of a poet. We have called him Beaudelaire.

He's spent the afternoon quietly following the hens around, as though gently wooing them, and tonight he's cuddled up with them on the same perch. The way he preens them looks as though he's murmuring gently into their ears, and they seem to be enjoying it.

I wonder if he'll wake us up tomorrow by crowing in verse...

Home. Monday, 28th July.

Hooray for sweet awakenings! Beaudelaire stirred at around six, and crowed softly, as though he was apologising for waking us. His crowing is lilting and melodic. This is more like it.

Big changes for Ben today – he had his first real meal at lunchtime. I was a little nervous about starting him off in life with my cooking, so I picked up a couple of jars of baby food in the supermarket. (I wouldn't have risked the village store, in case the baby food turned out to be fishing bait or rat poison, its main specialities.)

Well, the first jar might just as well have been rat poison. Ben spat it out, looking horrified. Eric read the label and said what did I expect – it was spinach. Most people spend their whole lives avoiding the stuff, and there I was trying to tempt him away from milk with it. I was bound to fail.

I opened the second jar, and as soon as he smelt the spoon he looked interested. Puréed bananas – just what a boy needs. I know you're supposed to start babies off with just a taste, but in three minutes flat he'd eaten half the jar. I thought he'd better not have too much, so Eric ate the rest.

Eric is MAD about bananas. Just the tiniest taste of one drives him, er, bananas. His fondest memory of the navy is of the months he spent in the French Caribbean – during the first three days alone he ate forty six bananas he picked from the wild palms. If Ben is going to be anything like his father, I joked, then we should seriously think of investing in some palms.

Eric laughed, and said he agreed. They are, by far, his favourite kind

126

of fruit. "But you're from Bordeaux! – You're supposed to like grapes," I said, scandalised. Eric shrugged, and said he's never understood why everyone's so crazy about them. "Nasty, pippy things," he said.

Well, we'll have to see whether we can plant a banana palm in the garden. There *are*, after all, plenty of them in the warm, sheltered gardens around Bordeaux. I phoned Lucienne to ask her whether she thought we could successfully grow one, and she said that one year in Bordeaux it was so hot the palms actually produced ripe bananas.

We'll never be able to afford a big palm, but Eric says he thinks he saw some small offshoots underneath the palm in Monsieur Beau's garden. It'll take time to grow though, and about ten years at least before it starts to produce anything even resembling a banana.

I think Ben might be weaned by then.

Home. Tuesday, 29th July.

Dad phoned this morning with bad news from England. My Great Aunt Lydia, Granny's sister, has just died. I can't believe it. Ninety-seven years – nearly a whole century of her being, and now she has gone. She has become part of our family's history.

I first sought her out as an adult when I came to London to go to University. Student London, was, of course, a very different city from my Great Aunt's. My London was one of pub-crawls and concerts and of 4am Christmas snowballing in Regent's Park. It was a 24-hour-a-day city, a city that rushed at breakneck speed. Exhausting and exhilarating – it made me feel more alive than I had ever felt.

Her London was bargain hunting in Woodgreen, popping into favourite bakeries and sipping tea in the sun in her garden. Her life moved at a slower pace; she had never even owned a 'motorcar', relying chiefly on her legs for transport. Somehow the delicate sweetness of the fruit from her garden, miraculously free of the acid taste of dense traffic, added to the impression that this was someone that the aging century had left behind.

I only really felt the need for that Other London once the exam season was looming. It had happened little by little, but I had to acknowledge that something was lacking. It was more than exam nerves, more like a kind of emptiness. I cut the umbilical cord that tied me to the Student Union and set off on the tube to Finsbury Park.

I remember how I sat, forlorn, in my carriage. It was so hot, heated by a summer sunburn of the passengers and perhaps in these dark depths by the heat of the earth itself. I closed my eyes and slipped into sleep. Sleep wound round with dreams, going back in my head, back to the time when I had first gone to stay with my sister at my Great Aunt and Uncle's.

We were going to stay a whole week without our parents, what's more in *London*, a place that seemed so very far away. We were not sure what to expect as we waved goodbye in the doorway. My sister was reassuring: at ten she seemed practically grown up to me. She was going to look after me and give me my night time cough-mixture. Everything would be all right.

I wasn't frightened of my Great Uncle and Aunt. It was just that up until then I hadn't really known them. They were two kind but terribly old people who arrived by train at Christmas and for one summer visit and were gone again a few days later. Their whistling, cantankerous hearing-aids discouraged conversation. Both of them had radiated kindness, though, and I was fond of them. When they did chat to us about the past, I used to struggle to understand; they still talked of weekends at spa towns to "take the waters" and asked me to put things away in the pantry. (Is that a room?? Is that a fridge?) My love for them was perhaps not one based on true understanding, but it was real and warm. A child's love.

Once or twice a year we would write to them. At first we would just draw a picture and try and sign our names, and later we would attempt a real letter. It was almost impossibly hard to write their names out in full, and letters to Great Auntie Lydia and Great Uncle George always started, " Dear A.L and U.G." Now suddenly we were going to stay with the *real* Great Aunt and Uncle, and on their territory...

It was very soon apparent that their house was no holiday camp. My Great Aunt especially did not tolerate idle hands, and immediately gave us jobs to do; brass cleaning, sorting wool, polishing glasses and suchlike. We didn't dare complain, but whispered to each other about our dire situation. It was worse than Brownies. It was worse than a labour camp.

It seemed that our 'holiday' was going to be pretty bleak, until our Great Aunt took us into her front room on our second afternoon. She led us to a huge and rather ungainly piece of furniture in the corner; we were both amazed when she explained that this was her 'gramophone.' This colossal dinosaur was so far removed from our neat hifi at home – how could music come out of it?

128

But music *did* come out of it. My aunt carefully wiped a thick black record clean, and set the needle. She took off her apron as the first notes floated out, and then she was flying, flying around the room. Her elderly body was feather-light, following feet that still remembered the steps she had danced as a young woman. She scooped us up in her arms and suddenly we were dancing too, whirling and spinning, all three of us carried by the music. Magic happened that afternoon. Her heavy machine poured out mad-giggling happiness, lifting us up and twirling us like tops until we collapsed, rocking with laughter, into one big and exhausted heap on the sofa.

My Great Uncle never danced. He was a much slower man. A steady man. His only 'folly' was his annual flutter of £1 on a horse for the Grand National. He never, ever picked a winner, but neither did he grumble when his horse fell at the first fence and when my sister's, chosen with the expertise common to ten-year-olds, went on to win. He took it all in his stride. He shrugged and pottered off into his beloved garden.

His real passion was his gardening, and it was a perfect reflection of his personality. There was no place for flashy plants or any showy decoration. Just a strip of lawn with a simple, stone birdbath that we would clamour to fill with water, eager to stand with our noses pressed to the cold glass of the kitchen windows and watch the sparrows dip and flutter. On either side of the lawn was the true glory of the garden, his pear trees, pear trees blooming with thick ruffles of pink blossom, and later impossibly heavy with fruit. Branches so laden that they would creak and lean to rest their tips on the lawn... their magnificent fruition the result of decades of careful pruning and loving care. My Great Uncle's *chef d'oeuvre*.

My Great Aunt brought her own, quick bright spark of life to the garden. She wouldn't wait patiently as the fruit ripened, but would wage an active campaign against marauding squirrels. My sister and I would be strategically placed on guard behind the kitchen door, and if ever a grey, fluffy creature climbed over the high garden wall, we would spring out onto the lawn, whooping and banging saucepans with wooden spoon. The poor animals would shoot back over the wall, fluffed with fright and, hopefully, resolved never to return.

Sometimes we followed my Great Uncle around the garden. He was no entertainer; he would talk about the past not as a story-teller, but as someone who had lived through it. He would tell us how it really felt when the war ended, or about the day when he cycled across fields (fields!) next to his London home to see the Hindenberg crash. We loved to hear about how he would push his barrow with my mother through wartime London, a London filled with horses, to collect manure for his garden. It was all so improbable, so magical this city of the past, that I didn't imagine *real* horses but brightly coloured carousel ones, half galloping and half dancing through the streets.

My Great Aunt also had her stories... about Girl Guide camping in High Barnet, when there were farms and meadows full of cows on the Northern Line. How they had slept on straw in tents with no groundsheets, and had awakened covered in slugs that had slipped in with the morning dew.

So we worked and listened and never really had the time to be homesick. We even forgot the cough-mixture. Once or twice we went to Priory Park. It was a time when my one fear was what would happen if my swing went right over the top of the bar. Swinging through the air, sick with terror but still wanting to see if I could get that high.

At night we slept in the back bedroom, overlooking the garden. There was just a big bed and one other piece of furniture; a heavy wooden cupboard. It had a thick key in the lock, and my sister and I fantasised deliciously about what could be inside. Virtually everything seemed possible, from griffin eggs to sleeping princesses. Finally we gave way to temptation and in what seemed like the dead of night (the sound of the nine o'clock news from downstairs failed to spoil the illusion) we turned the key, swung open the door and shone our torch inside.

The cupboard was filled from top to bottom with jars of jam, winking at us in the torch beam. Their colours glowed like jewels as the light played over them; burgundy, gold, ruby and amber. They shone with such intensity that it seemed they were lit from within, each jar containing the sunshine of an entire summer. They were labelled in sloping, antique-looking writing; my Great Aunt's hand. Apple and Blackberry, Gooseberry and Currant, and Pear Preserves. Those labels seemed like magical formulae, each containing depth and power. Some of them seemed not quite finished, and our imagination filled in the gaps. Thus bottled pears became "Sun shines and Pear Preserves." It became a kind of proverb for us, symbolising forever my Great Aunt's ability to capture warmth and light; a miracle greater than any alchemy.

All those years later I was oddly nervous when I rang the bell. I was no longer a child, and I felt awkward. What role could I play now that squirrel-watching was a thing of the past? Both of them came to the canary yellow front door, both smiling and eager to hug me. We went out into the garden, and drank milky tea and admired the first swelling fruit. I tried, in vain, to explain what university was 'for'. They were baffled – I was reading French, and my Great Aunt grumbled that in her day they had learnt French in Primary School, or at any rate, they could hum the *Marseillaise*. Why did it take modern kids years to learn it?

The afternoon ripened into evening as we chatted outside, and it was suddenly reassuring to explain my choices to somebody else. When it was time to go I was solemnly given a paper bag of homemade rock-cakes. Such things are rarely seen in student halls of residence, and I took a lot of stick over it. Visiting elderly relatives on a Saturday... hardly a cool way to spend one's time. I didn't care. My feet had touched ground and I was thankful.

The following autumn I helped with the jam for the first time. I picked and washed the blackberries and my Great Aunt lit the stove. She boiled and boiled the dark fruit, dipping in a quick spoon to see if it was ready. She dripped iridescent beads of it onto a cold saucer, pushing them with her finger to see if they wrinkled. Once the drops of jam were thick enough she sighed with satisfaction, and set about bottling and labelling. It was late when we carried the jars upstairs to the cupboard and I got my first official look inside. This wasn't just jam making, it was Initiation.

My Great Aunt was full of energy that year, but my Great Uncle changed. He had cancer. He no longer went out wearing his heavy over-coat and trilby to buy his paper. He sat in a chair wearing his faded pyjamas, and he was thinner and greyer every weekend. He was too weak to have his bet on a horse for the Grand National. Too weak even to get out into the garden.

He endured one year of the indignity dying can bring. Of spongebaths and commodes. Of pain. One Saturday I cut his nails for him. I hope I was as gentle as he had been years before, dabbing my grazed knees with gentian violet as I sat, tearstained, on the kitchen worktop. He watched me carefully as I held his hand to cut the nails. I saw that his skin had changed, as though his flesh was already dying. I was frightened and appalled, but was desperate to appear reassuring. I tried to think of something to say but his face, soft as a weary child's, quietened me. There was no need for words.

He died in the autumn; his death gentler than his year of dying. We had time to say good-bye, and it was a moment of love rather than of pain. When it was all over we stepped out of his room into the hallway. The sunshine was pouring in through the stained glass panel in the front door, such a feast of colour, so rich and cheerful that it seemed impossible that this day could be the start of mourning.

The autumn was golden and the garden was bursting with fruit, but that year my Great Aunt didn't have the strength for cooking, let alone jam-making. She lived on cup-a-soups. She tried to get out and go to her 'clubs.' She survived. She couldn't face the garden again though, and from then on even if the sun shone the fruit was left to rot on the trees.

I was afraid of how I would find her when I returned from my year out in France. I had feared the worst, but she had become strong again. When I went to visit her I was astonished when she suggested going out – she explained as she buttoned her coat that she had found a good bakery and was wanting to buy some cakes.

Three bus rides and a hike across Woodgreen later and we were at her shop. She didn't so much walk in as charge, wagging her finger at the teenager behind the counter.

"You're never going to sell all those cream cakes in the next hour, you know, and as it's Saturday you'll be closed then until Monday. They'll all be off by then. Go on, I'll give you fifteen pence for one."

The girl laughed, thinking it was a joke. My Great Aunt fixed her with a hard stare, and her laugh changed to nervous coughing. Finally, she opted for pity, and as I curled up with embarrassment she gave way, showing her kindness towards what she saw as a little old lady,

"All right then, but just this once and don't tell the boss..."

My Great Aunt grinned determinedly. "Thanks, dear. At that price, I'll take a dozen of them."

I left London after Finals. The years have flashed by for me, yet I know they went painfully slowly for her. Myself and others around us all moved on, and she was left behind. She even referred to herself as 'The Relic.' I visited her once more with my sister one Sunday. I was eight weeks pregnant with my Ben, and bursting with pride. We walked in Priory Park where there was a fair, an old-fashioned one with swing-boats and coconut shies. For the first time in forty years she stroked a real pony. It was white and wearing a brightly coloured bridle and saddle; strangely her real horse was the image of the carousel horses that I had imagined in London as a child.

Ben has been born, and yes, of course, photos were sent, but she never saw him. His birth made me feel more keenly the things I had not shared with her, the things I had not understood. She had lost her only child when it was just hours old. I don't even know whether it was a girl or a boy, or have any idea of how she lived through it. She bore electro-shock therapy, anything to jerk her out of her pain. Her life must have been overshadowed by that tragedy. At that time, of course, it was common to lose a child, yet it would be crass to think that because such a thing is common it becomes bearable. She spent the rest of her life battling to be brave.

Now Ben is lying beside me, tiny, soft and snuggled in milk-warmed sleep. The sun is streaming in, a French sun far from London. In just a few days she will be buried, but with a small baby I won't be able to go. I will never see her again.

I loved her, and I am sorry for myself, for it seems some vital part of my life has died, too. One of my last links to England has disappeared. I cry hot tears: a child's tears for a child's love. And I wish I could have something to remember her by – something simple: a jar of pears, one summer of our past.

Sun shines and pear preserves.

Home. Wednesday, 30th July.

Mum and Dad called in today on their way back to England for the funeral. It seemed a bit ridiculous to be showing them our new chickens, but Mum said Lyd would have understood such things. She used to keep chickens during the war, and she remembers taking hot potato peelings and bran mash out to them in the winter. She will always remember the warm, yeasty smell, and the way the chickens would scratch in the snow to eat up every last scrap. They were lean years – poor on calories but rich with memories.

Mum talked to me about that magical garden; of lying in the warm grass in summer and racing ladybirds between two freckles on her bare tummy. As she reminisced it was almost as if Lyd and George were there with us. I suppose that as long as we remember they *will* always be there.

Home. Thursday, 31st July.

The end of July.

A quiet day inside today. It's hot and I don't feel like going out. Eric studied while I took care of Ben. I cuddled him and sang him songs all day, and it felt right to be close to him.

Eric said I need cheering up, and that tomorrow he's taking us out for some air.

A walk has been announced...

AOÛT

Home. Friday, 1st August.

Hot! Hot! HOT! It really is *very* hot. It feels as though France has slipped down the melting globe and has settled somewhere near Africa.

I thought Eric had forgotten about the walk, or had put it off until it's a bit cooler. I was just filling the washing-up bowl for Ben (he's been using it as a paddling pool, it's the right size for him and keeps him cool) when Eric told me to get ready.

I wasn't sure what preparations he had in mind, other than packing a spare nappy for Ben and a drink for us. My walks in England were pretty simple affairs: one foot in front of the other, look left, look right and then head for the nearest pub. A walk *à la française* did not appear to be as straightforward...

To start with, a walk for me does not require any special clothing, other than a pair of reasonably comfy shoes (although these should not be so sensible that one would feel embarrassed if one met someone one knew on aforesaid walk.) Why oh why then was Eric digging out army boots and camouflage trousers???? Was this war?

It didn't just stop there. After a lot of rooting around in our remaining boxes from the move he produced a khaki coloured rucksack, a battered Ozzie hat and a gigantic army knife he acquired during his National Service days. A little apprehensively I rethought what I was taking, and put a large packet of chocolate biscuits in the rucksack. When in doubt take chocolate.

(As a teeny aside, I used to be quite into the Survival thing, actually. As a teenager I was forever packing wax-tipped matches, fishhooks and sugar cubes into shoe polish tins, just in case. I mean you never know, my school bus might have got lost and ended up in the Amazon. This, of course, was before a friend of Anna's – five years older than us and streetwise – informed me that the only things a modern girl's survival kit need contain are a credit card and a condom.)

Anyway, once Eric had got his stuff together he swung Ben up into the carrier, whistled for Dog and we were off. Eric strode towards the forest beyond our woods, and I pottered along behind, feeling anxious.

Once we were in the thick of the woods the walk really began in earnest. If I'd had Eric down as Biggles on our first fishing trip I now had to change my view of him. He was no longer Biggles; he'd graduated to pure, undiluted Tarzan.

He swiped right and left as the creepers, obviously imagining himself in that peculiar Hollywoodian jungle where African elephants and Indian tigers live quite happily side by side. Ben, it seemed, was cast in the role of Boy. My Tarzan was hell-bent on Initiation, giving Boy useful advice on everything from tree-house building to how to tie a tourniquet around your leg if you ever get bitten by a cobra. (Boy was actually asleep in the sling, but Tarzan didn't notice that. He was too busy keeping an eye out for those cobras.)

We didn't, of course, stick to the path, but battled miles and miles in the heat through bracken, tripping over tree stumps and brambles. Woods, woods and more woods. This, I knew, was a forest where you can walk for miles without seeing a house or a road, let alone a pub. We were hours away from Intelligent Life – there may have been a hunter around but they don't count. Mutinous thoughts came to mind – it was August – why couldn't we have gone to the beach?? Dog also looked Unenthusiastic, limping along behind and giving me soulful I'd-rather-have-watched-telly looks.

"What would Jane have done?" I asked myself. Apart from a couple of swimming scenes (where she mostly spent her time lounging about on outsized water-lily pads) I couldn't remember her doing anything much. Well, I suppose she did keep her tree-house spick and span, and used to sing a lot as she set the table with plates made from leaves. Just like Disney's Snow White – lots of propaganda about the wonders of woodland housework and nothing concrete to help get me out of the forest and back home.

Suddenly I was struck by a Brilliant Idea. "Eric!" I called after the hat that was bobbing along above the bracken somewhere near the horizon, "Why don't we have a weeny chocolate break?"

The effect of my suggestion was spectacular – he just can't resist chocolate. Tarzan stopped dead and waited for me to catch up with him. "In the bag" I gasped, sinking to the ground in an Exhausted and Very Hot Heap.

Once the chocolate biscuits were found things brightened up. Ben played happily with a Rusk I'd packed for him, licking it and wiping it on Eric's hat. I was revitalised, and soon stopped wishing Tarzan would fall into an elephant trap and be devoured by cannibals. As we munched our way through the packet things became more peaceful again.

After the chocolate we turned around and headed for Home, walking hand in hand this time. This was the Castanet family on an amble, and we actually enjoyed it. Thank heavens Eric was Eric again! Being Tarzan means that he really can't see the woods for the trees.

Home. Saturday, 2nd August.

Dog spent all day licking her paws after yesterday's excursion. I wish I could have licked mine.

Home. Sunday, 3rd August.

It's dead quiet in the village – the general store usually opens on Sunday morning, but today is has stayed closed. We drove all the way to Libourne to do some shopping in the market, but there were much fewer stalls. *Août* is pronounced here like a Cumbrian 'out', and that is where the French are in August. It is a month for holidays, not for making money. The country is deserted – everyone is at the beach.

Not quite everyone. Jean-Pierre came round today. He wasn't alone – there was a basket on the back of his moped. Inside was a poodle; his landlady is on holiday in the Pyrenees and hadn't wanted to take her dog, Bébé Béatrice, with her because she's worried she might suffer from altitude sickness. Bébé Béatrice, I should explain, is not an ordinary dog – she is his landlady's substitute for a daughter. She receives presents for her birthday and for Christmas and Easter, and has regular visits to one of the most expensive dog beauty parlours in Bordeaux. Bébe Béatrice is the most precious thing in his landlady's life, which made me wonder what an earth she was doing entrusting her to Jean-Pierre. I could feel dark, ominous clouds rushing in to darken the summer sky.

We hadn't seen Jean-Pierre for a while, as he's been busy watching the *Tour de France*. This was the first time he'd been out for ages, he said, and he wanted to give us a hand. He still hasn't found a job, but was keen to help us in exchange for something nice to eat.

Eric said he was planning to finish cleaning the barn, and I was busy painting the bathroom white. (I just couldn't live with the shiny blue any longer, so we bought a job lot of paint.) There *was* something Jean-Pierre could do though – the chicken man in the market this morning had mentioned that he had a friend with goats for sale. They wouldn't be expensive as they were really 'abbatoir material' but they would give us kids in the new year. We both love the idea of getting our goats now, and Eric suggested to Jean-Pierre that he start repairing the fence around the field.

He cheerfully accepted, as I promised him Orangina every twenty minutes, and a roast lunch. We all got stuck into our work, but after three Orangina breaks Jean-Pierre stopped coming into the house. I thought he'd just moved up to the top of the field, and couldn't be bothered to come down. It was lunchtime when I decided I should check on him, and just as I was stepping out the door the phone rang.

"Allo, allo!" said a worried voice, which I recognised (with some surprise and a great deal of apprehension) as Jean-Pierre's.

"You're supposed to be in the field!" I squeaked.

Jean-Pierre's explanation came rushing out. Bébé Béatrice, whom he had claimed was elderly and half crippled, had managed to give him the slip and race off. He'd run after her, and had spent the rest of the morning chasing her fruitlessly around the countryside. He was thinking about calling the *gendarmes,* but as his relationship with them has been a bit strained since the bank incident he hadn't dared to.

I've advised him to stay at home and wait – most dogs find their way home in the end.

Let's hope so, or else he'll soon be looking for alternative accommodation...

Home. Monday, 4th August.

Bébé Béatrice is back! Jean-Pierre rang this afternoon to say she turned up at last. She was so dirty that she looked as if she'd been through an oil slick, but at least she was safe.

Jean-Pierre said he had one other piece of good news. "It's the Job Centre. They've sent me a letter to apply for a job in the nuclear power station which supplies Bordeaux. This time next month I could be working there!"

God help us.

Home. Tuesday, 5th August.

We have three goats! I'm in ecstasy!

Eric rang the chicken man to find out the address of the farm this evening, and we drove over to see them. There were about forty goats in the goat-shed, and ours had been penned in one corner. They were so beautiful – silky white fur, intelligent eyes and horns like BMX handlebars.

All three of them were destined for the abattoir as they only produce a litre of milk between them, but that's plenty for us. They will also keep the grass down on the hill, and turn some of the brambles into milk. It seems like a good deal.

The farmer loaded them into his trailer, and explained he'd follow us home. His little daughter came out to say goodbye to them, and pointed out her favourite one to me. She's the goat with a dark patch over her eye, which makes her look positively piratical.

"*Au revoir, Houdini,*" she said sadly. As she walked around the other side of the trailer with her Dad I saw him crossly whisper something to her, and she shook her head stubbornly. "*Mais si, elle s'appelle Houdini, papa!*" she said.

Her Dad said, in a voice that we could all hear, that he was sure Marguerite, Rose and, er, Buttercup would be very happy in their new home. and then we were off.

We got home without incident, and put them in the barn. We don't have to milk them tonight as the farmer had done that before we left his farm, so we've left them in peace with a manger full of fresh hay.

Fresh milk for breakfast tomorrow!

Home. Wednesday, 6th August.

Buttercup *alias* Houdini is certainly living up to her real name. Eric went outside to milk the goats this morning, when I was changing Ben. I heard him open the barn door, and then swear loudly. Seconds later I saw something flash past the window, and I glanced out to see what it was.

It was Houdini. Eric explained later that she had climbed through the manger into the corridor where the door is, and as he opened the door she'd leapt past him. She looked at me coolly – her 'patched' eye was too dark to see, but I could swear she winked with her other one. That goat looks like she's going to give us a run for our money.

Eric finally got her back into the barn by tempting her with a handful of grain, and then he milked all three of them. Marguerite and Rose only produced a mug of milk between them, but Houdini produced masses. Eric thinks the farmer must have muddled her up with another goat, as milk yield really isn't her problem.

This morning we had over a litre and a half of milk – enough for all three of us – and at tonight's milking we'll have even more.

It's a pity I don't like the stuff, really.

Home. Thursday, 7th August.

More and more and more milk.

Lucienne has offered to send me a yoghurt maker she bought years ago, and I'm hoping that the milk won't taste as strong that way. We like yoghurt, and with a bit of luck we should also be able to make goat's cheese, which I adore.

I'm looking on the bright side, but Eric is gloomy. He doesn't like goat's milk, and I'm not sure he likes goats much, either. Well, things are going OK with Marguerite and Rose, who graze peacefully on the hill behind the house, but Houdini has done everything today to break out of her enclosure and into the vegetable patch. She has leapt over the fence, crashed through it and wriggled under it. It has finally dawned on us why she's called Houdini – she can escape from anything. I have a suspicion this is also the real reason the farmer wanted rid of her.

Tonight I'm cheering Eric up by saying we'll soon be eating yummy goat's cheese, and that I'm sure there's a way to keep Houdini penned successfully. I've suggested we invest in an electric fence, but Eric (still intent on being glum) says an electric chair is what that goat needs.

Home. Friday, 8th August.

Home alone.

Well, Ben's here but Eric is *en vacances* until tomorrow. Stephan rang this morning and asked whether Eric would like to go on a cycling/camping jaunt with him. They've planned to cycle eighty kilometres or so this evening together, then sleep under the stars on some haystack somewhere. Eric loves that kind of thing, and it's amazing to see how happy he is to exchange his bath for a dip in a stream. Maybe boys just never grow out of Scouts. They have compasses clipped to their car keys and at Christmas they buy each other strange devices to purify swamp water – I wonder if Eric still thinks he might accidentally end up in the Amazon? He's so into survival that he's even asked me whether I would eat my dead companions in the event of a plane crash, which makes me nervous when driving long distances in remote areas with him.

He milked the goats in the early evening, and then cycled off with Stephan. Véro had dropped him off at our house, and after they'd gone we both laughed about their 'luggage.' Eric has taken a light rucksack with a couple of cans of food in it – despite them being the pull-off top kind he's taken his Swiss army can-opener with him. Stephan packed an ultra light telescopic fishing rod, and a dozen lures he's whittled himself. He thought they should catch all their own food.

Véro and Théo loved our goats, and helped me close up the barn for the night. I don't want Houdini escaping when I'm all by myself. They stayed for tea and then left me to give Ben his bath and pop him to bed.

The house seems terribly quiet tonight, and what noise there is scares the life out of me. The sound of the water heater is one thing, but there is a noise like a rattling chain which is Disquieting to say the least. I wish Eric were here.

Home. Saturday, 9th August.

Got up to milk the goats this morning and found that they were all outside already. The chain on the door of the barn was right off. It took me ages (and many handfuls of corn) to get them in again, but the milking itself wasn't too hard. When I'd finished I carried Ben and the pail out, and carefully shut the door and put the chain on. Then, cuddling Ben, I crouched down behind it to see how the goats had got out.

The culprit, of course, was Houdini. Within two minutes I heard her climbing through the manger again, and then jump down the other side. Then I felt her pushing against the door, and it opened just a crack – just enough to let her get her horn through. It was extraordinary how she managed it really, but she jiggled the chain with the tip of her horn (it was the noise, I realized, that I'd heard in the night) until she lifted it right off.

I didn't let her get any further, but flung open the door and yelled at her. For a fraction of a second she looked apologetic, but I doubt it will last. She leapt back through the manger and hid behind a bale of hay.

I was worried about them having enough to eat, so I let them out for the day. Apart from a brief excursion into the radishes Houdini behaved herself, but she has a glint in her eye as though she's planning something Really Wicked. Oh dear.

Eric came back in time to milk them in the evening, and he looked hot, hungry and haggard. Not how one is supposed to look after a holiday.

The hot part of things was easy to explain, as the temperature is going up and up, and it is also becoming more humid. He was hungry because they'd eaten both the tins last night, and Stephan's fishing failed to provide today. Apparently he'd made a few miscalculations with his home-made lures – they either bobbed about on the surface or sank like stones. They pinched some sweet corn from a field, but apart from that they hadn't eaten all day.

Eric looked grumpy when I asked him why he was so tired, and he growled something about it all being the fault of the *anglais*.

I was a little nonplussed. Living in France when you are English is not always a *pique-nique,* as we so often get blamed for things – European financial problems, mad cows' disease, foot and mouth epidemics, harbouring terrorists and hooliganism – you name it, it's our fault. Despite the fact the area we live in *was* English several centuries ago, the locals are distinctly crabby with us. One old man in the village grumbled at me when I said I was from England, and said I just didn't realise how much France suffered in the war. I thought he was talking about World War One or Two, and was flabbergasted when he went on to say what a good thing it was that France won and threw the English out – in 1453. Some people have long memories...

Oddly enough, it turned out that this old war was why Eric was looking so exhausted. He explained (now looking a bit sheepish) that they'd settled down to sleep in a hay barn, but were woken half an hour later by what sounded like cannons. They both leapt to their feet and rushed outside, and saw the sky had turned red. There was a tremendous noise, shouting and screaming, coming from the village over the hill. They thought the end of the world was nigh.

It was Stephan who realised what was happening first. They'd camped next to Castillon-la-Bataille, which as the name suggests is a battle ground. THE battle ground in fact, where the English were beaten in 1453. Every year over 300 actors in the village re-enact the event, racing around on horseback and firing cannons – it is a *son et lumière par excellence*. They'd both forgotten about it when they picked their camping ground, and were awake half the night listening to it. Eric said he couldn't wait to get home and have some peace and quiet.

So much for the relaxing mini-break!

Home. Sunday, 10th August.

10.30am. Just had a call from Mum and Dad. They are on the way back from the UK, and are just a couple of hours away. Dad said the funeral was sad, but at least all the family were there. Mum saw cousins she hasn't seen since for years and years, and it was nice to catch up with them again. It's just so depressing that it should take a funeral to get everyone together.

Anyway, Dad said they are passing through our area, and would Ben and I like to come with them back to the coast for a little holiday? He knows that Eric will have to stay and take care of the farm, but I could probably do with a break...

Well, it sounded just too tempting, so I've packed Ben's nappies and my bikini, and I've already given Eric a big kiss goodbye. He looked a bit gloomy, but I've promised him I'll be back on Thursday. With a tan.

Back Home. Thursday, 14th August.

Hmmmmm – I love holidays. It's a shame Eric wasn't with us, but it was wonderful to laze about in the warm ocean with Ben. We swam every day, as Ben was just mad about splashing around in the shallows and blowing bubbles into the water. Not only has he made friends with the sea, but I've also saved a small fortune in nappies these past few days...

Mum and Dad were thrilled to have Ben to play with, and they liked taking him for long walks in the pushchair in the cool of the evening. Oh, and Ben got his first taste of Dad's barbecues – minced up, of course, but he found it Delicious.

We also took him to the park for the first time. We propped him up with a cushion in a baby swing, and he was ecstatic about it. We'll have to get one to have at home. The lime tree would be the perfect place for it.

I think Mum and Dad have cottoned on to one thing about Ben – they put huge amounts of energy into entertaining him – but however much energy they had Ben always had more. When we were all dropping in the evening Ben was still chirruping away in his pushchair, as though asking what we were going to play next. I think Mum and Dad are going to sleep for a fortnight to recover from these last few days.

Eric was suitably pleased to see us again. He says Ben looks twice the size he was on Sunday – must be the BBQs. He also admired my tan, although he says he still prefers the pale bits.

It's Dad's birthday tomorrow, and when he dropped me back at home Eric solemnly presented him with a homemade present – half a dozen goats cheeses! He'd asked around the local farmers for advice, and had bought some moulds and the yeasty stuff you have to put in the milk to make it all happen. He said it wasn't too difficult really – he just had to mess around with pipettes and thermometers. He thought it was probably easier than the home hair-colouring kit I used after my Disastrous Haircut, and that it had the added advantage of tasting much nicer.

The goats, chickens, geese and Dog have all been well-behaved during my absence, but I still wouldn't trust Houdini. Still, considering the scrumptious cheese she's just produced I won't say a word against her.

Home. Friday, 15th August.

BIG, BIG day in France. It is, of course, Dad's birthday, but this isn't the reason the whole country has a national *fête*. It's Assumption, an important date for Catholics, and it is also Napoleon's birthday. He declared it to be a day off, maybe so the country could have a little time off from military campaigns. I'm tempted to think that the *quinze août* is a holiday because it is slap-bang in the middle of the hottest, stickiest month, and that any excuse is a good excuse to have some time off, a big party and a few fireworks.

Any work which might have been accomplished during August is completely forgotten once the 15th approaches. It's quite impossible to get your car fixed, buy a pair of shoes or see your usual doctor. If you dare ask *pourquoi?* you'll be looked at as though you're an idiot and given the obvious explanation – *"parce que c'est le quinze août, madame!"* Even after the 15th the explanation is still valid – people need a recovery period after the party.

For us the 15th is a bit of a mixed blessing this year. The good thing is that the bank is closed, so our bank manager can't ring up and ask for money. Our overdraft is at its maximum limit, and we really need some money from somewhere. I'm not sure he'll accept fresh eggs in lieu. The bad thing is that our dossier for family allowance (which I am busy trying to transfer to our new address) is lost on some administrator's desk somewhere. Unfortunately it is impossible to get hold of anyone, as the entire government department has closed "for their customers' convenience." A likely story. They're supposed to be working away behind locked doors clearing the backlog of dossiers, but I bet they've all gone to the beach.

Well, if you can't beat them, join them. It's too hot to even sleep at the moment, so tonight we're going to the party in our village. *C'est la fête!*

Home. Saturday, 16th August.

Fabulous fun!

We got ready for the party in the early evening. Eric had an extra shave while Ben and I frolicked in a bath full of foam alphabet letters. Once we were clean and dry (and the panic was over about whether Ben had eaten the letter K) we put on our smartest clothes and drove into the village. There was a sit-down dinner on offer for the whole village, at only 50 francs a head. We haven't been out for dinner since prehistoric times, so we thought we'd join in.

We spotted Marie-Thérèse, deep in conversation with the local priest. Cathérine was also there, chatting to Monsieur Beau about the level of the river, trying to calculate already whether it will flood this winter. Cathérine had polished her rangers and Monsieur Beau was wearing a new beret for the party – he seemed to have bought the wrong size, as it kept slipping down over his eye. Huguette and Henri were nowhere to be seen – I asked Cathérine whether she thought they were busy with the cows. She shrugged and said they never come to the village, and they haven't shopped in the village store for over forty years. *"Que voulez*

HENRI HENRIETTE
+ THEIR BARN.

vous", she said, motioning towards the tables full of villagers, "their cows are clever than that lot. And kinder."

It seemed harsh, but when we sat down at the trestle tables we were struck by the oddness of the conversation around us. One man, the village hairdresser, was giving anyone who'd listen a lecture about AIDS. His theory was that AIDS was invented by the Chinese and sent to Europe via satellite. Anyone with a satellite dish could pick it up. We blocked off our ears to that conversation, but the group of men next to us were discussing local wildlife, and that wasn't much better. Their conclusion was that everything with fur or feathers is better off in the freezer, where it won't damage crops.

Happily the conversation mellowed as the wine began to flow. People became friendlier, laughing and joking together. Wonderful cooking smells began to curl around the village square where we were sitting, and music started to play. The *apéritif* had taken some time, and now the villagers were merry enough to dance to the endearing sounds of the local brass band and "Le Mégamix" which was playing on an ancient sound system. There was something for everyone, and everyone danced. Even Ben jiggled in his pushchair.

At around ten o'clock dinner was served. There were sea-food platters to share for starters. These turned out to be a little disconcerting as virtually everything on them was still alive. Usually the killing is done some while before the eating, but here there were oysters to be opened, cockles to be cracked and whelks to winkle out of their shells. It was tough for an ex-vegetarian, even if it was delicious. I tried to rescue a baby crab which crawled out from under a pile of seaweed, but Eric said there was no way we were going to drive 80 kilometres to the seaside to set it free. He's so mean sometimes.

I left him to finish off the seafood (literally) and chatted to the person sitting next to me – a glass of wine really helps my sociability. "In England," I said, waving my arm in the direction of the band, "we don't have this 15th August thing." He looked utterly bewildered, and asked quite seriously, "What, do you go straight from August 14th to August 16th then?"

Fortunately the main course arrived then (some kind of rabbit stew) and we were all too busy eating to converse. Ben tried little bits, and seemed quite keen on it. After that there were huge slices of crusty bread and pungent cheese. Eric took out his penknife, which he usually uses to whittle bits of wood into strange canoe shapes, something to do with the survival thing again, I suppose. This time he used it to cut tiny pieces of cheese for Ben, which he quite liked. What he really adored, though, was dessert – a rich, creamy *crème caramel*. He ate nearly all of mine, and used quite a few teaspoons as facepack as well.

Absolutely full up we sat back and sipped cognac as the dancing got underway under the trees. It was dark, and the square was lit by candles on the table and multicoloured lights in the trees. As the dancers twirled they were lit up green, orange, red and blue. I said dreamily to Eric that it looked as though rainbows were whirling around the square, but he just told me to go easy on the cognac.

Ben, suddenly, was very quiet, and we saw that he'd fallen asleep in the pushchair, both arms wrapped tightly around Teddy. The first fireworks started a few minutes later, but as firework after firework exploded into the starry August sky Ben just hugged Teddy tighter and let out a gentle snore. I won't bother walking around on tiptoe anymore if I get up at night – this child can sleep through rockets.

At midnight we went Home, a little sad that the party was over but safe in the knowledge that it will all happen again next year. In France, *heureusement*, we never go straight from the August 14th to the 16th...

Home. Sunday, 17th August.

I thought there were a few stray fireworks going off again in the early hours, but it was just the first of the seasonal storms crashing its way across the country. By the time we got up it was all over – the sun was out and the grass was gently steaming dry.

We went out to see how the rain had watered the garden. It had really chucked it down, and some of our plants had been flattened. Eric didn't mind though – he was too excited by what the storm had brought out from dry walls and other hidey-holes – there were hundreds of snails everywhere.

He raced into the barn to get a bucket, and persuaded me to collect some. In just an hour we had over two hundred. Eric said his Mum has a fabulous snail recipe – we would be able to have a gourmet meal absolutely free.

I thought we were going to have snails for lunch, but apparently they have to be purged first. This means they have to spend a week with nothing to eat except flour. I did have other things in mind for my bag of flour other than flushing out snails' intestines – I rather preferred the idea of an apple pie. Still, Eric said I had to try a traditional French dish, so the apple pie will have to wait. This time next week we are in for a treat.

Instead of snails we had nettle quiche for lunch, courtesy of our hens and of the huge mounds of nettles on the hill. We had fresh salad and tomatoes from the garden with it, and goats' yoghurt for dessert. We are eating well, even if our meals have to be earned. Self-sufficiency is HARD WORK!!!

We both worked together on the vegetable garden in the afternoon, only breaking off our work to repair more damage caused by Houdini. She'd leapt over the fence and come into the garden, where she'd found Ben's baby blanket drying on the line. She had nipped the end of it to see what the wool tasted like, and then walked away, unravelling the blanket as she went. By the time we found her she had virtually unravelled the whole thing, and the garden was full of blue crinkly wool. I'm not sure if chains around her body – Houdini style – would stop her, but I have positive proof that having wool wound round and round her doesn't slow her down one bit.

Tonight we're both feeling a little despondent. We are totally knackered from the physical work, and Eric is going to have to study all evening so he'll be ready for his first '*stage*' in September; this is a compulsory week-long course that everyone doing the diploma has to attend. I am frantic as the bank opens again tomorrow, and we are going to have to come up with some cash.

I'm going to sleep on it and hope for an answer in the morning.

Home. Monday, 18th August.

A Good Idea. I rang Véro today to see if she knows anyone who wants English lessons. She knows stacks of people and could well come up trumps. If Eric looks after Ben (between feeds!) then I may be able to earn a bit of cash.

Fingers crossed...

Home. Tuesday, 19th August.

HOORAY!!!!!!!!!! SUCCESS!!!!!!!!!!

Véro rang back this morning. She has friends of friends (of friends) who have a big wine *château*, and their fifteen-year-old boy needs some "*cours de rattrapage*" – remedial lessons to boost his level before school starts again in a September. Véro is wonderful.

I rang the boy's mother, and she said as he goes back to school in a fortnight, could I possibly come tomorrow? Charles-Henri would *love* to get started.

We've agreed to do ten hours of teaching over five days, and she's offered to pay me 1750 francs. Riches indeed!!

Tonight I am sorting through my clothes, desperately looking for something smart enough to wear. I'm not sure how well army trousers would go down in a *château*...

Home. Wednesday, 20th August.

I set off to the *château* at eight this morning – despite the early hour I was already boiling hot. The only passable thing I had to wear was a black wool suit, and it was stifling. I'd had to shave all the bobbles off it with Eric's razor to make it presentable, and as the temperature rose I began to wish I'd cut a few ventilation holes in it as well.

It was complicated finding the *château*, and I was relieved to spot its huge, golden gates-like something you'd see at Versailles. I rang a big

149

bronze bell, and the gates swung open all by themselves-quite eerie, really.

I got back into Virginie – just in time. Two absurdly large dogs belted down the drive, foaming at the jowls and baying like wolves. I drove what seemed like several kilometres up to the front door, while the dogs from hell leapt wildly at my tyres and windscreen. My wipers were going full tilt, trying to keep the windscreen clear of rabid slobber.

Madame was waiting at the door, wringing her hands. "Do be careful of the dogs, they are pedigrees..." she cried. It took a lot of courage getting out of the car, and I had to grit my teeth when she told me not to step on their paws. I was more concerned about not being eaten than about damaging one of their plate-sized tootsie-wootsies.

Madame knocked on the front door – she must have come out of some other door, as it was locked on the inside. It was made of dark oak with iron studs, and it must have had countless chains and bolts on the inside because it took the best part of five minutes to open. I wondered vaguely why she didn't just show me in through the way she'd come out. I found out once the maid (a real French maid, I thought that kind of thing only existed in sex shops) finally got the thing open. Madame had wanted me to see the hall so that she could impress the hell out of me.

It was a gloomy place. On the walls there were the heads of some of the animals the family had shot in their spare time – deer, foxes, wild boar and other furry creatures. One wall was entirely devoted to a painting of their family tree, which she showed me with great pride. It went back generations – all the way back to Asterix, I think. It had a big gap in it around the period of the French Revolution, but I didn't see any of her ancestors' heads among the boar and the chamois.

I followed her through to Charles Henri's bedroom. I didn't see him at first, as he was slumped behind an enormous computer, in the middle of playing Tomb Raider. It took veiled threats from his mother to make him turn it off. I seriously began to ask myself whether she had just been lying through her teeth when she said how he would love to start as soon as possible.

His Mum left me to it, and I sat down beside him at his desk. He couldn't quite bring himself to look at me, let alone say hello. A fine start. He was obviously feeling a bit sulky about being dragged off the family's golf-course and into an English lesson in the middle of his summer holiday.

To break the ice, I asked him brightly in English what he liked to do during the summer. "Golf" he growled. "Er, how about a verb?" I said, although I would have settled for a friendlier sounding monosyllable. My suggestion was met by sullen silence. Seeing that he wasn't going to open up on the subject of summer I asked about the winter instead. "The mountain," he said, expansively. This was getting to be a real conversation.

In desperation I opened my "Let's teach English" book – also known as "Help me get through the next hour without strangling my student" or as "Please give me a few pointers, I'm in dire need of cash." It is full of games, quizzes and puzzles to try and get students to speak. It's difficult to use because nearly every page needs to be heavily edited, but it's got me out of a tight corner before now. I turned to the quiz about dreams for the future.

"What would you do if you were a millionaire?" I asked. He looked at me stonily, and said that as he was one already he'd never thought about it. I moved swiftly on to question number two – "What will you do if you pass all your exams?" (Ha! I thought, got him there.)

"Maman and Papa will buy me my very own wine *château*," he said, with a smirk.

"So what will you do if you fail all your exams?" I asked, viciously.

"*Je sais pas.*" he said with a shrug, "I think I wait. One day I have this one."

I snapped the book shut, and spent the rest of the lesson revising the preterit. Charles Henri sagged lower and lower in his chair, while I battled on. I was uncomfortably hot in my suit, and it was a great relief when his Mum popped her head around the door and said it was time to stop. I practically bounded out, and saying a rapid *au revoir* I was away, speeding past the guard dogs and heading for home. It was melting in the car, and I ripped my jacket off before I even got to the end of the drive. As it was thick wool that I hadn't dared to wear anything under it except my bra, but what the hell, I was hot. It had to come off.

As I got to the gates they opened in front of me. I thought I must have triggered off some kind of automatic sensor, but it was only when I glanced in my rear view mirror that I discovered the truth – on each gatepost there was a large camera. My presence, and my bra, had been noted by someone in the house.

And I've got to go back tomorrow.

Home. Thursday, 21st August.

Charles Henri was waiting outside to greet me today. I have a sinking feeling he might have been the one who opened the gates. He kept grinning at me during this morning's lesson – most unnerving.

I was more comfortable today as I'd borrowed one of Eric's work shirts from when he was a salesman. There was no way I was going to put that suit on again. My skirt was a bit worn, but I hid it under the desk. At least it was cool.

Today we looked through some more of his syllabus, and to lighten things up at the end of the lesson I got out a crossword from the English teaching book. It was all about food in England, and was quite fun. There was one clue which I thought he might find difficult, which was, "Meat the English eat with mint sauce.(4 letters.)"

I was amazed when he said "easy" and confidently scribbled down something. I glanced over his shoulder to see what he'd written, and was a little bemused when I saw he'd written "catt."

"Er," I said, swallowing, "perhaps you might like to think again?"

He scratched his head and answered in French, "Nope. It was a cinch, that one."

"Look," I replied, trying to keep calm, "for a start you don't spell 'cat' like that. Secondly we don't eat cat. Not ever."

"Well," he continued, quite unabashed, "you never know. I mean England's a big place isn't it? Someone may be eating cat(t) somewhere."

"It isn't a big place!" I said, trying to stop myself exploding, "And even if it was, it wouldn't mean that we'd eat cat! Australia is gigantic, but cat isn't usually on the menu."

"If you say so," he grumbled, so obviously unconvinced that I wanted to slap him around the ears. It wouldn't have convinced him, but it would have made me feel better.

I left him with a whopping great lump of homework instead – an composition to write about the differences between French and English cuisine. Ha.

It was good to get back to my own lunch with Ben and Eric. Eric had already given Ben some mashed potato and gravy, but hadn't quite managed the breastfeeding. I sat in the garden and fed him while I told Eric all about the morning's lesson. Eric had also had a tough morning – chasing Houdini round and round. He did have some good news though – Scramble is sitting on a clutch of eggs! Soon we'll have our first chicks!

Home. Friday, 22nd August.

Here is Charles Henri's essay. It was such a classic that I thought I'd reproduce it in its delicious entirety.

"'The difference between the Inglisch and the French cuisine.' by Charles Henri Du X.

"In my cuisine in France the sink is under the window. In my house for the holidays in Ingland the sink is not under the window. It is the difference."

It was hard to know what to say, really. I patiently explained that I hadn't meant 'cuisine' the way he'd taken it, and with mighty proof of my ability to keep cool we started rewriting the essay together. We'd looked at tons of recipes so that he could learn the words for different sorts of food, and I thought that he had more than enough material to write a few lines. I started him off with 'In France people sometimes eat frogs' legs, but in England..." He shuffled through is papers before answering, "In England you also like this." He shoved a piece of paper at me to prove his point.

It was a recipe for toad-in-the-hole.

Home. Saturday, 23rd August.

Wonderful, wonderful rest from Charles Henri. I don't have to go back until Monday – phew.

Spent the day pottering about the place with Ben and Eric. Kept going to check on Scramble – we've put ten eggs under her, and she is so fat that she covers all of them like some voluminous feathery tea-cosy. In three weeks' time she'll be mother to ten chicks. It must be so great laying eggs – no need for ante-natal classes, epidurals or any of that jazz. These birds have it sussed.

Home. Sunday, 24th August.

Spent the best part of the day preparing the last four hours of lessons for pupil from hell. I have selected a guessing game about English speaking authors tomorrow, which I have high hopes for. Mind you, Charles Henri does have a talent for spoiling things.

Home. Monday, 25th August.

As predicted, he put a spanner in the works. He had never even heard of Shakespeare, and when I asked him about Oscar Wilde he asked whether Kim Wild was his Mum.

I though I was going to lose it, so we changed the subject to British pop groups instead. He said he'd liked music, and I was quite astonished when he started writing away. He wrote for five minutes non-stop, and produced a mini-essay about the Spice Girls. As it turned out it was mostly about Posh Spice ("I like Posh – she very nice!") but it was a start. Maybe there's some hope....

Home. Tuesday, 26th August.

Actually, as long as there's a pay cheque (and there is!) I don't care whether there's hope or not. I don't feel much like Robin Williams in 'Dead Poet's Society.' I mean he really LOVED his pupils and was broken up when one of them shot himself, whereas I actually fantasized about taking a gun to my student's head. Oh dear.

My last lesson went OK. I was at a psychological advantage, as the whole family at the *château* were depressed today. It has been storming on and off since last night, and the heavy rain is bad for the grapes. I had to struggle to stop myself smiling, and at the end, when I collected my cheque, I found myself humming, 'singing in the rain.'

Maman, as it turned out, was delighted with my teaching – she even gave me a 500 franc tip in cash. She has recommended me to all her friends, so I will have some more teaching work soon. I'm going to cheer myself up by thinking of the money I'll be earning.

Tonight Eric and I are talking about all the different things we could spend the 500 francs on, from new clothes to an electric fence. Hmmm. It's hard to decide.

Home. Wednesday, 27th August.

Well, we paid the cheque into our account, and the decision about what to spend the tip on was made for us. We had to pay our electricity bill.

Home. Thursday, 28th August.

More light at the end of our Dark Financial Tunnel – my teaching may prevent our Noah's ark from becoming a sinking ship. Had a phone call from another *châtelaine* this morning; could I come round tomorrow and give her son an emergency day-long course before school starts back? She sounded much nicer than Charles Henri's Mum, and also promised a generous chunk of cash. I was easily persuaded.

I think we should get an electric fence with the money, so we can keep Houdini out of the veggies. She may be living her last few hours of freedom.

Home. Friday, 29th August.

I had my faith in teaching restored today.

The whole family were waiting to meet me at the *château* this morning, Mum, Dad, my pupil (Pierre), the baby and the family dog. I really felt welcome, and that feeling increased when I was shown into the kitchen where the lesson was going to take place and given juice and biscuits. I was thanked profusely for coming at such short notice, and Pierre shot off to get all the revision notes he'd taken during the summer.

We sat down together, and the rest of the family left us to study. His English was not only passable, it was also polite. He was only fifteen but he was amiable and eloquent.

We looked through some of the problems he'd been having with the language, and he also asked me to take a look at the essay he'd been given to complete during the summer. Sometimes I wonder what the teachers are on when they dream up essay titles – I mean can you imagine asking a group of teenagers to write 1000 words on the title "What comes into your head when you close your eyes and think of England?"

I know the teacher who gave out the essay title, and she does seem to make a habit of such mistakes. She once told me she'd had a problem with an 'A' level class when she set them a general knowledge quiz about England. "In what county did the Battle of Hastings take place?" was the question which had them all stumped. She thought she'd give them some clues to help them come up with the right answer of "Sussex". "It begins with an 's'" she said, just to give them a hint, and when no-one found the correct answer, she added, "and it ends with a rude word." Immediately one pupil's hand shot up. "Suffolk!" he cried triumphantly.

Well, I helped Pierre with his essay, and every time I explained something he thanked me. It was really gratifying, and at the end of the day I'm sure he'd learnt a lot. I wouldn't mind a few more pupils like him...

Home. Saturday, 30th August.

Yesterday's teaching was fun, but it was nice to spend the day with Ben and Eric. We were milking the goats this morning when I suddenly had an awful sinking feeling. We'd completely forgotten the snails we gathered nearly two weeks ago.

I couldn't face opening the bucket, so I got Eric to look. Fortunately he'd put a good dose of flour in it, so they were all still alive – but not for much longer...

Eric rang his Mum to ask her what to do with them, and she gave us precise instructions. We had to boil them, take all two hundred and eighty snails out of their shells and chop bits off them, and then stuff them back in the shells again. Then we had to squash sausage meat and home-grown garlic into the shells, cover them with bay leaves from the garden and roast the snails in the oven.

It took all day.

We had a delicious dinner tonight, but what a palaver. Snails from our own field may be a fine example of living off the land, but I'm not sure I'll prepare them again. I know Stone Age people survived entirely on hunting and gathering, but considering how long it took to prepare one meal it's not surprising that it took them a few million years to get around to inventing the wheel.

Home. Sunday, 31st August.

It's the end of the month and we haven't even celebrated Ben's fifth month birthday. We've been busier than ever and we never got around to it. Wicked parents! Never mind, in September we will have a cake for his half-year birthday.

We went out today to celebrate my starting work again. My latest family have promised me more hours, and they also have friends who are looking for an English teacher. It could really help us out financially.

Ben must have known that we were planning an outing, because he got up at 5am, just to be sure he wouldn't miss it. Eric looked after him for two hours while I played dead – the man's a hero.

We hit the road at eight o'clock, and as we drove north towards the village we wanted to visit we passed through another one where people were preparing a village fair. It was early and we had plenty of time, so we stopped off to have a look.

The fair was only just opening – the only people there were either selling produce or else they had babies with them, just like us. It looked as though the fair was going to be a real treat for the taste-buds. There were stalls selling lavender, acacia and *mille-fleurs* honey, dried sausage flavoured with walnuts and peppercorns and cheese studded with truffles. There were also umpteen stalls where we could have tasted wine, but we didn't really feel like it at that time in the morning. In the middle of the square there was a gigantic ox roasting on a spit – there was going to be a banquet in the evening for over seven hundred people!

We took our time to look at everything, and came away with bread, fruit, smoked ham and apple juice for our lunchtime picnic. We decided to eat on the sandy bank of the river Drone, and *aussi tôt que possible* as we were starving.

It only took half an hour to find a good spot to eat, and about sixty seconds later we'd installed our picnic blanket on the sand and had unwrapped all the food. We watched a pair of kingfishers dipping in and out of the river as we ate, and when the meal was done we washed our hands in the cool clear water. I tried to dip Ben's paws in, but he lunged forwards, plunging his head and body under water. He came up smiling though – he's a real water-baby. Lunch just took a little longer than planned as we had to lay his clothes out to dry on a warm rock.

It wasn't a bad spot to be stuck, so we stretched out on the picnic blanket and played with Ben until his clothes were wearable. He was so sweet, chuckling at us and playing with his toes. He is getting so much more sturdy – soon he'll be able to sit up all by himself. Then he'll be crawling and after that, Véro has assured me, I won't ever have five minute's peace again.

Once he was dressed in dry(ish) clothes we drove to the village we were both wanting to visit – Aubeterre, a village a little to the North of us in the Charente. The guide books rave about it, and once we got there we could see why. Really they hadn't exaggerated at all, it's a beautiful place. Aubeterre is one of the stops on the St Jacques de Compostelle pilgrimage route, and there is something a little saintly in the air. Maybe it's the old stone and the medieval architecture, but there is something there that makes you feel the place is important.

We parked Virginie and walked down through the village to the monolithic church we'd read so much about. I didn't think I'd like it that much, but, well, it blew my socks off. A monolithic church is cut out of the rock rather than built out of blocks of stone, and the entrance to this one was at the bottom of a cliff. We paid to have a guided visit, and it was well worth it – as we walked through into the dark, chill interior it was immediately apparent we were in a mysterious and marvellous place.

It was *huge*, with 20 metre high vaults hewn out of the rock and a vertiginously high gallery where bats have lived peacefully for centuries. A spring runs down one of the mossy walls to fill a font, near stone tombs that date from the fifth century. Many of the tombs face Jerusalem, others are angled towards the church's very own reliquary. There are many human bones on show – apart from having tombs, it was also a place where people were buried *en masse* when most of the village's population was wiped out by the plague. Some of the walls have been scraped – during the French Revolution the saltpetre naturally present on the rock was 'harvested' to make gunpowder.

We thought we'd seen it all, but underneath the church things got even stranger. Avoiding the deep pit near the door (where the first Christians were baptised by immersion) we made our way down to the crypt. This was only discovered in the latter part of this century, when a heavy lorry put its wheel through the road and into the crypt below. This place goes back to the Grecian cult of the bull, and here followers were also baptised. In bull's blood.

It was a bit sinister, so we went back up to the vaults above. It was so ancient and peaceful – until Ben started up. He let out a load squeak, and when he discovered his echo he couldn't resist doing some more. He got louder and louder, and we were getting such stern looks from the other tourists that we had to leave. The guide glowered at him as though he were a lager lout.

Back home again now, and we feel mystically enriched. Ben, I think, was untouched, but he's found out about echoes, and that's something. His tan has also deepened – he's lying in his cot next to us looking absolutely beautiful. Our golden delicious.

SEPTEMBRE

Home. Monday, 1st September.

It's hard to believe that the summer is drawing to a close. Today is just tropical, and it difficult to imagine the garden full of mud and puddles and autumn leaves – the leaves on the lime tree have been burnt to a crisp by the sun, rather than rotting away as they do in England. Autumn is just three weeks away, but you'd swear it's the height of summer.

I think the temperature must have got to Eric's brain, because he's suddenly started talking about having a banana palm again. I've promised him we'll go and visit Monsieur Beau tomorrow, and see if he has any smaller palms that could be dug up.

I put Ben down for his sleep inside this afternoon, as it was sweltering in the garden. These old stone buildings do keep wonderfully cool in summer, and I was tempted to have a little nap myself. I think siestas are a fabulous idea. Unfortunately Eric had other plans – we worked solidly in the hottest part of the day driving stakes into the hillside for the electric fence. Eric wanted the enclosure to be as big as possible, and it was Absolutely Knackering banging the acacia posts into the rock hard ground. Eric did most of the hammering, but I risked life and limb steadying the posts. The noise of a sledge hammer whistling past your ear and crashing into the wood next to your fingers is Disquieting, to say the least.

At least the wood for the fence is in place tonight, but this week we'll have to find the cheapest electric fence to string around it. I still have to convince Mum and Dad that this is the best way to keep them in – Mum has come up with good inexpensive solutions, but these are more often that not difficult to put into practice. (Besides, I worry about Mum's ideas. I remember when she wanted to make a cage to protect our soft fruit in England, 'if we make quite a strong structure we could also keep little birds in it...') Anyway, we don't have any thin whippy bits of willow from coppiced trees to make fencing, and even if we did the goats would eat it. Dry stone walls are also out of the question, as we don't have any stone. We have thought about asking Jean-Pierre to be our shepherd, but as he couldn't even manage to keep his eye on one elderly poodle I'm not sure he'd be the best man for the job. So electric fence it is.

Tomorrow, though, my main mission has already been decided. My men-folk need bananas.

Home. Tuesday, 2nd September.

Mission *accomplie*.

We walked to Monsieur Beau's house today in search of aforesaid palms. We found him sitting out in the garden, under a gnarled old plum tree. Despite its age it was laden with golden plums, which kept plopping down and landing beside him like oversized syrupy raindrops. There was a cloud of wasps around the tree, and Monsieur Beau was sitting perfectly still so as not to attract their attention. He was wearing the stereotypical beret, but his Nike (Just do It) tee-shirt was a bit incongruous – especially as he was absolutely immobile.

We said 'hello', and Eric pointed to his tee-shirt and asked if he was *sportif*. He laughed and said he was working, and that he was far too busy to do sport. We were puzzled – he didn't seem to be slaving away too hard. By way of explanation he pointed up into the branches of the tree, where there were hams strung up to dry in the warm sun. He was watching his hams cure.

Eric explained why we were there, and he got up carefully and led us over to his banana palm. Eric said how much he liked the fruit, but Monsieur Beau said he would be better off planting grapes – at least they would ripen in this climate. He said this year has been one of the hottest on record but he still won't have any bananas. Eric argued that everybody has grapes – in Bordeaux, 'grapes' and 'Bordeaux' have always been linked, it's just too obvious. He was wanting to us to do the self-sufficiency thing a bit differently. 'Bananas' and 'Bordeaux' – well, that is different. Monsieur Beau found it funny, and said Eric was more of a dreamer than a farmer.

Still, I married Eric for his dreaming qualities rather than his farming ones, and so I didn't feel worried about asking whether there were any baby palms we might procure.

Monsieur Beau chuckled and went to the shed to get a rusty old garden fork. He used it to part the red brambles which snaked over the baked earth, and in their midst we saw a miniature palm growing. He tried to stick his fork into the ground, but the clay had been all but fired by the sun, and was impossible to break through. Eric tried, but a prong of the fork snapped off. I'm not sure where all the water has gone from the couple of storms we've had, but it looked like it had just slipped through the cracks in the earth and disappeared.

We found a solution in the end. We watered the palm with buckets of water (drawn from his deep well) until the earth was soft, and then we dug and levered the tree out.

Now we have our own banana palm! Tonight it is storming, so we don't need to water it. All we have to do is wait for it to bear fruit...

Home. Wednesday, 3rd September.

We drove around all the shops which sell electric fences this morning to find one we could afford. Eric wants the fence to be ready for this weekend, as he has his course next week and doesn't want me to have to spend my time running around after Houdini. Anyway, we bought one for just 500frs, and spent the afternoon fixing it between the posts.

It didn't take that long to put together, and at the end of the afternoon I held Ben while Eric opened the door to let the goats out. We all stood together and watched them explore their new pen.

The two older goats stayed in the middle, grazing quietly, but Houdini made straight for the boundary. She is much more interested in escaping than in eating. She approached the fence looking a tad apprehensive, and stretched out her nose to sniff it. Instantly we heard a powerful *zing!* and she leapt back, bleating wildly. Eric rubbed his hands together and laughed with satisfaction as she went to join the other goats. For the moment he has won, and Houdini seems resigned to her fate.

We let them graze until late in the evening, and then shut them back indoors. It seems nice to be the ones in control, for once...

Home. Thursday, 4th September.

In control *mon oeil*. We let the goats out to graze this morning, and then got on with our other jobs. Eric was making cheese and I was bathing Ben when I heard an odd noise in the garden. I wrapped Ben in a towel and we went outside to investigate.

All three goats were racing about the garden, Dog in hot pursuit. How they got out was a mystery to be sorted out later, as getting them back in was my main priority. I unhooked a section of fence and was going back to get them when they came charging past me, followed my Dog. She herded them expertly into the barn. Dog is a first-class goatdog!

I called Eric so that he could help me find how they'd got through the fence, and we sat behind the bramble bushes observing them. Houdini came out of the barn followed by her pals, and looked right and left as though to check if there was anyone about. She nipped over to the fence, and to our amazement she lay down on the grass and lifted up the bottom string with her horns. What's more she didn't go right under, but stayed like that until the two other goats had ducked underneath. Only then did she go through herself. It was breathtaking, if irritating.

We hadn't bargained on her discovering that her horns insulated her from the electricity. The only way around the problem seemed to be to put another string around the fence, just skimming the ground. We have spent our afternoon doing just that, and now our hands are full of blisters and we have sunburn. And we are severely p***ed off.

I wish some of the goat books had told us about how hard they were to keep. Really there should be a warning in the first chapter (right alongside the paragraph which explains how to equip their shelter) saying, 'be prepared to tie their legs together' or 'So you've seen the fences in Jurassic Park? Well that ain't nothing'.

Well, now they are safely inside, but I touched wood before writing that...

I thought our menagerie was big enough, and that we already had enough problems looking after everyone, but tonight Eric has said we need some more animals. I'm not sure if he's joking, but he said we are about to have a few thousand more souls on our farm, and that they won't need an electric fence.

I am mystified. And alarmed.

Home. Friday, 5th September.

Woke up to the sound of rain. It was actually chilly when we opened the shutters this morning. The dust in the garden is muddied, if not real mud. There I was only on Monday thinking autumn wasn't going to happen, and now (wham, bang, thank-you Ma'am) it's suddenly, brutally here.

Ha! I bet Charles Henri's parents are tearing their hair out! Winegrowers always say lots of rain so close to the grape harvest is a *désastre*, but I'm cynical about this. All it really means is that we'll pay more for bottles from the other years. What's more I recently came across a chart which rated all the Bordeaux vintages from one to twenty, and none scored under 18.5, so I'm sure this year's score won't be too *catastrophique*. It may just be classified an average year instead of (the usual) *année miraculeuse*.

I may have a slight denial thing about autumn, but Eric just flatly refuses to admit the season is changing, as he does every year. He is always the last person in Bordeaux to swap shorts for jeans, and he is downright stubborn about not putting his flip-flops away until it actually freezes. Last year he so wanted it still to be summer that we went to an aqua-park as the temperature plummeted. I sat there under a plastic pineapple by the pool (pregnant, cold) as Eric splashed about. *"Regarde, chérie,* we are the only ones here, isn't it lovely!" he cried. The only other creatures which might have enjoyed that water were penguins.

This year he's doing it again. Absolute Blindness to the fact autumn is here. The weather has just broken and Eric has announced the new hobby he wants to take up, the one which involves the new animals for the farm. He is obviously remembering the sunny lavender fields of Provence (where his parents now live) and the creatures which make all that lavender possible – they symbolise the sun and flowers for him, and he thinks we need some. He wants to keep bees.

"Oh God!" was my first reaction. Why bee-keeping? Images of a bigger Ben toddling off to peek into a hive set my alarm-bells ringing. Eric calmed me down by saying that Cathérine won't object if we put our hive on the edge of our field, near her cottage. The bees would be far from the house, but we would be able to have our own honey, and they would fertilise the trees in our future orchard.

To get me more enthusiastic about the idea he persuaded me to come

163

and see a wild bee colony he'd discovered in the woods when he was out mountain biking. It wasn't too far from the house so we walked there – me cuddling Ben protectively in my arms. The bees were so close that it only took a few minutes of hiking through the dripping trees to get there. Their home was an oak tree, cracked right open by a storm of yesteryear. It was still raining – which had quietened the bees down – but we could see some small, black wild bees buzzing in and out of the fissure in the trunk. I had to admit it was positively *charmant*, especially as honey ran in dark, shiny rivulets down the bark.

Eric said if I was interested he'd already done some research, there is a bee-keepers' meeting in a local village tomorrow. We will be able to learn how to clean a hive and harvest honey, and it sounds interesting. I think we might go along and have a look.

8.30pm. Guess what's on TV tonight – a documentary about killer bees...

10.30pm. I shouldn't have watched that – now I'm in two minds again. To bee or not to bee? That is the question.

Home. Saturday, 6th September.

I was still vacillating about going to the meeting this morning, but Eric so wanted me to go that I did. We agreed, though, that we would drive a few miles beforehand so that Ben would fall asleep in the car. I thought he'd be safer in his car seat than in the thick of the hives.

Well, we drove around for an hour and Ben did go to sleep, so when we parked next to the hives where the bee-keepers had gathered I was quite relaxed. I hadn't realised, however, what a macho lot these bee-keepers were. There were fifteen men and one woman (Muggins herself) and many of the men were glowering at me.

"We're opening the hives," one of them growled, "and women's hormones get them all stirred up. Just the smell of a woman's urine will drive a hive crazy."

I wasn't sure what to say. Did he think I'd wet my pants or something? I tried to pass it off by saying cheerfully that I was fully toilet trained, but this didn't seem to relax them one bit.

"It's not just the hormones," said chief bee-keeper, "it's the smell of fear. It gets the bees all agitated."

I explained that I wasn't afraid, but several of them snorted loudly.

"Women are afraid of everything" one of them said. I thought they ought to have worried about an English feminist going berserk and attacking them, but I thought that a cool, calm image might impress them more. "Just open the hive," I said coldly.

I was looking on interestedly as they began to puff smoke into the hive when I felt a sting on my neck. "I am not afraid" I told myself firmly, but twenty seconds later there was another sting on my arm. I wasn't going to lose face and I was thinking I'd grin and bear it, when suddenly Eric took off, running faster than an Olympic sprinter away from the hive, wailing like a banshee. He went in mad circles, screaming a high-pitched scream, like a blown-up balloon deflating. The only thing that slowed him down was that he was trying to rip off his shorts at the same time. The bee-keepers looked on with cruel smiles as he tried to swat the bees that had flown up his Bermudas and, in a most unsporting fashion, had attacked him below the belt.

I said a speedy *au-revoir* to the beastly men, and went to help Eric. He'd killed the bees and was sitting, pale and trembling, in Virginie. He didn't say a word all they way home, but as soon as we got back he went to our room, and emerged a few minutes later wearing trousers.

The onset of autumn may not have made Eric give up his shorts, but a couple of bees certainly did the trick.

As for the bee-keeping idea – I think it's been filed.

Home. Sunday, 7th September.

We went into Libourne to have a look round the market this morning. Ben was fascinated by the big rabbits, the giant kind you see on Tellytubbies (I thought this diary ought to have a few cultural references) and I must say I'm tempted to invest in a couple. Of rabbits, that is, not Tellytubbies. We were standing looking at them when it started to storm, and we dived into a bistro as the heavy raindrops began to pelt down.

It was full of Brits! These were sad, disappointed Brits who'd waited until the kids went back to school before taking their holiday. Yup, France is quieter in September, but it's also wetter. This lot were all arguing about whose idea it was to come out in the autumn, and they were so cross that it sounded as though they were going to write to *Watchdog* to complain, or try and sue the French tourist board. We sat quietly, sipping our hot chocolate and enjoying the fun.

Well, tonight is Our Last Night – Eric is off on his course tomorrow. He has got to go to Angers, and I am going to have to run the farm alone for a week. I'm a bit nervous about the milking etc... but I'm sure I'll cope. He'll be back on Saturday, after all.

He is packed up and ready to go, but he keeps giving me bits of advice about what the geese like to eat, or how much grain to give to the goats. I'm not sure this is the way couples are supposed to spend their last hours before parting...

Home. Monday, 8th September.

11.30am. Going, going, gone. Ben and I are all alone, but apart from feeling a bit lonesome all is well. The milking went fine, and I have done tons of work in the veggie garden, picking beans and so forth. The rain has stopped today, and it is cooler but sunny out – perfect weather for gardening!

One piece of garden work I'd really like to tackle is the fallen-down ruin at the end of the garden. It must have been stone pig-sties or something, but now it has no roof and is full of brambles. Some of the rafters are still in place, and I am having a vague idea about covering the top with wire-netting and making a rabbit pen. There appears to be a solid floor which would stop the foxes getting in, and the walls are intact. All the rabbits would need is a warm nesting box inside. Hmmm, I think I might ring Jean-Pierre to see if he'd like to come over and help me clear it out.

6pm. Great surprise! A Renault Espace swooped up the drive a few minutes ago. Guess who? Charles-Henri's mother, pearls and all, in our farmyard. She got out of the car carefully, and daintily avoiding the chicken poo with her calf-skin shoes, she came up to me and shook my hand. "Merci!" She said, and explained that her son had come top of the class in his English test. I did my best to hide my astonishment – I thought her son would need either a miracle or a brain transplant to improve his English, but apparently the course had done the trick. His Mum gave me six bottles of her *château*'s best, and departed as quickly a she'd come.

I wonder if I should wait for Eric to come home before I try some??

Home. Tuesday, 9th September.

I rang Jean-Pierre after I'd milked the goats this morning, and he said he'd come round later on. True to his word he arrived at 1pm – with another furry animal. Not Bébé Béatrice this time, but a tiny kitten that was somewhat precariously lodged in an old binoculars' case around his neck.

Jean-Pierre introduced Ben and myself to Miu Miu, and said this small animal would help him on his way to fame and glory. His application form was rejected by the nuclear power station (thank God) so he had to find an alternative career option. He got an *idée fantastique* while watching the circus on daytime television; one performer had trained cats to do all kinds of tricks, and he thought he'd make a fortune doing the same.

Happily, the cat had a few hours off from its training program, so Jean-Pierre could help with the brambles. Ben was ready for his afternoon sleep, so we had two hours or so to hack away at the undergrowth. Jean-Pierre cut with the shears, and as he cleared each section I shovelled out the dirt and washed the floor with the hose.

I remarked to Jean Pierre that we can't use hose-pipes in the summer in England, because more often than not they are banned due to the shortage of water. "But it's an island, and it rains all the time – surely there's enough?" he queried. It is a bit hard to explain.

Anyway, we are weary and bramble-torn, but the ruin is clear. It is quite big, about 3 metres by 7, so there will be bags of space for rabbits. While I made us dinner (and he tried to teach Miu Miu to do somersaults) I told him all about my plans to breed them.

He's promised to come back tomorrow, and we will try to cut some poles in the wood to replace missing rafters. I have planned to frame up the roof tomorrow, nail the netting to it on Thursday, cement up any holes in the walls on Friday and fix up nesting boxes before Eric gets home on Saturday. That way we'll be able to buy two bunnies in the market on Sunday.

How's that for organisation?

Home. Wednesday, 10th September.

Back-breaking day. For a start, milking the goats twice daily with Ben on my back isn't easy...

Jean-Pierre came over in the morning, and we went up to our wood armed with saws and an axe. Climbing the hill with all the gear was tough, but as ever the wood is well worth the trip. The badgers have been busy again; they have dug out a mountain of sand. Still, we didn't contemplate for long, but got on with the job. Jean-Pierre cut down half a dozen young chestnut trees from a thicket – they grow tall and strong, and were the perfect size for the roof. I chopped off the branches, and we carried three trees each (and Ben!) back down the hill.

Fortunately, Ben fell asleep on the way down, so I put him down in his cot. I wanted to get on with the work while he was in Nod Land, but Jean-Pierre insisted it was time for Miu Miu to be put through her paces. I left him to it, and fixed the poles on the roof while he relentlessly (and fruitlessly) tried to teach her to leap through a small hoop he'd bought. Poor Miu Miu – she just isn't circus material. (I could see Jean-Pierre as a clown, though.) In the end I did manage to get Jean-Pierre to leave her alone, but he said she'll have to do a double training session tomorrow to make up for it.

Jean-Pierre had lunch and dinner with me, but I felt a little relieved when he left. He started to tell me all about the European tour he is planning with Miu Miu – he is sure her amazing stunts will pay his way. I tried hinting that Miu Miu's tricks won't get him as far as Bordeaux, let alone Rome, but he's so caught up with his project that he won't listen. We all need dreams, but I was glad when he got on his moped and set off home.

This evening, despite the fact I ache all over, I have been gardening again. We are doing everything organically in the vegetable patch, and I am a bit appalled at how much weeding work there is. Every day we have to weed for at least two hours – the raspberry canes and currant bushes were almost buried by nettles. It is hard growing fruit, etc. It doesn't just grow on trees, you know!

Eric rang tonight. All is well in Angers, and he's enjoying the course. I kept quiet about what I'm doing here, but I can't wait to show him...

Home. Thursday, 11th September.

4pm. Went out to the hardwear store this morning and bought wire-netting. It was horrendously expensive (I'll probably have to teach for the next twenty years just to cover the cost) but at least it does the job.

Jean-Pierre hasn't turned up – Miu Miu must really be suffering – but I've clambered about on the roof and nailed the wire to the new frame. It is looking really brilliant – just the cementing to do tomorrow and it will be practically finished.

7.30pm: Wow! I just went to milk the goats, and checked on Scramble. The poor thing has been sitting on her eggs for ages now, and I thought they'd maybe gone bad. When I looked in the manger I saw a whole pile of eggshells and no hen, and I thought she'd abandoned the nest. The most likely explanation for the broken eggs was that they had been eaten by rats. Suddenly I heard a cheeping noise, and there in the corner of the barn was Scramble with nine gorgeous, fluffy chicks. One seems to have not made it – there were ten eggs – but the ones that have look healthy and sweet. It is amazing to see Mother Nature at work on our farm!

Home. Friday, 12th September.

Jean-Pierre came round at ten o'clock this morning, looking miserable. Miu Miu is not living up to his expectations, and while she is in her learning period she is costing him a fortune in cat food.

"If she carries on like this I'll have to find her a new home," he said, giving me a Meaningful Stare. "*En plus*, Bébé Béatrice keeps sneezing, and my landlady thinks she may be allergic to cats. I'm not sure about keeping Miu Miu."

He has gone right off the circus idea, and my rabbit project didn't have him enthused, either. Today cement was on the menu, so to speak, and he looked even gloomier when I explained that I had a sack of cement, but no sand. I thought there wasn't much point in buying any as we're surrounded by the stuff – all we had to do was go up to the badger set with a bucket and *voilà*, Bob is your *oncle*.

He sat on a rock in the garden, smoking Gitane after Gitane, as I went up and down the slope with Ben and a bucket. It was physically exhausting – I just hope I'll have muscles like Madonna's to show for it.

Mixing the cement wasn't hard, but Jean-Pierre just sat there, the odd tear rolling down his cheek. I carried on and plugged the holes in the wall, washing my hands every five minutes so that I could take care of Ben. While I was finishing the roof I heard Jean-Pierre roaring off on his moped, and climbed down to wave good-bye. He'd already gone, but

169

he'd left his binocular case – which was moving.

Miu Miu, it seems, is now a Castanet cat.

Home. Saturday, 13th September.

12pm. Have finished the nesting box! There was an old crate in the barn which I think will do, and I've put roof tiles on top of it so that it will be waterproof. All we need now is the rabbits themselves.

3pm. Eric is due home at 5pm, and I'll go and pick him up at the train station in Libourne. I'm so excited that I think we'll leave now. Libourne is only half an hour away, but never mind – I can't wait.

7pm. He wasn't on the train. Oh my God. I waited and waited and checked every carriage, but he wasn't there. Ben and I hung around on the platform for a while before setting off home again. There isn't another train for hours so we'll just have to sit it out. Where is he?

Midnight. He's back. It turned out that he was so worried about being sick on the train (yup, Eric is even train sick) that he'd taken two sea-sickness tablets. They'd made him sleepy, and he only managed to stay awake for twenty minutes before falling into a semi-comatose state. He woke up hours later when the guard came to check his ticket. He hadn't changed trains when he should, and was miles from home – he told me all about the different trains he'd had to catch to get back, but I won't tell the whole story. He's hours and hours late – but at least he's here.

I could strangle him.

Home. Sunday, 14th September.

Woke up at 4am when Eric screamed. He'd felt something small and furry in the bed, and thought it was a rat. I had completely forgotten to introduce him to Miu Miu last night. I tried to explain that she was a failed circus cat, but it was probably a little early for explanations. He booted her outside – come to think of it, she may actually have done her first somersault.

I properly introduced them at breakfast, and I think Eric has quite taken to her. She is beautiful, and I've assured him that she'll stop mice from coming into the house – that part went down well. I'm sure they'll be friends.

When we went out to do the milking I showed Eric the new chicks. He

was really thrilled that we have managed to produce our own livestock. Our long-term aim is to rear all our chickens from eggs, and nine chicks is a great start.

My *pièce de résistance*, of course, was the rabbit enclosure. Eric asked whether it was an outdoor playpen for Ben, but I hope he was joking. He admired the roof beams and the netting, and seemed impressed (modest cough) by my cementing. He agreed that it was ready for the rabbits to move in, so we went to the market to buy a breeding pair.

Well, the loving couple are now in their new hutch, and they seem to like it. The only problem is that they don't seem to like each other very much. Whenever the male goes near the female she tears mouthfuls of fur out of him. Let's hope they can work it out.

Home. Monday, 15th September.

The rabbits seem to have sorted something out, because they were both in the box this morning. Rabbit on the menu soon! That sounds harsh, but we are trying to run a farm here.

Eric seemed pleased with his course, but I can tell he's glad to be home and back in his Farmer Giles role. I even caught him giving Houdini a hug and playing with the baby chicks. There seem to be animals everywhere these days – geese, chickens, rabbits, Dog, Miu Miu and the goats, but soon there will be even more. Eric has telephoned the man who sold us the goats, and has arranged that he'll pick them up on Friday and keep them for a couple of days. They are off for a dirty week-end with his billy-goat. Soon we will hear the pitter-patter of tiny hooves...

Home. Tuesday, 16th September.

I was struck by a strange compulsion this morning. Maybe it had something to do with the fact that Eric's parents are going to visit us soon, or perhaps it was because we could no longer see out of our Disgustingly Grimy Windows, but whatever the reason I was seized by the desire to clean the house. Just like Mole from Wind in the Willows I wanted to scrub everything and make our Humble Abode sparkle. This kind of thing doesn't often happen to me.

Eric was disconcerted when I whisked away the breakfast things and began hunting for the various nozzles of the vacuum cleaner, last seen in Ben's toy-box many moons ago. "What on earth are you doing?" Eric asked, looking anxious. "Spring cleaning!" I replied, giving up on reviving our asthmatic vacuum cleaner and opting instead for a witch's broom.

Eric followed me as I began sweeping the bedroom floor. "Er, it's not spring, *chérie*..." he tried to tell me, but as far as I was concerned I'd started so I'd finish. As I abandoned sweeping in favour of turning out cupboards he got really worried. "God, you're not pregnant are you? I mean this isn't about nest-building is it?"

Nope, nothing like that – it was just one of those odd moods that occasionally make me want to don an apron, clean the house and then do a spot of baking. It was scary, but suddenly the only thing I could concentrate on was getting every last rattle and soft toy out from under Ben's bed.

I dusted and tidied and washed and wiped. This was more tiring than circuit training... and it didn't stop there. Once everything visible was clean I attacked the bits that weren't on display. I washed out the inside of the microwave, which had previously looked like the interior of Lascaux. I scrubbed away at the red, black and brown galloping patterns and dislodged the stalactites and stalagmites – and then I set about

Supermodel cupboard's make-over.

I took everything out of it and washed the shelves, and then I thought I'd line them with paper – Lucienne would be so impressed. I began pulling pages out of our local paper, but I couldn't bring myself to use them in the cupboard. As is the way of so many French local papers, it was all smashed cars once again. The only page which made me smile was one which featured a picture of the local fire brigade; the photographer's flash had reflected off the fluorescent stripes on their uniforms, so the entire photograph was just white aureoles. The gore of the rest of the paper really got to me – our local paper in Bristol was a NEWSPAPER at least, not just a body count. There were features in The Evening Post that I used to look forward to reading – though the thing I loved most of all were the Classifieds. Every other day I'd skim through the 'Dogs, cats and pets' section and try to persuade my parents to adopt another animal. I suppose it's not surprising that I've ended up surrounded by furry companions. Anyway, I gave up on lining the shelves and used the paper to light a fire in the stove instead. I could feel a crumble coming on.

Well, we had an apple pie at lunchtime (I couldn't think how to make it go crumbly) and then I carried on relentlessly washing while Eric took Ben out for a walk. Housework has become a lot harder since we've started his weaning – I have to chip bits of Rusk off his chair and wash apple purée off practically every surface in the kitchen. That stuff gets everywhere.

I'm all in tonight, but at least the house is clean. Eric has asked (a little nervously) whether we can expect the same again tomorrow. Hmmm. I think the housecleaning poltergeist which has possessed me all day has gone, but you never know. I'll have to wait until tomorrow to find out for sure.

Home. Wednesday, 17th September.

Eric took one look at me this morning and said he was going to study in the village library rather than at home. I wasn't even considering doing anymore housework, but he said that I had my Determined Expression on my face, which he always finds alarming. He did the milking and set off with his books.

I didn't actually do all that much cleaning – I just washed the floor in the bathroom and then I took Ben out for a little walk. As we made our way along the lane I couldn't help but notice all the glistening, heavy clusters of blackberries in the hedgerows – now there was something homely to do that was a lot less tedious than housework: Jam making.

Eric came home at lunch looking vaguely guilty – I'm not sure what about. He can't have been up to much at the library; the librarians alternate but their average age is about a hundred and seven, and I think they are more interested in their crochet than in Eric. Maybe he was feeling bad about leaving me alone this morning. Hmmm. Mysterious.

Well, after we'd eaten I persuaded Eric that blackberrying was a *très bonne idée*. Ben could sleep in the pushchair as we worked, and between us we were sure to pick kilograms. Eric wasn't hard to win round, and we were soon combing the hedgerows.

The blackberries were sweet and juicy, and it was hard not to stuff dozens into our mouths. Our lips, tongues, cheeks and fingers were stained purple but oddly enough when we set off home, our tummies full to bursting, the fruit bowl was practically empty. We'd sort of forgotten to put any blackberries aside for a rainy day.

Oh well, I'll make jam another time. I'm planning to spend tomorrow relaxing with the boys – to hell with housework, homemaking and other chores! After all, the boys are really what makes my house home.

Home. Thursday, 18th September.

No work today – hooray! (Well, just childcare, cooking, egg-collecting, rabbit feeding, milking and weeding.)

Eric is still looking guilty. He isn't saying anything but he's definitely acting shifty.

Home. Friday, 19th September.

SIX MONTHS OLD TODAY!!!

9am. Little Ben has already had rice pudding with half a candle on it, and we have sung Happy Birthday six times. He actually SAT UP all by himself in his chair when we were cutting the cake, as it were. Half a year together already! We are going to have to spend the whole day celebrating.

10.30am. Goat man (I really must find out his name) just came round with his trailer to take the goats away for the weekend. They are in for fun, and we are also free for a couple of days. No milking – phew! Eric has suggested we go to Bordeaux tomorrow, and then on to my parents' for the weekend. I can't wait to leave – it is wonderful here, but it will be nice to get away. Bright lights tomorrow and beaches on Sunday – bliss!

3pm. I've just found out why Eric is looking guilty. I thought we would celebrate Ben's birthday tonight and maybe go out, but it turns out he has 'volunteered' us for a library committee meeting. Apparently Gladys (chief librarian) made him an offer he couldn't refuse on Wednesday. She also mentioned how it would be nice to have some 'young, handsome blood' amidst the library staff. What is it about getting old which makes people think they can flirt so brazenly?!

Eric has asked me to go with him (I'm a Gladys deterrent) but I'm a bit worried about it; my pedigree does not lend itself easily to committee work. Mum once did a very short stint for a Healthy Teeth campaign which advocated adding fluoride to water. At the first committee meeting she lost her temper with the Pure Water campaigners who were also present – she told them all to go and suck on their dentures. She gave up committee life after that.

I have also had a brush with Gladys from the library already. Ben and I popped in to say 'hello' to Eric the other day. I happened to pick up a new novel, and said what a fabulous photograph it was on the front cover. Well, Gladys came strutting towards me, squawking like a mad chicken. I didn't get what she was saying at first, but it was something about Young People of Today judging books by their covers. She was so scary that I didn't even speak up for myself. It was only on the way home that I started saying *zut alors* – I mean I did do a degree in literature for heaven's sake, and anyway what I read and like is my business. I did think of some more wittier, more cutting comments, but only in the bath several hours later. Oh well.

Anyway, Eric has asked me so nicely to accompany him that I won't let him down. It won't be that bad.

11.30pm. It was. And it went on until eleven o'clock – hour upon hour of irritating discussion. Every daft point had to be voted on – it was maddening. I'm not even sure if any of the motions (you could take this as a synonym for *merde*) were voted in. I'm not convinced I grasped the full complexity of the conversation, but it seemed like we spent all evening talking about the problem of shelving.

When we arrived at seven thirty the battle was already in full cry – one half of the committee wanted more books, the other half wanted to chuck some away so there would be more room for the books they already have. We were ignored at first – I got the impression that most of them didn't have the foggiest idea that Eric and I were also part of their committee *extraordinaire*. This feeling was confirmed a good hour and a half later, when one of the older members asked me how long I was on holiday for out here. *Mon dieu.*

Well, we watched them getting more and more worked up about the 'book storage problem' until Eric stopped them all in their tracks by offering to build a new bookcase. I was a touch miffed that no one even said *merci* – they just spent another hour faffing about what wood it should be made out of.

I should really have sat tight and said nothing, and then we could all have gone home earlier. Sadly my Big Mouth opened and I offered to lend them a pile of English paperbacks, so that we could start a Foreign Language Section. Once again, no one looked very pleased; they just launched into an Enormous *polémique* about whether we should really favour English over and above other languages. One lady even said that it would be racist of me not to offer books in other languages and dialects. Bloody Hell.

Their clinching argument against accepting my offer was that my books would clutter up their shelf space. Eric was about to offer to make yet another bookcase when I gave him a Warning Look. Enough was enough – and Ben obviously thought the same thing too because he began to cry. Muttering our apologies we left them all to it and came home.

The rest of the committee is probably still arguing points, but Birthday Boy rescued us. Six months old and he's already bailing his parents out.

Bassin d'Arcachon. Saturday, 20th September.

It feels very strange to be away from home, and to have missed out on all our usual routines. Not having to milk the goats is one thing, but tonight is also the first night we haven't shut the chickens and geese away. They are used to roosting in the stable and I'm sure they'll be all right, so I am refusing to worry. Dog is here with us but we have left Miu Miu overnight – I hope she's OK... oh God, there I go again, worrying.

It will all be FINE, and we really needed a day off.

We got up early this morning to go to Bordeaux. I thought we were just going into town and then on to Mum and Dad's, so I didn't understand why Eric was sneaking his trainers and running shorts into Virginie. He's been running as well as cycling recently, but I couldn't see why he was going running in town.

As we set off Eric explained – there was a hidden item on the agenda. His shorts weren't in the car just because warm, sunny weather has Mysteriously returned to Bordeaux – no, the shorts were there because he had entered himself in a FunRun in Bordeaux.

'FunRun' to me has always seemed to be a bit of a contradiction in terms, as I have too many school memories of gruesome cross-country runs to ever connect the word 'run' with 'fun.' Eric, on the other hand, loves running, and he explained that today it was for a good cause – raising funds for cystic fibrosis research.

Well, I wasn't going to grumble, as the race was for a good cause and was 'only' 10kms long. It took place in one of Bordeaux' suburbs, and was really well organised. The runners had their running thing, and for their families there were jumble sales, roundabouts, pony rides and, most importantly, coffee and cake. Ben and I gobbled down a *tarte aux pommes* as Eric set off, and then we had a browse around the jumble. (Dog, by the way, stayed in Virginie as I didn't want her to do her shepherding with two hundred or so runners.) By the time Eric finished the race Ben was sharing his pushchair with a jug, a milk churn and an antique picture frame – all things we couldn't possibly live without. Ben didn't seem put out at having so many things in with him – he was having much too much fun banging on the lid of the milk churn.

Eric was all smiles as he had done well in the race, and he'd raised over five hundred francs for research. Content with our morning we drove to the Bassin.

Mum and Dad found that Ben had grown mightily, and Mum also spotted a tiny tooth just about to break through. Teeth! Already! I was beside myself with excitement, but Mum said that getting teeth isn't a 'Develop-Mental Milestone.' Huh! Paediatricians! Still, the granny part of her was pleased.

We had lunch and did the traditional tour of the garden, admiring their new water feature made out of a dismantled washing machine drum and a length of hose ("I couldn't believe it," said Dad, "some idiot had actually thrown all this into a skip.")

After that Mum and Dad took Ben out for a spin in his pushchair, and we did what we haven't done for A Long Time – nothing Naughty – we just sat in the garden in the autumn sun and did just the 'nothing' part. We flicked through magazines, drank our drinks and chatted. It was lovely.

Tonight we are tucked in our Wondrously Comfortable Bed Mum always makes up for us, enjoying that on-holiday feeling. Tomorrow we haven't planned any further than a walk along the beach, but that is already sounding nice. I think I'll try and go to sleep ASAP so that I can wake up with the sun – and my son.

Bonne nuit!

Home. Sunday, 21st September.

Well, he was up before the sun – hours before. He must have been looking forward to going to the beach...

We all strolled down to the sea at the end of the morning, when the tide was just starting to rise. The Bassin is quiet again now the tourist season is over. Undisturbed by holiday-makers the seabirds pick over the sandbanks for shellfish. Boats bob about gently, their motors silenced and sails furled now their skippers have gone home. We sat on the white sand in the sun... Mum and Dad watched Ben balancing in a sitting position – this is a Big Thing for parents and grandparents alike, and got a good deal of applause. Next he started experimenting with licking the sand – which didn't go down well with us but which he loved. I can't believe he's finicky about the stews and purées I cook for him, but that he will eat handfuls of sand, grit and broken shells. He's worse than a chicken.

We thought he shouldn't consume too much of the beach, so we picked him up and pottered down to the wet sand. We tried to show him his shadow, and Eric drew him pictures of dragons in the sand. We didn't get so much as a flicker of interest, all his attention was focused on the water. The sun was flashing on the surface, and he stretched his arms out towards the bright light. Paddling with Ben can oh-so-easily turn into swimming, but we thought we'd let him get his toes wet. The sun was really quite hot, and the tide was coming in over warm sand and heating up nicely.

Eric held Ben, and took him into the shallows to splash about. I waded out a bit further with Mum and Dad – the water felt refreshing, and I was just turning around to say so to Eric when I slipped on a patch of clay. I never, ever fall over, but this year I've managed two falls – both times of the full-blown Laurel and Hardyesque variety. This one involved a half cartwheel and a good dunking. When I surfaced my family were all shrieking with laughter, clutching their sides as I sought to recover my dignity and my contact lenses. What a supportive lot they are – well, as Mum used to say when I was little, families are there to prepare you for Life – if you can survive your family you can survive anything.

I was soaking wet, so Mum and Dad looked after Ben while I went with Eric to get changed. I had been so busy packing stuff for Ben that I'd forgotten to bring anything for me, so Eric offered to lend me a tee-shirt and a pair of shorts. The tee-shirt was fine, but the idea of wearing shorts in public and in broad daylight was a little disheartening. When I was breastfeeding full-time I could eat what I liked, but now that Ben is complementing his diet (with handfuls of sand) I am not getting rid of all those calories. Eric didn't help when he launched into a conversation about drawing up a diet plan. Repressing the memory of yesterday's *tarte aux pommes* I promised to follow it to the letter. I felt too insecure to argue.

Still, I don't see why I should be overweight – it's so unfair. If you eat too much you get fat – but I don't eat much at all. Mum says that if you under-eat you also get fat; your body stocks whatever food you do put into it, in case there are hard times ahead. As soon as I even think about going on a diet I start stockpiling enough to feed an army throughout a long siege. In my left thigh alone there is plenty enough to nourish a battalion.

So, over-eating and under-eating both make you fat, and Véro told me that eating just the right amount can also lead to obesity... if you are *bloqué* by *problèmes psychologiques*. This, she has explained to me many a time, means your body will be fat if your brain doesn't want you to be thin. This really gets me – I mean I am sure my brain wants me to be thin, and my brain is supposed to be running this ship. If things carry on the way they are this ship seems destined to become a galleon. And I so want to be a dinghy!

Still, we are back home now, having had a hearty dinner at Mum and Dad's. The diet starts tomorrow, but I can't feel too despondent when the

179

weather forecast has predicted another glorious day. Maybe my fat will just melt away in the sun.

Home. Monday, 22nd September.

Terrible shock today.

It was dark when we got home last night, so we just closed the barn door and left the animals to it. Sadly, it seems we locked the door some time after the horse had bolted. Or more to the point, after the fox had done its job.

The geese, Omelette and Scramble are still alive, but five of Scramble's chicks and most of the young pullets have gone. Apart from our sadness at their dying, we also have to face the fact that we will have to rear more all over again. It was depressing to see the mounds of blood-stained feathers – Eric was kind and cleared out the corpses and the bloody straw while I stayed well away. I couldn't bear to watch. Such disasters are part of farming, but losses like these are hard to deal with.

I tried to make lunch with what was in the garden. The fright has put the chickens off laying, so we have nothing available apart from a slug-chewed lettuce and a few beans. I am very down about self-sufficiency today. You do have to do everything yourself; all the rearing, watering, killing (more so for animals than for lettuce, I must admit) and preparing for the table. Processed food is Bad, but I would love a little bit of pro-cessing to be done for me at the moment. What I wouldn't give to go out into the veggie garden and find a pizza... Oooh, I'd kill for a Deep-pan!

Still, with half a lettuce for lunch the diet plan is definitely on course.

Home. Tuesday, 23rd September.

Still feeling traumatised. Chickens are feeling better though – two eggs today.

The goats came back this afternoon, and it cheered us up a lot to see them – Eric was even pleased to see Houdini. They are on top form (their weekend obviously did them good – they have the misty, far-off look in their eyes of the love-struck.) We are glad to have found our four-legged friends again, and we have also got our milk-supply back. At least we'll be able to have a bit of cheese with our lunch tomorrow.

Home. Wednesday, 24th September.

Hope on the financial horizon!

The grape harvest in in full swing, and a neighbour has just asked Eric if he would like to pick grapes with his team. Eric was brought up in this area, and like all the Bordelais he knows all about grapes – it's a kind of unconscious *savoir-faire* they all have. He doesn't like grapes much, but he does know about pruning and flowering, when it's time to pick off surplus leaves and grapes and when it's time for harvesting. To be a part of that harvest is to participate in one of the most important economical, agricultural and cultural activities there is in Bordeaux.

A successful harvest improves the quality of life here far more than any law voted in a European court. Wine is the lifeblood of Bordeaux, and if the harvest is to be good the climatic conditions must be right. It's strange to think that something as unpredictable as the weather makes a good deal of difference to ordinary people's lives... in modern times it is somewhat humbling to see that we are still at the mercy of the elements.

The harvesting takes place over several weeks, depending on whether the wine is red or white and on the ripeness of each individual vineyard of grapes. Eric gets all nostalgic when he talks about the *vendanges* of his youth – children went back to school only once the harvest was in – sometimes even at the end of October. There weren't the harvesting machines around which you see now, but instead all the family (greatly extended at this time of year!) would work together, bringing in the grapes from dawn till dusk. To keep things cheerful the harvesters would sing and tell jokes, and everyone would look forward to the traditional feast at the end of the *vendanges*.

Eric hasn't been a part of all that for years, and he's excited about going grape-picking tomorrow. There should be about four days of work at this *château*, and he should earn enough to buy me a pizza, at the very least...

Home. Thursday, 25th September

6am. Eric has just left, looking all eager. There are storm clouds in the sky though – showers are common at this time of year. He's taken his cycling cape with him. I hope he won't get drenched – mind you, he deserves to, considering the way he laughed when I got my dunking on Sunday.

181

8pm. The Man Himself is back, weary and aching. Here the harvest was going to be brought in by hand, and the team was divided – as per usual – into pickers and carriers, the women picking and the men carrying. For Eric this meant hauling up to 50kgs of grapes at a time in a basket on his back from the picker to the trailer. Back-breaking stuff.

Eric said he enjoyed it anyway. The vineyards were so beautiful at first light when he arrived; the mist was rising, and there were wild boar tracks in the mud between the vines. It had been raining, and despite the fact they all had waterproofs the harvesters were soon soaked. No waterproof will stop water from the vines running up your sleeves.

The team were all great fun. There were twenty-five people, a few of them from Paris and the Mediterranean, and a German student. They all seem to get on well, and despite the physical difficulty of the task and the frequent showers Eric said the *ambiance* was great. He is looking forward to tomorrow.

Home. Friday, 26th September.

Lucienne's birthday today. I remembered! Phew!

Eric got home looking even more knackered than yesterday. He said the work seemed harder than ever, and that by lunchtime his aching shoulders stopped him appreciating the atmosphere. What's more, if the work hasn't changed in 30 years, then neither has the repertoire of jokes.

Home. Saturday, 27th September.

Good news! I got a phone-call from the headmistress of a local primary school this morning. She'd heard all about me from Pierre's parents, and wanted to know if I'd be interested in an afternoon a week teaching English to children. I'm more than interested, I'm ecstatic! It will be fun working with kids, and it will also be nice to have a regular pay packet, however small. I may even be able to withdraw money from the bank without worrying the manager will yell at me.

Eric is thrilled about my new job, and he's also jolly because it is the end of the harvest tomorrow. That means a pay-cheque and a feast. *Vivement demain!*

Home. Sunday, 28th September.

7.30pm. It's the end-of-the-*vendanges* feast tonight! Can't wait! Ben and I are ready for the fun, and are waiting for Eric to pick us up. I expect we'll be back late, so more anon...

Home. Monday, 29th September.

Got a headache. What a party! Will write tomorrow.
Where is the aspirin?

Home. Tuesday, 30th September.

I've never had such a good time. I think I've just about recovered enough to describe it...

Eric picked us up at eight o'clock, and he was tired but happy. The work had been harder than ever as everyone was worn out, but they all felt relieved and proud to have finished. He drove me round to the outbuilding of the *château* where the feast was to take place, and I was introduced to the team. They were very friendly, and the German guy was particularly pleased to see me – he didn't speak any French but his English was quite good, and he had his first conversation for weeks.

When we arrived everyone was busy tasting the first grape juice. It was hot off the press, and there was much discussion about its colour and taste. A show of hands proved that the general feeling was that it was going to be an exceptionally good year. (As per usual, I thought, but I also thought it wise not to say anything.)

There was a gigantic oak table at one end of the building, and a roaring fire in one of the largest fireplaces I've ever seen. Ben's eyes were wide when I settled him into his pushchair – there were so many new sights and sounds that it must have been hard for him to take it all in. We sat down – more than thirty of us at a single table – and Ben looked more relaxed as the adults began to laugh and joke, and once I'd given him a piece of freshly-baked bread to suck.

Our meal came soon after – huge helpings of some of the most delicious food I've ever tasted. I forgot the diet plan as I tucked into wild mushroom omelette, shrimps from the Gironde estuary, steak cooked over the fire and potatoes sautéed with oregano and garlic – this was too good to miss. I savoured every course, and there were many. We washed our food down with wine or grape juice, and I think I ate more than I ever have in my entire life. When I was pregnant I ate for two, but at dinner last night I ate for twelve, at the very least.

Throughout the meal (and it lasted well into the early hours) we told stories and sang and made merry. The whole group felt like old friends by the time it was over, and everyone swore to come back and do the *vendanges* together next year. It was a harvest and a party to be remembered.

Little Ben, this diary is also for you, so I should say now how good you were. You fell asleep before we even started the main course, so you kind of missed the party. Thank-you for giving Mummy a chance to let her hair down, and thank-you even more for sleeping until eight thirty in the morning when Mummy was weary.

OCTOBRE

Home. Wednesday, 1st October.

Déjà Octobre! At the beginning of September there was a hint of autumn in the air, but now it's really here. Eric lit the stove to keep the kitchen warm this morning, and I lit our first fire in the hearth in the end room. The fireplace is so huge that I think most of the heat went up the chimney, but it was cheering nonetheless.

I spent a lot of today planning lessons for the primary school. The head teacher wants me to start on Friday, so I'm at panic stations. To be honest I'm a bit nervous about teaching three classes of thirty children or so. I will have an hour with the 8/9 year olds, another hour with the 9/10 year olds and I'll finish up with the 10/11 year olds (if they haven't torn me to shreds.) Yup, I know, they are just children, but I can remember how horrid I was sometimes as a child, and I'm worried this lot will be as bad...

Home. Thursday, 2nd October.

I popped into the school this morning to meet the staff. They were all very *sympas*, and I feel encouraged about tomorrow. They actually have a English method already – cassettes and books about an alien coming to earth and learning English. It looks quite jolly. On the way out I met some of the children who were coming into the yard for break time. They were absolutely adorable, asking me all about England, offering me their break-time biscuits and wanting to carry my bag. Yesterday I was so worried about teaching them, but now I can't wait to start!

Home. Friday, 3rd October.

Success! I left little Ben with Eric this afternoon, and drove off to the school. The children were all waiting for me at the school gate, and were eager to start. I needn't have worried about whether I'd manage to keep their attention – they were quite captivated. This had less to do with my teaching skills than with my nationality. I thought they might be interested in the alien from space, but what they really wanted to know about was this strange person from England. Did I eat *le pudding* every day? Did my Dad wear a bowler hat? Did I drink only tea? Their questions kept us all amused, and we got on like a house on fire. I taught them how to say their names and ages, and at break time it was sweet to see the older children trying to teach what they had learnt to the younger ones in the *maternelle* class. I had a really fun afternoon, and it was also ego-boosting to be a Big Hit. I can't wait till next Friday!

Home. Saturday, 4th October.

Back to my other rôle – just as much fun. I cooked us all *crêpes* on the stove this morning, and then we went outside. It was sunny but the temperature was crisp, so I wrapped Ben up. We watched Eric dig over the garden, and talked about where we'll plant our new fruit trees. Gilbert and Lucienne are coming to see us next month, so we will be able to plant the orchard together.

After our planning we cleaned out the rabbits, giving them fresh straw in their nesting box. The female looks decidedly plump – either she's been eating too much or she's pregnant. I am looking forward to having some more babies on the farm!

In the afternoon we drove off to find some hay. The grass is not so rich in nutrients at this time of year, and the goats really need a few bales of some of this summer's grass – especially as they are expecting. We didn't have to go far to find what we wanted; Marie-Thérèse's neighbour is a farmer and sold us a bale. He also treated us to a few tales about country life, a weather forecast and finally an *apéritif* – the people here are so welcoming.

I rang Véro this evening and I described our meeting with the farmer, and said how friendly he was compared to average English people. I was a bit bemused when she exploded on the other end of the line. "You Brits," she yelled, "you move from London or some other city to the *trou du cul de la campagne* (literally the 'bottom hole of the countryside') and you talk about 'the French' as though we were all like your farmer. You don't seem to realise you are sampling a tiny percentage of the population – the *paysans*! What about people like me – a Softwear designer who wouldn't be seen dead in Wellingtons? I LOVE my job and I couldn't bear to spend all day swinging on the garden gate yakking with the neighbours and drinking endless *apéritifs*. We aren't all peasants, you know! And although you think the *paysans* are kindly, I can assure you they devote a good deal of their time to spreading rumours, killing each other's livestock and poisoning their neighbours' wells. Don't put all French people in the *panier*."

I apologised, and she did too for flying off the handle. She said she didn't mean to be snobby about the rural French, but that she was just feeling irritable because Stephan had used her silk knickers for polishing his bike. Apparently he thought they were 'just an old rag.' She had been grumpy all day because of it.

Come to think of it, Eric also polished his bike this afternoon. I'd better check what he's using.

Home. Sunday, 5th October.

What is it with these men? Eric had also used a pair of my knickers to shine his handlebars. What's more he added insult to injury by saying he'd only used them because they looked far too small for me. *"Regarde!"* he exclaimed, holding up my underwear which was now smeared with chrome restorer, "you'd never get into these." Hrmphh.

After a little tiff (I refrained from beating Eric about the head though) we set off on our traditional Sunday trip to the market. Today we bought a roast chicken, chestnuts to cook on our fire and two bottles of *bourru*, a deceptively alcoholic drink made from the first fermented grape juice. It is yeasty and sweet and seems to smell of the grape press and the vineyards. It washed our chicken down nicely.

We were cooking our chestnuts in the ashes of our fire when Eric remarked that we were a bit daft to buy them. The woods around here are full of chestnut trees – we could take a basket and gather our own. We had our goats' cheese to make and a dozen other farmyard tasks to do today, but we have planned a picking trip tomorrow. I ADORE chestnuts, roll on tomorrow!

Home. Monday, 6th October.

Up at six for milking, and then we got ready for our Expedition. We thought we'd drive a few miles to woods a little further up the valley, as here we are mostly surrounded by oak trees – not renowned for producing good chestnuts. We brought the carrier so that Ben could sit on Eric's back, and I had a big wicker basket to fill (hopefully) with chestnuts. The gods did seem to be with our Expedition – it was clear and sunny and it made us feel optimistic.

My mood changed somewhat when we got out of Virginie and headed into the woods. It was beautiful – the reds and golds of trees in autumn has always left me spellbound. The problem was the signs which were nailed to the trees. Most of them looked as though they had weathered a winter too many, as often the only decipherable word was a mysterious and rather menacing *interdit*. I'd decided they must be about trespassing when I saw a rather newer sign which had a more complete and alarming message – *cellulite interdite*!

What could it mean? I felt the message was aimed at me and not at Eric and Ben – not that I take these things personally, of course, but the Eves of this world are more often afflicted by this malady than the lucky Adams. It's as though getting us chucked out of the Garden of Eden wasn't punishment enough – we had to suffer a good dose of cellulite to boot. Paradise was where women could run about naked, happy and without any complexes, the Real World was a cruel place where we would torment ourselves with diet and exercise to make our thighs look like something more attractive than pillow cases stuffed with ping pong balls.

Well, was this forest trail an exercise track? Had I been wrong to wear shorts with a thick jumper? Was the diet not working??? (I have been making an effort to cut back on calories.) A dozen questions came to mind, but in the end all I could manage was a pathetic "Eric (sob) why does it say No Cellulite?"

Eric looked at the sign and then at me before bursting out laughing. He sensitively observed that my dieting has obviously zapped more of my brain cells than my fat cells. He explained that it wasn't *cellulite interdite*, it was *cueillette interdite*. Still in the dark I waited for him to explain. "No picking!" he said. "Of what?" I asked, fearing for my chestnuts. He showed me another sign, *champignons interdits*, and the light dawned. No mushroom picking.

So that was what it was all about – I should have guessed. The French rave about wild mushrooms, and anyone who owns land in this area wants to keep their mushrooms for themselves.

It's a little hard for Brits to understand what all the fuss is about – after all, a mushroom is, well, just a mushroom. I used to think a mushroom was something you bought in a plastic box in the supermarket. The idea of going into the countryside and picking them myself would never have occurred to me – let alone choosing which variety to pick. I considered anything that didn't look like a supermarket mushroom to be a toadstool, and thought that anyone daft enough to eat one would probably have dropped dead on the spot.

In France ordinary mushrooms – *champignons de Paris* – are used in everyday cuisine, but it seems that most people here can recognise at least half a dozen wild sorts. What's more they are not afraid of gathering them; if they are not sure that the variety they've chosen is edible they can always drop in and ask at their local pharmacy. Pharmacists are all quite competent at distinguishing between poisonous and wholesome mushrooms.

I still find fungal culture, as it were, a touch bewildering. Véro (even though she swears she dislikes country pursuits) can pop into the woods for an hour and emerge with her basket overflowing with bright yellow frilly *chanterelles* and bulbous, russet *cèpes*. Whenever I've tried mushrooming I blither about with my mushroom guide, never sure of what I'm picking, and always end up looking silly in the pharmacy with a handful of muddy (and more often than not, toxic) specimens. Today it

was a relief NOT to be looking for them, and I felt relaxed and happy as I filled my basket with shiny chestnuts. Ben tentatively touched the spiky cases, and we brought some of those home too to jolly up my dusty bowl of *pot pourri*.

Maybe as the years go by I'll acquire that French knack for mushrooming, but tonight as we roasted our pickings I was glad we stuck to chestnuts. They were truly *délicieux* – and they had that other endearing quality of not being *venimeux*. Safe isn't necessarily boring...

Home (half dead). Tuesday, 7th October.

Cathérine came round at lunchtime. We were having an *apéritif* together (a purely alcoholic event as Ben had eaten all the little cheese biscuits which usually accompany such things) when Cathérine announced she had a little present for me. I was touched and a little baffled when she presented me with a necklace – a weird thing made of string threaded with black, knobbly beads. I hadn't thought Cathérine was into jewellery making, but this was obviously homemade.

"It was my mother's," Cathérine said, "she died last year and this was one of the things she left me. I would like you to have it."

It wasn't a thing of beauty but I was very moved that she'd offered it to me, and thanking her profusely I slipped it over my head. Cathérine's reaction was somewhat surprising: she snorted with laughter. *"C'est pas pour toi, c'est pour l'omelette!"* she said between guffaws.

She explained this was a string of wild mushrooms that her Mum had dried and prepared. They were too strong to be eaten whole, but a bit of one grated into an omelette would give it a subtle, woody flavour. I said hesitantly that I was nervous about wild mushrooms, but she assured me these were tasty. I was planning to make an omelette for lunch anyway, so I thought we would try some – but I said I thought Ben was too little to have any. That really made her shake with laughter, "We were weaned on mushrooms in my family!" she said. I wasn't reassured, as I was sure she'd mentioned on a previous occasion that two of her twelve siblings had died in infancy... and anyway, what had her mother died of????

I insisted on Ben having an ordinary omelette, but Cathérine stayed for lunch and we grated some of the 'necklace' into ours. The mushroom flavour was *extraordinaire* – it was quite the finest omelette I've ever tasted. Cathérine left after a dessert of goats' yoghurt and homemade jam, and Eric went to study. I was clearing up when I suddenly got a sharp pain in my stomach, and five minutes later I had to dash to the loo to be sick. I have been ill all afternoon with terrible sickness and stomach cramps. Eric is fine and has been taking care of Ben, but I am shaking with sickness and fright. I hope I haven't poisoned myself. I feel perfectly awful, worse than I've ever felt. I am going to sign off here and try and sleep it off.

Home. Wednesday 8th October.

9 am. Worse worse worse I feel worse. I don't even dare ring Mum because then I'd get told off. Thank God Eric is OK and has taken Ben out. I'm going back to sleep.

11 am. Can't rest because I'm worrying so much. I'm not sure who to call for advice. My big brother Ian is a vascular surgeon in London – he'd give me sterling advice if I had a leaking aneurysm but I'm not sure he'll be able to help with a possible case of poisoning. He usually diagnoses anything I get wrong with me as a "bad case of Grot." Ah ha! I know – I think I'll try an old school friend who is now a GP in Bristol.

5 minutes later. Oh no oh no oh no. Managed to get hold of Liz, and described my symptoms. "What have you been eating?" she queried. I remembered what Cathérine had called the mushrooms, and replied (with more than a slight sense of foreboding) *"les trompettes de la mort.* That means Trumpets of Death. They're a kind of wild mushroom." (Toadstool! Toadstool! Shrieked my English half.)

I heard her breathe in sharply and then breath out again very slowly. "You must be bloody mad," she said, comfortingly.

Squeaking with alarm I asked her what might happen to me. "Well," she answered, "we could be talking upset stomach, or liver transplant. Or death, of course. I should see a doctor if I were you."

That's friends for you. I thought she'd reassure me, but now she's got me thinking the Grim Reaper's about to bang on my door. I'm done for.

I'm in two minds whether to ring the doctor for an appointment or just get on to the undertakers.

2.30pm. The doctor was out for a long lunch, and when I finally got hold of him he sounded very strange. Different, anyway. There was a good reason for that – it wasn't the same doctor. Mr Badger is off on his hols and he has an Italian locum. He seemed very unstressed by my story

– he doesn't think it is anything serious or else Eric would be ill, too. I have a *rendez-vous* for tomorrow at ten. If I'm still here.

Home. Thursday, 9th October.

Sick all night, so I went with the doctor's with nothing in my stomach except a numb feeling of panic. I was surprised to find the waiting room chock-a-block full – and that the patients (apart from me) looked really healthy. Curiously enough, they were all women, and were all wearing tons of makeup. They looked more as though they were waiting to see the hairdresser than the doctor. I asked the lady next to me what the locum was like, and she sighed a deep, sensual sigh, licked her lips and said, "you'll see."

I had a long wait, punctuated by trips to the loo. The other women sat there sleekly as I tripped over their high heels for my umpteenth visit. Eric held Ben, looking uneasy and embarrassed. He whispered in my ear that there was no sound-proofing between the toilet and the waiting room, so everyone there could hear my every retch and gurgle. It was awful, but I was too ill to worry about it.

Eventually it was my turn, and I staggered in to the consulting room. Yup, even though I was all in I could see what those other women were looking so dreamy about. He was darkly, sexily gorgeous. Not the kind of man whose wastepaper bin you'd want to be sick in on your first date. I wish I hadn't done that.

When I felt well enough I explained what was wrong, and that I thought the *trompettes de la mort* were the cause of it. He checked me over, and told me I just had a dose of gastric 'flu. "What, my days aren't numbered then?" I said, sighing with relief.

"Definitely not." he said. "Those mushrooms haven't done you any harm at all. You can even eat the rest if you like."

He must be joking.

Home. Friday, 10th October.

Started to feel much, much better last night, and even had a light tea. I told Eric in the afternoon that I wanted a little something to eat, and he said he'd buy me some fresh fish. I was glad my stomach was in better shape when he emerged from the kitchen with a steaming platter for me at 7 o'clock. He said the fish hadn't looked too good at the fish-stall, so he'd bought me something else instead. A whole kilo of steamed whelks. He was so sweet that I couldn't refuse, even if they were the last thing I felt like eating. Happily I've managed to digest them. The one good thing about this episode is that it's really helped with the diet; I've lost half a stone. *Victoire!*

This morning I put Ben on a rug to play in front of the fire, and I sat beside him and planned the afternoon's lessons for the primary school children. I thought we wouldn't start the 'alien' method, and that instead I'd teach them their numbers and then do a fifteen minute activity for fun at the end of each lesson.

Well, the kids can now count to twenty in English, and in the last quarter of an hour I told them how to make scones and launched a mini competition for next week. They are thrilled – and I am cheerful, too. It is wonderful to have so many enthusiastic pupils!

Roll on next week's teaching – and to tasting and judging the scones. I have a feeling that half stone will be back before long...

Home. Saturday, 11th October.

Did the usual egg collecting, whisk around the veggie garden and milking this morning, and then we went out for the day. I have been feeling so ill all week that I needed a treat to cheer me up.

We went to Bordeaux, to the lovely *jardin public*. It a park which is caught in a kind of time warp; as you walk its shady paths you think you are still in the 19th century. There are old fashioned swing boats and a traditional Guignol puppet show, and a gondola glides under the ornate iron bridges on the park's very own artificial river. The Victorian feel continues in the *jardin botanique*. There is an extraordinary variety of plants, and an ornamental pond where Lucienne used to fish for tadpoles as a child during the war. The centre piece of the park is the Natural History Museum, which houses an astonishing collection of animals. All dead and stuffed, of course, but that's the Victorians for you. It is well worth a visit.

I was looking forward to visiting the collection again, and was surprised to see that there was also a temporary exhibition at the museum, all about saving the sturgeon. I can't say I was very familiar with this creature, and I certainly didn't know that it was on the endangered list. To be honest, the only thing my brain could come up with on the subject was a poem I'd heard (and failed to understand) as a child:

'Have you heard of the virgin sturgeon?
Virgin sturgeon very fine fish.
Virgin sturgeon needs no urgin'
That's why caviar's a very rare dish.'

I had already linked the sturgeon with eating, thanks to the graffiti on the posters advertising the exhibition. Many of the 'Save our Sturgeon' posters had 'at least for special occasions' added to them by someone more interested in gastronomy than ecology. Although attitudes are changing this is still a prevailing sentiment in Bordeaux! I haven't yet forgotten my first (and last) attempt to buy dolphin-friendly tuna in a supermarket. "Don't worry, Madame, of course they don't net dolphins when they catch tuna... I mean there wouldn't be any point, would there, as dolphins don't taste very nice..." So we went into the exhibition expecting the sturgeon to be treated more as a Supertanker of Caviar than as Flipper King of the Waves.

We couldn't have been more wrong. Of the 24 species of sturgeon we were introduced to Léon, an enormous replica of the European species, *acipenser sturio*. He looked like a cross between a dolphin and a crocodile, with a long, pointy beak and an exterior like a tank. This Gentle Giant (his diet is made up of tiny crustaceans and molluscs) was Big, but not as big as the Beluga variety, which can get to be the size of a bus. Sturgeons are an ancient kind of fish, and there is something reminiscent of fossils about them. Each one may live for a hundred years or more, and can migrate over untold distances during their long lives. A Léon of this century, swimming up the gravely bed of the Dordogne river, could well have seen the D-Day landings...

Sturgeons look indestructible, but the exhibition explained that (as is all too often the case) people are responsible for their near extinction. Over-fishing, pollution and the destruction of river beds where they breed are wiping them out. Dams across rivers prevent them from swimming up river to reproduce. Many die because of litter in the waterways and the ocean – some have even been found with condoms over their heads, which proves Safe Sex isn't good for everybody. It is a sad fact that arbitrary planning decisions about river and waste management may destroy a species that was swimming in the river in Bordeaux when we were still messing about with bananas in the treetops.

The conclusion of the exhibition was that whether we love Léon just because he's Léon, or because sturgeons are like geese which lay golden eggs, all Europeans should fight to save him. We should campaign and sign petitions if we want to see this creature preserved other than in a jar.

Despite the fact that only about thirty sturgeon have been seen in the Gironde estuary since 1981, we thought we'd drive to a local vantage point and have a look. We went to the *village des troglodytes*, on the right bank of the Gironde near Blaye. It is a tiny, vertical village hewn into the chalky cliffs that flank the estuary. People still live in these cave dwellings. There are miniature windows and doors cut into the rock, and gardens of wallflowers grow up the cliff face. Rabbit hutches and chicken coops have been hollowed out above, below and alongside the houses. We climbed to the top, and found a good spot between the clay chimney pots that poke charmingly out of the wiry grass.

We sat alarmingly close to the blue sky, hugging Ben tightly and watching the sunlit waters. There was a wonderful view of the estuary, where fishing boats scudded about. In the spring they fish for the *piballe*, tiny eels which sell for the price of gold dust. The boats have nets which swing out on booms, and which makes them look like butterflies. Beyond the water was the Médoc: Wineland. We watched for Léon, and as monster observation goes it beat watching the drizzle on Loch Ness. We didn't see any of Léon's offspring any more than we spotted Nessie, but sitting quietly on the cliff in the evening sun helped the dreams about the mighty fish sink in. Eric and I held hands as the sun set and Ben dropped off. This was pure happiness... better than the finest jar of caviar.

Home. Sunday, 12th October.

After the market this morning I went for a walk with Ben while Eric went out on a photographic expedition. He is an excellent photographer, and was hoping to capture the kingfishers which bring a dash of colour to the river bank. He came home with a few shots of them, but as they are constantly ducking and diving he said he hadn't managed to get the picture he wanted. I persuaded him to take pics of Ben insead – what better subject matter?! He did seem to enjoy being photographed, grinning up at the camera and showing off his new teeth. I think he could solve our financial problems by becoming a model for Pampers or Petit Bateau.

Home. Monday, 13th October.

Mr Badger is back in his surgery, and I took Ben along for his check-up today. He is as healthy as anything, and the doctor says that if he continues on his present growth curve he'll be six foot six and light as a feather when he's eighteen. There you are, the kid really does have a future in modelling!

Home. Tuesday, 14th October.

My brother David called. He's coming out here for a holiday – I can't wait to see him! He is staying at Mum and Dad's, but will come and see us for his birthday. Could this just be a ploy to get a birthday present?!! I'm sure it isn't, even if he used to give us a six month countdown to his birthday when he was a child just to make sure we didn't forget. Up until last year, in fact... no, just kidding. David and I were the only siblings who didn't follow a medical career in our family, and that made us close. I remember us both retching while the rest of the family dissected medical magazines, and discussed nasty diseases (particularly ones you could catch from food) during family dinnertimes. We would try and talk about books instead. Salmonella? Give me Salman Rushdie any day.

I'm really looking forward to seeing David, but I'm not sure that with a farm to run and Ben to take care of I'll have the time for our Literary Discussions of old. Oh well. It will be wonderful to see him anyway.

Home. Wednesday, 15th October.

Oh dear. Poor Eric now thinks he has dangerous supernatural powers. He said he spent his entire photographic session on Sunday wishing the kingfishers would stay still, and what do we now have on the kitchen table? – A dead kingfisher. Dead is about as still as you can get.

The tale started this morning. Monsieur Beau came round to see us, saying he knew we were interested in bird-life and that a strange parrot had flown into his window and died on impact. He thought we'd like to see it.

The parrot was a kingfisher. I'm often surprised by how little people know about their rich ecosystem, and Eric explained to him what kingfishers eat and where they live. I have heard villagers say that lizards have six legs, toads make you blind if you touch them and that salamanders have a bite which burns you. They can mostly identify the animals in the *manuel de chasse* but their knowledge of the rest is shaky. It is a shame because they are surrounded by fabulous wildlife they know almost nothing about.

Well, Eric has photographed the dead kingfisher from every angle, although these weren't the kind of photos he'd had in mind. Now he wants to preserve the skeleton. His idea is to leave it outside in bowl on the grass, where the ants will strip it of its flesh. In theory it isn't such a bad plan, but I have a few misgivings. It sounds like a messy business.

Home. Thursday, 16th October.

Mum rang this morning to say that David had arrived safely. He is coming to us on the 21st. Let's hope the weather stays nice.

I went outside and sniffed the air to see if it smelt of coming rain. I quite fancy myself as a weather prophet sometimes (although I am not a Mighty Sorcerer like my husband, who can will a kingfisher to die at fifty paces). The morning was crystal sharp and bathed in sunshine, just the kind of weather I adore. There was a smell of autumn leaves and bonfires, and a hint of grapes and wine. After the grape harvest the stalks, skins and pips are dumped around the countryside in great purple heaps. They wild boar love to dig about in these alcoholic piles, and I love them because they add their delicious perfume to the air.

I am sure that if I sniffed deeply enough I could have got a faint whiff of oestrogen. What with the goats and the rabbits expecting, there must be measurable amounts of stuff around the place! I am really excited about having our first litter of rabbits, and ecstatic when I think of baby goats in our barn.

Home. Friday, 17th October.

Busy day today.

To start with there was planning my lessons this morning, and then the actual lessons themselves. The children had all taken the scone competition very seriously, and in the first class alone there were thirty lunch boxes filled with scones to taste. They all varied tremendously in shape, taste and size, and we had great fun trying them. One little boy held out a box filled with a sticky, gooey mess, saying Mummy hadn't understood what sort of 'flowers' to put in the mix. As it turned out, all the scones were worthy of praise, and we learnt lots of words like 'excellent', 'wonderful' etc...

By the time I got around to the second class I was feeling a little queasy though, as children expect you to taste their offerings wholeheartedly. When I tried to taste just a crumb they looked so disappointed that I had to have a bit more. Well, the second class had baked just as many scones, and once more I had to be chief judge. The children wanted me to eat an entire scone for each of them, and that meant thirty scones. At the end of the third class I was decidedly pale about the gills, and I had to stop off on the way home to get some air. Groaning and green and with a grossly distended stomach I vowed to stay off the subject of food for at least a term.

It took me all the end of the afternoon and the beginning of the evening to feel a bit better, and at eight o'clock we had to go out. It was the monthly library meeting. I was not keen on going, but Eric said it was important to contribute to the local community and help village committees.

When we arrived I settled myself near the door with Ben, so that I could make a quick escape if he cried. The discussion was already underway – they had got back onto the subject of shelving. I couldn't bear to listen to it all again, so I thought I'd have a bash at changing the subject. Inspired by the success of my scone competition, I suggested we launch a writing competition. Eric thought it was a great idea, and said excitedly that people of all ages could contribute something – a poem or a story. We could involve the school and the Old Folks' Home – it could be a real village event. There is so much hidden writing talent, and it would be wonderful to discover it.

We were surprised to see the rest of the library committee turn pale. The *présidente* was horrified. "All that reading! *Mon dieu!* Especially if it's poetry! *Alors là, non!*"

We tried to find out who was interested in the idea, and found that the organising team/jury was quickly whittled down to Eric, myself and one of the secretaries for the village hall. This could go the same way as the scone competition... I have a feeling we'll get overloaded.

Eric tried once more to get the rest of the committee interested, but they all shook their heads sternly. We left shortly after, with Eric grumbling "s*d the committee" all the way home.

"The problem with working with other people," he said later as we were going to bed, "is the other people."

Home. Saturday, 18th October.

Pooooooh! Eric's kingfisher is really starting to pong. It's October so there are fewer insects to clean it off, and it just seems to be getting smellier every day. Miu Miu kept trying to play with it when Eric left it out on the lawn, so now he has put it in an old saucepan on the window ledge. The kitchen window ledge. There is an awful stink coming through the gaps around the window, and it is making a ghastly odour inside. We are going to have to have words about this.

Home. Sunday, 19th October.

Ben is seven months old! Three teeth and counting!

We went to market this morning and bought some baby fruit trees. We have an old-fashioned variety of apple, a peach tree and an apricot. They are tiny (about forty centimetres high) but they look healthy and should grow quite quickly. We have already planted them along the edge of the veggie garden, where they will be watered by the spring. We have an orchard!

When we went inside for a late lunch even Eric had to admit that the kingfisher was stinking out the kitchen. Poor Miu Miu used to sit on the kitchen window ledge, but the rotten smell has driven her away from her favourite spot. (Instead she has been balancing on the fence next to the kitchen. It is narrower than a tightrope along the top – maybe she could have been a circus cat after all...) Anyway, the corpse really is giving off an AWFUL stench. I tried to be reasonable when I talked to Eric about it, but ended up saying that either the kingfisher goes or I go.

Home. Monday, 20th October.

9am. The kingfisher has gone!

The mysterious thing is that it wasn't Eric who got rid of it. It has just vanished into thin air, taking its bad smell with it. Eric looked really freaked when I said it had gone, and clutched his head with his hands. "I was willing that smell to go away, and it has!" Now he is back in sorcerer mode.

10am. Went out with Eric to milk the goats and solved the kingfisher mystery at the same time. Dog pottered up to see us, and I was the first to noticed bright blue feathers stuck to her fur. Dog had managed to knock down the saucepan containing the poor bird, and had eaten it up. Dog has eaten many strange objects in the past, but this was by far the most disgusting. I'm going to have to keep her at arm's length because her breath smells so fetid.

Home. Tuesday, 21st October.

David is here. It is really nice to see him, and he was pleased to see us – always a good start to a successful visit. Ben really stole the show – David is mad about his little nephew. He played with him for ages, and said he wants one just the same...

He seemed to like the farm, esp. the site and the buildings. I'm not so sure about the animals. When he saw the chickens in the barn he said there was 'shit everywhere!' and was definitely not keen on Dog. I adore dogs, but he doesn't like them at the best of times, let alone when they smell of rotten flesh. Poor Dog spent the day under the lime tree moping – or maybe she just had a stomach ache.

We had a slap up, pre-birthday meal in the evening, and he was amazed that his little sister could make goat's cheese and other such wonders. We had one of our home-grown chickens roasted in garlic and honey and stuffed with chestnuts and herbs from the garden, accompanied by our own vegetables. Although we are poor in the financial sense of the word, we can still have feasts fit for a king. And fit for a brother.

Home. Wednesday, 22nd October. David's birthday.

Gave David his present this morning. I think he was worried that with all this self-sufficiency going on around him he'd end up with a hand whittled whistle, or a scarf knitted out of sheep's wool we'd recovered from barbed wire fences. He was pleasantly surprised when we gave him a nice book instead.

Dog was looking so miserable that I made a bit of a fuss of her. The smell is wearing off and she has paid for her sins quite enough. I tried to persuade David to stroke her, but he has this thing about dogs being vicious. I was trying to persuade him that she was quite the opposite when the post van arrived.

Patrice is on holiday, and Dog went berserk when she saw an unfamiliar figure coming up the drive. Patrice's stand-in had a letter for me to sign, but before I could warn him or catch Dog she had leapt at him. She usually looks like Dougal from 'The Magic Roundabout' but now she bore a striking resemblance to a grizzly bear.

The postman panicked (as well he might) and threw his entire bag of mail at her. She disappeared under a snowy mountain of letters, emerging teeth first and sinking them into his ankle.

I yelled at her and she fled into the barn, and David, the postman and I were left in an uncomfortable silence. David retreated into the house, 'to get back to his book.' I think I have failed to convince him that dogs are an asset to any household. The postman rolled up his trousers, and we saw that he had just a tiny scratch where one of her teeth had got through his trouser leg and sock. Fortunately no blood had been shed. He was very nice about it, and I invited him in for a cup of coffee.

He said he was a dog lover himself, and that his dog had also bitten the postman who delivers to his house – still, it was very embarrassing, and Eric and I apologised profusely. He munched cake with us while we talked and drunk our coffee. He said that he wouldn't do anything about the incident, but that French law still stipulates that a dog which has bitten someone must be seen by a vet to make sure it isn't carrying rabies. We promised Dog would see a vet straightaway, and that we'd keep him informed.

I have telephoned the vet, and we have an appointment for tomorrow morning. I'm sure she doesn't have rabies, but the thought of it is frightening. I mean we make horror films about rabies in the UK! Eric is less panicked than myself and more philosophical – rabies, *la rage*, is fantastically rare in this area, but it should still be taken seriously.

We were determined not to let Dog's misbehaviour spoil David's birthday, so we all went out together on a forest walk. In the end we had a enjoyable day, and although David has to fly home tomorrow I'm sure he'll soon be back for more.

Home (David-less). Thursday, 23rd October.

Took Dog to the vet's at nine o'clock. She was very nice, and tried to set my mind at rest by saying there hasn't been a case of rabies in the area since the 1980s. The French part of me was reassured, but the English part shrieked, "My God! Rabies! In my backyard!"

She examined her and it was my turn to be reassuring. I explained that she had never, ever bitten before. The vet said that such things do happen, and not to worry. She showed no signs of having rabies, but she would have to have another two visits to make sure. The three post-bite visits are compulsory, and are going to cost us about £50. Dog has made an expensive mistake.

At lunchtime we took David to the plane at Merignac airport in Bordeaux. It was sad to say goodbye, but he has promised to come back soon. We will see him at Christmas over here (at my parents) and I'm sure he'll be out in the summer. I said he should come and have his birthday again with us – it was nice to give him his present in person. I said he will get a bigger present next time, just to tempt him back.

"Just don't buy me a dog," he said, firmly.

Home. Friday 24th October.

Back to school today.

I made the mistake of using my old teaching guide when I was casting around for ideas. It had a chapter of games, and one of them looked like good fun. I had been wanting to teach the children the names for clothes in English, and this was a game to help with that. It looked great on paper...

My lessons had been swapped around at school, so I had to start with the top class. We drew pictures of people, and then dressed them with photos of clothes we cut out of catalogues. Then we stuck the English labels next to each item of clothing, so soon they could all say what they were wearing in English. When I announced that we were going to play a game it was greeted with great enthusiasm.

The book had said to sit all the children in a ring. This wasn't as simple as it sounds, as most of them were so pleased to leave their seats that they pinged off around the room in all directions. Rounding them up was harder then herding wild goats. Still, I managed to get them into a (fairly rowdy) circle, and it was at that point that things went wrong.

The book said to ask each child to put an item of clothing in the centre of the circle. Then each child in turn should say the English word for it in order to reclaim it. Well, as soon as I explained the game the sky just went dark. Shoes, socks, jumpers and skirts flew through the air, and I even spotted a junior bra. I just had the presence of mind to pull the blinds down... the headmistress's office looks directly into my classroom, and I wasn't sure my teaching methods would impress her.

It took some long while to get all the kids dressed again and back in their seats. I was five minutes late for the next class, but that was just as well. The cutting and sticking lasted until the end of the lesson, so there was no time for the Dreaded Game.

I thought my mistake was going to pass unnoticed when the last hour of the afternoon slipped by uneventfully. No such luck. As I cleared up the classroom at the end of the day I saw one Mum collect her little boy at the school gate and march him straight to the headmistress's office. She was angry, and complaining loudly. I didn't catch all of it, but it did have something to do with why her child was wearing odd socks, neither of which were his, and a girl's blouse. *Oh là là.*

It's a bit of a relief that I'm not there every day. With a bit of luck it will all have been forgotten by next week. Fingers crossed.

Home. Saturday, 25th October.

Monsieur Beau came around early this morning to invite us for lunch. It is really wonderful to be on such friendly terms with all our neighbours. We feel absolutely at home – it's as though we've lived here for ever.

The feeling that we've always lived this way grew even stronger during our lunch together. We ate his delicious mutton stew (Ben had it cut into tiny pieces and mashed in with the vegetables and adored it) and as Eric chatted with Monsieur Beau about his plantations in the veggie garden I couldn't shake off the idea that we've always been living like this. As they got onto the subject of clipping the goats' hooves I found it harder and harder to remember what Eric looked like as a salesman in a suit. I have got used to my student/farmer husband and wouldn't have him change his rôle(s) for the world. I love this place and our life, and it seems we are here to stay.

Home. Sunday, 26th October.

Well, yesterday Monsieur Beau invited us, and today Marie-Thérèse asked us round for a drink. We are being spoilt.

Marie-Thérèse is a delightful lady, full of fun. Although she tragically lost her husband five years ago, she is still full of wit and sparkle. I was surprised to see that she had decorated her house with pumpkins, and commented on it. She said that this year (despite stern warnings from the old-fashioned parish priest) she had decided to celebrate Halloween with her children. She found the bright orange pumpkins brought a touch of colour to her house, and she thought Halloween was *rigolo*. I'm sure her priest would have been shocked if he'd have seen the fake cobweb and plastic spider on the crucifix over the mantelpiece... We'd had Marie-Thérèse pigeonholed in our (narrow) minds as being a very straight-laced Catholic, but she surprised us with her spontaneity and humour.

She was also crazy about Ben, and I like anyone who loves my son!

Anyway, we were chatting about Halloween when she explained why she liked it so much. She used to spend her summer holidays in America as a child, and is interested in all aspects of American and English culture. She said that she regretted not having the chance to speak English more. It was too good an opportunity to miss, so I asked her whether she'd like conversation classes. She looked thrilled, and asked whether she could bring some friends along to form a small group. She said that if they all chipped in a bit it would pay me for my time.

So now I have four more pupils! Conversation classes should be fun, and I'm looking forward to our first session which we've scheduled for Tuesday evening. I'll have to find some good ideas for the lesson – no scones, or clothing games...

Home. Monday, 27th October.

Feeling VERY clever today. I've just finished *Sophie's World*. I would have liked to have discussed it with someone, but Eric gave up after chapter one, and Véro flaked out at some point during chapter five. I got to the end! I won!

Home. Tuesday, 28th October.

Hmmm. Something is afoot. Caught Eric on the phone today talking about flights. He looked guilty, so I went out of the room. Privacy is important for couples, but guess what I did? – I legged it down to the other end of the house and picked up the extension. I know, I'm despicable.

Anyway, I didn't get to hear anything except my Dad's voice saying goodbye and replacing the receiver. Burning with curiosity I cross-questioned Eric, but he is doing a good impression of a being clam at the moment. There is absolutely no budging him, so I'll have to wait and see.

I didn't have the time to dwell on it as it was my first group lesson tonight with Marie-Thérèse and her three friends Isabelle, Martine and Françoise. I needn't have worried about what we would talk about, because the hour and a half flew by. We had stories, jokes and even songs in English. Their overall level was very good, and it was great fun for everyone. They felt like old friends at the end of the lesson!

Home. Wednesday, 29th October.

HOORAY! Got the information I needed out of Eric. He and my parents are such loves. They have arranged a little break for me and Ben in the UK. My big sis' Anna really wanted us to come and stay with her so she could see Ben (and me!) a bit more, and Eric thought I needed a holiday. It is the half-term Toussaint holiday next week, so I am free. They have booked me a flight out on the second of November, returning on the sixth – that means we're off in four days!!!!!!! Anna has borrowed a car-seat and cot, so I won't have to carry too much stuff. Ben will get to see England! I'm so excited.

Home. Thursday, 30th October.

We have baby rabbits! I went out to check on them this morning, and saw that the nesting box is full of fur plucked from the female's chest. It looked warm and cosy in there, and as the fur was moving I am sure the babies are alive. I said to Eric that I can hardly bear to fly off and leave them, but he pointed out that they won't even have their eyes open for another ten days. They'll be here when we get back.

I spent much of today doing laundry in preparation for our trip. I thought I'd hand-wash Ben's babygros as the washing machine has been playing up. The problem was that there were so many of them that it seemed destined to take forever. Then I had what I thought was a Brilliant Idea. Ben was having his sleep so I had a bit of time, so I ran a big bath, put all the clothes and a squirt of shampoo in it, and then took off my clothes. Then I got into the bath and started trampling them, as people used to trample grapes. I thought this was this best way of moving them around in the water so that they would get nice and clean.

After a good fifteen minutes of 'foot-washing' the clothes Eric came into the bathroom. He looked at me and burst into hysterical laughter. He asked me what on earth I was doing, and whether I'd gone completely mad. As is the way with geniuses, we are never understood by our contemporaries and are often dismissed as being insane.

Tonight all the clothes are washed and drying in front of the fire. Yup, foot-washing took up most of the day, what with the rinsing and wringing, but at least it worked. So there.

Home. Friday 31st, October. Halloween.

Taught my schoolchildren all about Halloween today. It's the first year that it's been so big in Bordeaux; there are pumpkins, paper witches, ghosts and ghouls in every shop window, and most people seem to have hollowed out at least one pumpkin. No one seems to know about trick-or-treating yet (thank God) but the rest seems to have really caught on.

Usually this time of year is utterly dominated by La Toussaint, but this has had to shrink down a little to make room for the 'new' Halloween. Toussaint, All Saints, is a time for remembering people we have loved and lost, and for flowering their tombs. When you aren't French you could easily mistake it for a flower festival. I did when I first arrived in France as a student. Enchanted by the rainbow colours of the chrysanthemums for sale on every street corner, I bought a big bunch for Véro who was in hospital with an appendicitis. She was appalled. Pale and trembling she explained that in France chrysanthemums are the flowers of the dead – every November French people take them to the family tomb, but they NEVER offer them to friends in hospital. Ooops.

It takes between eight and ten months to prepare the many tons of chrysanths for Toussaint. At the beginning of November it is often chilly and grey, especially in the austere graveyards, but the bright flowers set the place ablaze with colour. Everyone is expected to give at least one bunch, and families can be torn by feuds of 'Dallas' proportions (yes, we still get 'Dallas' here) if anyone forgets. I know one family where two sisters haven't spoken to each other for ten years because one of them didn't take flowers to their mother's grave. La Toussaint is a serious business; if you forget the remembering other people will certainly remember...

Well, Eric dislikes Toussaint as he finds it morbid. He much prefers Halloween. Tonight we sat around our open fire, eating chocolate goblins and telling each other scary stories. Once we went to bed Eric told me some 'true' ghost stories from Bordeaux. Unfortunately I'm a total wimp as far as horror stories are concerned, and I was petrified. In fact I have refused to turn the light off until Eric tells me he made them all up.

I have also told him that we are never doing Halloween again in this house – it's just too frightening. Next year we won't have any pumpkins around the place. Although on second thoughts I might buy some more chocolate goblins.

NOVEMBRE

Home (last day!). Saturday, 1st November.

Leaping about with excitement. I think I've repacked our bags a dozen times. What can I have forgotten? Passport – check! Tickets – check! Money – stony broke as usual...

I think that's about it. I even have Ben's teddy-bear. I'm sure I haven't forgotten a thing.

Home again. Thursday, 6th November.

I forgot my diary...

Now I'm going to have to try and remember the essentials. The main thing is that we had a Splendid Time. Ben and Anna absolutely charmed each other, and Anna had him all to herself while I went out shopping. Whoever would have thought that the English shop I'd miss most would be Oxfam?! I picked up some paperbacks which I'm dying to read – it is so rare to get my hands on English books. I also got some interesting toys for Ben. They look as good as new and he loves them.

I was a little amazed at how much of an outsider I felt in the UK. When I overheard other people's conversations in town it really struck me that the Brits and the French just *do* conversation differently. In France ideas are gathered and the conversation gets broader and broader (and rowdier!), but in England everyone I heard seemed hell-bent on winding up the conversation, ending up with the one (often tiny!) point they were trying to make. All their conversations seemed funnel shaped. I don't want to seem like a traitor, but *honestly* guys!

The other thing I felt was that the conversation tended to focus on two subjects. The first, Seriously Nasty/Fatal things that had happened to them or someone they know, however slightly. Secondly, long and protracted arguments about some consumer issue. I *know* being diddled by a double-glazing company is awful, but it did seem to be one of the MAJOR topics of conversation in England this time. If it wasn't double-glazing it was mobile-phone companies or some such, and everyone seemed to be talking about breaking contracts and how to get one over the sales team etc, etc... There were TV programs and news reports featuring disgruntled customers all the time, and by the end of my stay I felt like pleading with people to change the subject – or else whopping them over the head with one of their consumer magazines.

Anna, of course, was much more fun. We have always got on brilliantly, and it was great catching up and showing off my son. We also got the chance to drive up to London and see my biggest brother, Ian. He is a surgeon and was madly busy at the hospital, but he came out to eat with us between two operations (he washed his hands first, never fear).

He was looking as handsome as ever, but very tired as his work is exhausting. He was constantly looking at his watch to see when he had to go back to work. It was, in fact, rather a gorgeous watch, and I told him how lovely I thought it was. Without a moment's hesitation he took it off and gave it to me. He is always so generous and I was really touched. Come to think of it, maybe I should have said I liked his car as well. I could quite fancy myself flashing around in a sleek BMW... mind you, it is possibly not the best car for transporting goats and hay bales.

Ian held Ben and told me about London life, but I felt a bit awkward talking about the farm. We live so very differently that is a little hard to understand each other, despite everything we have in common. He used to pick me up in his arms when I was tiny and frightened by the planes flying over our garden, and now I longed for the time when feelings were so easy to express. Despite my *maladresse* I hope he felt how pleased I was to see him, how proud I was to show him Ben, and how dearly I love him.

The holiday was all too quickly over, but once the (tearful) good-byes were said I was so dying to see Eric that I couldn't think of anything else. Ben was an angel during the flight, and even enjoyed airline food (he was the only one, I think). When the plane started its descent I saw the orange lights of the city shining in the darkness, and my heart leapt. It was Bordeaux. Home.

Home, Friday 7th November.

A quick PS for yesterday. I forgot to say Eric took Dog to the vet's for her second visit. No rabies – phew.

Well, it is good to be back. I have had a happy day pootling around the farm, making a fuss of Miu Miu, Dog and the goats. I had a look at Scramble's chicks, but they are not the fluff-bundles of old. They are all feathery now, with legs that look like they need a good dose of Nivea.

Mum and Dad drove over to see us this evening – this was the second part of the surprise they were all planning for me. I have not only had a wonderful stay in England, they have also planned to 'farm-sit' for us for the weekend. It is the big book fair in Brive tomorrow and Sunday, and Mum and Dad know how much we enjoy it. They had plotted with Eric to take care of the farm so that we could go. They know how to milk goats and shut away the chickens etc... and I think they are quite looking forward to it.

I can't believe I'm going on another mini-break! With Eric! Life is *magnifique*.

11pm. Change of plan. Mum and Dad aren't just going to look after the farm, they are going to look after Ben as well. Mum has promised it will be fine, as he knows them both well and they love spending time together. I am still breastfeeding him in the evening and at breakfast, but Mum says I won't lose my milk supply in one night, and it won't curdle and turn into cheese either. It feels very strange to be going somewhere without him, but I am looking forward to having some time with Eric.

I'm also sure that I won't miss out on anything Ben does this weekend. Mum and Dad are doting grandparents and record his every smile and sneeze on videotape whenever they see him. My parents know how to make epics – James Cameron's are puny in comparison. So I'll know what he's been up to, and if I want an immediate update I can always telephone home.

On the way to Brive. Saturday, 8th November.

9.30am. We've just set out, having given Ben his last breast-feed until tomorrow. Actually he looked more interested in his baby rice than in me. Hrmph.

Will phone to see if he's OK. Thank heavens for the mobile.

9.35am. He's OK.

10am. Does Mum know where I keep the Rusks? Will ring.

10.05am. Phew, she'd found them.

10.25am. Time for Ben's nap. Did I tell Mum what time I put him down?

10.30am. Well. Mum has just told me to stop ringing. She used the argument that she is (a) already Mum to four kids, and (b) a qualified paediatrician, so I should stop worrying about Ben and enjoy my weekend. I'm going to put my diary and 'phone away and concentrate on Eric.

Brive, 10.30pm. It took us two hours to get to Brive. The countryside was gorgeous, the castles and cliffs of the Dordogne flashed past us as we drove, and quite distracted us from our conversation. Still, we managed to talk about Ben all the way to the Corrèze, where Brive is.

When we got there we saw a massive queue outside the book fair, so we thought we would look around the town itself today and visit the fair tomorrow. There should be fewer people if we get there when it opens.

We had a good time exploring the town. The centre is beautiful – old but with a touch of the modern; smart new shops, restaurants and delightful ancient buildings. We bought ourselves a kilo of roast chestnuts and walked through the cobbled streets, looking at everything from Benetton to an exhibition about restoring antique books.

This evening we ate in a cheap and cheerful restaurant and then wandered around the corner to sample a half pint of Guinness in an Irish pub. All things Irish are fashionable in France these days, and it does make me feel chirpy to know that I no longer need to take an aeroplane to drink something other than *bière blonde*. Sadly, Eric and I didn't see any of the pub's regulars, as we drank our Guinness at nine o'clock, ages before anyone else arrived. French people start their evening at around ten thirty (my bed time!) and don't leave the pubs until the early hours.

After our drink we checked into an hotel. At only thirteen pounds a night we could just about afford to splash out instead of facing the misery of camping in November. Our room is simple but clean, with a toilet and sink. The shower is out on the landing, and this was the cause of Major Embarrassment this evening.

Eric showered first, and I let him back into our room. Then I stripped off, wrapped myself in the Indecently Small towel supplied by the hotel, and nipped across the landing for my shower. I had a lovely long one (as we weren't paying for the water!) then I wrapped the towel around me again and raced back to our room. I knocked but there was no answer, and I couldn't for the life of me remember the code for the lock on the door. Where was Eric?! I panicked when I heard another guest opening their door, and hid behind a conveniently placed ficus plant. I couldn't hide all of my naughty bits with that towel, and I didn't want to be charged with indecent exposure.

Eric took ten minutes to turn up. He'd been downstairs checking the breakfast window, and nearly jumped out of his skin when a large plant hissed, "Eric, you bastard!" at him. Happily he had the presence of mind to let me back into the room.

Tonight we are lying in bed, and like all self-respecting parents on a Romantic Break together we are busy yakking about our son. We have also been playing with the TV set – our one at home died some while back. Oddly enough there seems to be exactly the same thing on TV as last year in Brive – a strange film about a magic goose and a girl with a very short haircut, who seems to be a bizarre mix of Joan of Arc and Cinderella, and on the other channel there is a dreary documentary about lemurs. Hey ho! It's a good thing we have other things to do...

Eric has just told me his Deep Thought for the day – we are about to have our first night of un-interrupted sleep for over half a year!

Home. Sunday, 9th November.

Un-interrupted sleep! We must have been dreaming. At three in the morning there was banging on our door; it was the *pompiers* coming to evacuate us from our room. I panicked and thought there was a fire, but in fact there was a water leak and water was flooding the electricity supply. We were shown to a room in another part of the hotel, which was bitterly cold as the electric heating wasn't functioning. It was much colder in Brive than at home, and the temperature had dipped below freezing.

Our 'new' bed was damp and *glacial*, and we took ages to get back to sleep. The only good thing about our new accommodation was that it had a bathroom with a proper bath, and as I lay in bed shivering I fantasised about the hot soak I was going to have in the morning.

We got up at six, too cold, stiff and tired to lie there any more. I went to run a bath, only to find there was no water. We couldn't even brush our teeth. We thought we would find ourselves some breakfast, but when we went downstairs we found the lobby full of complaining guests. We hadn't seen any of the hotel staff during our 'evacuation' and I was a bit shocked when the manager of the hotel explained to guests that the technical hitch wasn't his fault, so that instead of asking for a refund the guests could all take a running jump. I would have settled for a cup of coffee on the house, and his attitude left me outraged. Maybe I could get into those English programmes about consumer rights after all!

Well, guess what we did. We packed our bag and left without paying. Just like that. No one had taken our details the previous evening, so I don't think they'll come after us. What we did now feels Positively Daring, but this morning we were too annoyed to worry about it.

We picked up a *croissant* each in a bakery, and had coffee in a bar while we waited for the book fair to open. We were the first to go inside, and it was a treat to chat to the authors and get ourselves a signed copy of our favourite book. There were so many different kinds of books to see – novels and cookbooks, cartoons and children's stories – and we had a happy three hours browsing.

We had a sandwich for lunch and then set off home. Eric suggested we take a different route, down through the Vézère valley, so that we could glimpse Lascaux and other *grottes*. We hadn't planned on visiting any caves, but when we saw a sign for a prehistoric site we couldn't resist it. We usually have Ben with us so we can't easily visit such things, so we both wanted to take advantage of this opportunity.

'Our' cave was Stupendous. We sat on a little train to go around it, to prevent tourists from damaging the floor or touching the paintings. There were umpteen pictures of mammoths, deer, rhinoceros and horses. We were allowed to get off the train and explore the cool, circular 'room' at the end of the cave, which was literally covered in animal paintings. The drawings of each species were generally separated into different areas, and the guide explained that the whys and wherefores behind this were unknown. It is not even certain what the cave was used for.

And then guess what? I, *historienne extraordinaire*, single-handedly solved a mystery which has baffled the Greatest Scientists for more than a century. That cave was a fridge; it's dead obvious. It was far cooler in the depths of the cave than outside, so much better for storing recent kills. Even one dopey guy at the narrow entrance would have been able to prevent scavenging animals getting in to steal the meat. The cave paintings were just to divide the 'fridge' into its different sections – antelope over here, mammoth at the bottom on the left. And as for those human handprints on the walls – you should take a look in my fridge, it's covered with grubby paw prints. So there you are, mystery solved. Give me a Nobel Prize.

Got home in the early evening, and found everyone safe and sound. Ben had a huge breastfeed, so now I look less like a page three model. He seems to have had a fantastic time with Mum and Dad... what's more, we have the video to prove it!

Home. Monday, 10th November.

Mum and Dad have just gone home. Ben impressed them before they left by his first real crawl! I always knew the child was a genius. It is brilliant to see him crawling about, although as he headed for the Dangerous Area below the kitchen sink I began to wonder whether his increased mobility is a bit of a mixed blessing.

2pm. Have spent all day putting away bleach bottles, protecting sockets, and picking up small objects which he might put in his mouth and choke on. I was in the bathroom hiding away Eric's razor when I turned around and found Ben playing with the loo brush. This is going to be difficult.

10.30pm. During Ben's sleep I designed posters to advertise 'our' writing competition. My literary cells have all been fired by Brive, and I'm looking forward to reading the manuscripts. Eric has taken care of putting an advertisement in the local paper, so I'm hoping we'll be inundated with replies.

Home. Tuesday, 11th November. Armistice.

An important day. I thought people would be wearing poppies, but apparently only the Brits do that. Here the poppy has no special significance; my English conversation group tonight said they were shocked that people would place common weeds on war memorials. In France they are bedecked with chrysanthemums, *comme il faut!*

Eric and I talked a bit about the war, but it ended up as much the same discussion as on the 8th May. Our argument about who did what during the world wars goes back years, right to the very first November when Eric and I were together. I remember him getting very shirty when we played our first Truth game. He thought I was going to ask him something of a sexual nature, and was Furious when I asked, "Eric, do you *really* think France did *well* in the war?"

We have still not resolved the question, so we stayed off the subject. (Well, I only asked him once why there are Arches of Triumph all over France when they've had so few 'triumphs'. Except the World Cup, of course.)

Today was brightened up by our first manuscript coming in. Marie-Thérèse shyly gave us a slim volume of her poetry. We have just begun reading it tonight, and it is really good. If all our competitors are of this standard we're going to enjoy the judging.

Home. Wednesday, 12th November.

We saw the baby bunnies for the first time this evening. Two of them came out of the nesting box at dusk, although I think it was accidental. Their mother soon pushed them back inside, but we did have a chance to admire them. They are SO cute, soft and grey and velvety. How will we ever be able to *eat* them?

Dog had her last trip to the vet's. It has cost us a fortune – I hope she's learnt her lesson. Anyway, vet gave her the once over, and assured me she was healthy. As we left I promised she would never bite again, whereupon (to my mortification) Dog turned round and bit the vet on her bottom. It was awful. The vet, fortunately, suffered no harm, and she said Dog was probably stirred up because she's about to come on heat or something. She was really nice about it, but I was scarlet with embarrassment. What on earth has got into Dog?????

Home. Thursday, 13th November.

Lucienne and Gilbert are coming tomorrow. It will be good to see them, but at the moment the house looks like a bomb has hit it. Eric is in the middle of an essay crisis, so I have been slaving away by myself all day. I have washed the house from top to bottom, but it is still messy. (I have a feeling it always will be.)

Nb. Must clean the fridge. Eric assures me that not everyone's has fingerprints inside. I hope that doesn't rubbish my cave/fridge theory.

Home. Friday, 14th November.

My in-laws surprised us by arriving at 8 o'clock in the morning. They had driven all night to avoid traffic, which meant they were here hours earlier than predicted. It was really nice to see them, but I wish I had had a chance to clean the fridge or even put on my clothes before they came...

We had coffee and then we showed them around the farm. They were really impressed by all our animals, and enjoyed milking the goats with us. When Lucienne was a little girl she used to spend her long summers living on a farm in the Pyrenees, taking care of a flock of geese. This was years before child labour was frowned upon, but (as was often the case) there were too many children in her family for her parents to look after, and those that could went out to work. She was only tiny – her age wasn't even in double figures – but she worked from dawn until dusk. It was tremendously hard, but she said that seeing our geese still brought back some happy memories.

I had to leave in the afternoon to go to my lessons, and Lucienne was delighted to look after Ben – they were both beaming when I left (and when I got back, I hasten to add).

My afternoon's teaching went well. I have such a good time at school now, I wish I'd loved it that much when I was a child.

In the evening I came home and found that Lucienne had made tea. It is great to be looked after! Eric and his Dad have been busy digging holes for the fruit trees they are planning to plant this weekend. The orchard is really taking shape.

Home. Saturday, 15th November.

Tree-planting put on stand-by as our 'bird' friend Philippe telephoned to see if he could come and see our farm. We had talked to him about our kingfishers and barn owls, and some other large and unidentified owls we'd glimpsed in the wood.

We managed to spot the kingfishers, and we looked at the barn owls in the attic through the round window. There was only one up there, sitting on a beam and glaring down at us. He looked very beautiful and quite regal.

Later in the afternoon we went up the hill to see if we could see the other owls. Luck was with us, and we saw the large, brown bird up in a

216

tree. He had orange eyes and his amber stare was quite disconcerting.

He was not the only one of his kind we found – there were several in the wood. Philippe was wildly excited; we had our very own *dortoir* *(*dormitory) of *Moyens-Ducs:* Long Eared owls. Their ears are really two feathers sticking up on either side of their head; it makes them look terribly appealing.

We collected some of their rejection pellets (little balls full of bones, feathers and fur which they spit up when they digest their prey) and Philippe and Eric took photos. We also had another good look at the badger set. It is rare to see such a large set that has been left undisturbed by the hunters.

Let's hope our wood stays a wildlife haven forever...

Home, Sunday 16th November.

Had a Castanet outing to the market this morning, and brought home a bootload of little fruit trees. We had great fun putting them all in, it feels like a historical event to be planting trees which will be here when I am an old lady.

I found some photographs of an orchard in one of our gardening books. I can't help but think a mature orchard is one of the Most Beautiful things on our planet. This one had trees laden with tiny red apples, and sheep grazed between the trees. The article explained that sheep keep the grass down and stop insects moving in which might damage the trees.

I showed the article to Eric and his Mum, and they both simultaneously said the same thing. We need some sheep. Goats are too destructive and kill trees, but sheep can live in orchards – although we will obviously have to protect the little trees with chicken wire while they are growing.

Lucienne told us all about the sheep on 'her' farm in the Pyrenees, and Eric also enthused about this variety. They *are* the sweetest kind of sheep, I have to admit. They have fleece which hangs in snowy ringlets, an angular shape and noses like Julius Caesar's. The ewes are milked in the mountains, to make delicious *brebis* cheese. It would be interesting to experiment with our own cheese-making. I think we are all now persuaded that we should buy some.

The best person to ask about Pyrenean sheep was my friend Danièle.

Her family are farmers and although they have cows and corn, they probably know someone who could find us some sheep. We rang her after tea, and she invited us on the spot to come down and see her. She was really wanting to see us and meet little Ben, and she promised she could help us track down some sheep. She said they were right in the middle of the *pelère* (forgot to ask what that was) at the farm, but that she would love to see us ASAP, and suggested we come tomorrow.

I hesitated, but Lucienne and Gilbert urged us to go. They are good at looking after animals, and Gilbert is a master gardener. The farm would be more than just safe with them overnight.

So there you are, tomorrow we're off to the mountains!

Small farm in the Pyrenees, Monday 17th November.

Happy trip down south. We got to Dany's at the beginning of the afternoon, and little Ben stretched his arms out to her straightaway. It's wonderful to see that he's such a good judge of character already.

Dany made us a late lunch, and teased me about whether we were planning a trip down during the skiing season. She knows I'm terrified of skiing – I think I was traumatised by watching *Ski Sunday* as a child. All those horrid hundred-mile-an-hour accidents – it does seem unwise and unhealthy to crash with two long sticks attached to your legs and two poles attached to your arms, with only a pine tree or a cliff to break your fall.

We chatted over lunch about Pyrenean wildlife. You can see vultures and eagles lazily circling the *pics,* and marmosets popping in and out of their burrows. If you are fantastically lucky you could come across the trail of a bear – I say 'fantastically' lucky because there are only a handful left. (If you can fit bears into your hands.)

Dany said that most people in her area are far from thrilled at having bears in their mountains. The general reaction is, '*merde, c'est dangereux!*' In reality the bears spend their 99.9% of their time trying to avoid people, esp. hunters.

We pottered about the farm after lunch and relaxed. We also talked to Dany's uncle about the sheep, and he said he could find us some orphan lambs to adopt at Christmas. Bottle rearing lambs is a tough job, and most farmers are only too glad to 'get rid' of them.

We are having an early night as we're tired and we're both looking forward to trying the Phenomenally Comfortable spare bed. Dany has just knocked on the door, and asked whether Eric could take care of Ben while I go with her to the *pelère*. The word is not French, it is a regional dialect called Béarnais, so Eric and I are both in the dark about what it is. We've said a wary 'yes'. I wonder what it's about...

Home. Tuesday (Wednesday, I suppose), 18/19th November.

2.00am. Too late and too knackered to write. Home safe. Will explain *pelère* tomorrow.

Home. Wednesday, 19th November.

10.00am. All is rosy on the farm. Lucienne and Gilbert have had a thoroughly good time and the animals are all looking jolly. The baby rabbits have been out for a play – all nine of them.

Right, back to the *pelère*. Yesterday morning Dany banged on our door at six am, yelling '*vite! vite*...or you'll miss the killing.' Not wanting to wake Ben I opened the door and asked in a whisper what she was talking about.

I listened with alarm as she told me that the *pelère* is when they kill the pig they have reared over the past year. The whole family gathers together to prepare traditional dishes afterwards, and then in the evening there is a feast to celebrate and to taste the meat.

Well, as I've already said, I'm a lapsed vegetarian. Although I'm interested in regional cooking, I was not burning with desire to see the poor beast get shot in the head, be hung up and have its throat cut. I told Dany I'd get dressed and be down in an hour. I fumbled about in the dark for my clothes, and opened the shutters as I left the room. I accidentally dislodged a hibernating lizard, which dropped unpleasantly from the lintel into my hair. The day hadn't started well.

I had my breakfast and then walked slowly down to the barn. The pig was dead, that much was obvious. It actually looked as though Hannibal Lecter had gone beserk in the barn; blood was boiling to make black pudding, brains were simmering in a cauldron to make pâté, shoulders were severed to make hams and the intestines were being stuffed with leftovers to make sausages. All the family were there, working hard to turn every scrap of pig into something tasty – nothing is wasted. The *pelère* is all about economy, family and tradition – fine values, but I found the blood and guts side of it hard to handle. I sat (a little queasily) on an upturned bucket, and as I looked around I noticed *six* trotters hanging from a beam. Was this a genetically engineered pig? ???? I anxiously cross-questioned Dany, and she burst out laughing and explained that two of those trotters were from last year's porker.

I left the family to it, and found Eric and Ben. They were having breakfast together, and we planned our day. We had all sorts of ideas, but in the end visited the stunning *château* in Pau, which overlooks the Pyrenean mountain range. The tapestries in the castle were fabulous, and we loved the cradle which had belonged to Henri 1 V; it was a turtle shell. It was an original and interesting way of making a baby's bed, although it's a good thing for turtles that the idea never really caught on.

In the evening we were invited to the feast. It was at the neighbouring farm, which belongs to Danièle's grandparents. The older women prepared everything, and there was enough food for a whole village. I would have helped, but I was having a hard time stopping Ben from crawling away to play with the farm dogs. We ate by candlelight; electricity is still treated as a new-fangled thing here, and many older people prefer to do without. Twenty bloodstained and battered people sat up at table, forgetting the day's cares as they drank their honey-sweet Jurançon wine, made by the family.

We ate an awful lot, and I was surprised to see that it wasn't all pork. We were each given a huge plate of white-bait *en entrée,* which I found a challenge. I have always had a problem when my plate gazes up at me with so many eyes. I looked up and concentrated on the man opposite me. He was also staring at me fixedly, and I couldn't help but notice that he had a glass eye.

Dinner continued into the night, and we left at eleven o'clock. Ben was fast asleep, so our 'goodbyes' (or *adiou* as they say in the Béarn) were muted. I made the same promise I always make to Dany; 'next time I'll bring my skis...'

Well, I am feeling very washed out after last night's excesses, and I half wish I didn't have my conversation group this evening (which we had to swap from Tuesday night.) I'll have to make it especially interesting, because if they start falling asleep I certainly won't be able to stay awake.

Home. Thursday, 20th November

Ben was eight months old yesterday, and we forgot to wish him Happy Birthday. We are such Bad Parents.

It seems we got back just in time from Pyrenees. The roads all over France have been blocked by angry lorry drivers, and I think we're in for a long 'siege.' Eric and Gilbert have both been to fill up the tanks on the cars, because if the strike holds we'll be without fuel in a couple of days. I've been out to buy some necessities, especially nappies. Being without them would be a Nightmare.

Home. Friday, 21st November.

Drove to school along empty roads. As soon as the lorry blockades are in place the traffic stops, as everyone has to conserve their fuel. I hope this dispute won't last too long – if I have no fuel next week I may have to miss a teaching session, and I couldn't bear that. I really love this job.

The children were as sweet as ever, and learn English so quickly that it is a joy to teach them. All too soon it was time to come home. Back in our village I was amazed at the queue in our local filling station; people were not just filling their tanks, they were also pouring fuel into jerry cans, buckets and even ice boxes. I think it is a bit unfair to take too much – if we make do with a bit less petrol than usual there will be more to go round.

When Ben was in bed we all sat in front of the fire and

listened to the news on the radio. We had to turn up the volume, as Miu Miu's purrs on Lucienne's lap kept drowning it out. Well, the strike is holding. Lorry drivers are badly paid, and are often forced by their bosses to break the legal limits on the number of hours they drive. Some work as many as fifty hours a week, which is dangerous for them and for other road users. The bosses are pushing them harder and harder, as their rising costs (fuel prices etc...) mean they have to transport more in less time. It sounds terrible, and we are sympathetic, but it does mean that other French people are being prevented from going to work.

All we can hope for is that the negotiations get a good result quickly, so that the country can get back to normal.

Home. Saturday, 22nd November.

Telephoned my siblings first thing this morning. They all sounded a bit concerned – is France heading for another revolution? I said I think it will all be sorted out soon, and that I don't think anyone will lose their head.

Off to the library for the monthly meeting after. It was nice to have it on Saturday morning instead of deep into Friday night. The president of the library handed us a pile of manuscripts – the competition has taken off! There was a wad of stuff from the school, and lots of individual entries. It means there is a great deal of reading to do, and I remarked to the secretary that it is a good thing that there are three of us. I had a sense of foreboding when she blushed and looked hard at her shoes. She mumbled an apology, which was something about her boss wanting to submit a manuscript, and her not being able to vote for any other competitor. The 'jury' is now down to two members; Eric and myself.

Came home and found Lucienne all pleased. She called me into the kitchen (which smelt of her delicious cooking) to see what Ben had starting doing while I was out – he can pull himself up to standing! She assured me she hadn't made him do non-stop press-ups all morning, he'd just suddenly stood up while she was getting lunch. Ben is a vertical person!

Home. Sunday, 23rd November.

Left the hubbies and went off to the market with Lucienne and Ben.

The atmosphere was very strange – people were buying huge chunks of meat, incredible quantities of bread and buckets of potatoes. It's all because of the lorry siege; basic essentials are getting scarce, and what's left is being rapidly bought up. It doesn't look as though a Revolution is in the offing – it's more like France is preparing for a war. I can't believe the lorries will stay on strike much longer – surely it can't last?

Home. Monday, 24th November.

Lucienne and Gilbert made the decision to drive home early this morning on their tank-full of fuel. Using the car for short trips around here would have used up the precious liquid, and left them stranded. We hugged each other goodbye at 6am, and they were safely back at Nimes this afternoon – but only just. They'd had to take a complicated route to avoid the lorries, and had been just a drop away from an empty tank when they got home.

We avoided using our car today, and we walked into the village, pushing Ben in the pushchair. It felt like a Public Holiday – the place was full of people. The commuters no longer have enough petrol to get to Bordeaux, and had stayed in the village. The atmosphere, however, was far from that of a holiday. Many people who can't get to work will not be paid, and if the strike holds this could have severe consequences on the monthly pay packet. Also the temperature is dropping – it is close to freezing. Most houses in the country have oil or gas heating, and deliveries of either are impossible. We have hardly any gas left in the tank in our garden, and we won't be able to heat our water for much longer. We are feeling a bit miserable tonight.

Home. Tuesday, 25th November.

COLD. Cold water, cold house, cold garden, cold toes, cold everything.

The temperature plunged below zero in the night, and everything froze around the house, including the drinking troughs. Ben whooped with surprise when he saw the chickens slipping about on the ice this morning like overweight skaters. They didn't seem particularly at ease, and they kept falling onto their feathery *derrières*, but their performance (certainly not worth more than a 5.2) impressed little Ben. I'm not sure what it will do for their laying; I don't think they'll produce any eggs for a while that aren't scrambled.

As for the goats, well, they licked the frost, looking for grass and looking none too thrilled about the new addition to their diet. At least their milk wasn't frozen.

The fires in the hearth and in the stove burnt all day and they certainly look nice, but don't give out much warmth. We rely on the radiator in the bathroom to keep that room cosy, but this morning it was horribly cold in there. Our gas had run out during the night, so now we have no radiator and hot baths are off.

We have decided not to get too depressed. We heated water in a cauldron over the fire (witch style) to pour into the bath, so we all smell wholesome. We have no more money worries than usual; we won't lose out on our pay if we don't go to work, as our work is here. And it *is* interesting living like this, almost as though we've slipped back in time.

Eric went off to the village on his bike to buy a few things in the local store, and came back grinning. The old guy in the shop had made him laugh – he said he was worried about getting deliveries through, and was wandering whether he should stock up now on mole traps...

Eric was also pleased to see how many people were on bikes in the village. Now fuel supplies are dwindling the trusty *vélos* are being dusted off and brought out of garages. He *loves* bikes, and says it is great to see a whole previously unknown population of them coming out to play. He thinks this strike will be a great opportunity for his bike to make new friends.

My conversation lesson was cancelled tonight, as all the women wanted to economise their petrol. Marie-Thérèse said that she does, of course, have a bicycle, but explained that it isn't nocturnal and that she prefers not to venture out with it after dark. Never mind, we'll catch up next week.

Home. Wednesday, 26th November.

Ben's upright balancing has turned into cruising. No, not the American kind (driving around in a car hoping to pick someone up) I'm talking about walking around the room holding on to things. I'm pretty surprised he's doing this already; at this rate he'll be walking before Christmas, riding a bike in January, and he'll have twelve A levels by the time he's four.

He must take after me.

Home. Thursday, 27th November.

I think I could just about dig out my old Filofax. My lessons tomorrow have been changed from afternoon to morning, and I could have written this into my planner. I am a working woman once more!

Eric studied and we did our usual jobs this morning, and then he persuaded me to come out on a little bike ride in the afternoon. He fitted a baby seat to my bike some long time ago, but we'd never tested it. We thought that if we wrapped Ben up in many layers he'd enjoy the air and the sensation of riding along the country lanes.

I was terribly nervous about it all. I like cycling, but I am not at all skilled at it. In fact I freely admit to being a total and utter dunce. I have never managed a hand signal, let alone riding with my hands in my pockets. (Even hand signals in the car make me go wobbly.)

Still, we all put our cycling stuff on, and I put lots of fleecy clothes on Ben, plus an improvised cycling cape made out of an old blanket. To begin with our cycling went (er) swimmingly, and as we bowled along I began to feel more and more confident. Little Ben yelled with excitement, I was brimming with happiness... I thought I'd finally discovered a sport which we could do as a family.

After about five miles Eric told me he'd poured some warm tea into a drinking flask, which he'd clipped to the frame of my bike. "Just pull it out and have a swig," he said, as though getting that bottle out was a mere trifle. Well, as I said before, I'm terrible on a bike, and I refused to take my hand off the handlebars without stopping.

Eric wouldn't believe me. He said *anyone* is capable of having a drink on a bike (even Jean-Pierre) and that it was just a question of confidence. Through gritted teeth I explained I have a balance problem, but he wouldn't listen. We were having such a lovely time that it seemed a shame to argue, so plucking up all my courage I reached my left hand down for it.

I'm not sure what happened next. One moment Eric was there, cycling along beside me, and the next my front wheel had whirled round, bashing him broadside. Ben and I were absolutely fine, but we watched horrified (well I was, Ben thought it was funny) as Eric catapulted through the air into the deep and very wet ditch.

Rather unkindly, I did hope for temporary unconsciousness and total amnesia, but Dearest Loved One was fully conscious and Really Angry. I could hear him splashing and yelling insults down in his hole, and for just a second I felt like running away rather than helping him out. Fortunately the good side of me triumphed, and I got off my bike and pushed it over to the verge. Eric and his bike had totally vanished from sight. He was right at the bottom of the ditch, amongst the mud and the hibernating frogs, shaking his head in disbelief. He seemed to be muttering something about me being *handicappée*.

He was all right, but he wouldn't accept any help getting out of there. He said icily that I wasn't to touch him – I'd already done enough damage for one day. We cycled home in silence, except for Eric saying, *"c'est pas possible, elle est handicappée"* from time to time. I did feel very guilty, especially as he was soaking wet, freezing cold and covered from head to foot with evil smelling slime. And we had no hot water at home.

When we got back Eric took all his clothes off while I made hot tea. He sat by the fire and sipped it as I apologised profusely. In the end he accepted a pack of babywipes as a peace offering, and I helped him to scrape the worst off. Then we boiled water over the fire so he could scrub off the rest.

Tonight I think I'm forgiven, and I hope we can put this behind us. Eric still smells like a drain, but he hasn't come to any real harm – the only thing which has really suffered is his image of me. He said just now that we will go out cycling as a family again, but on one condition... I get stabilisers for my bike.

Home. Friday, 28th November.

Dear, dear, dearest darling Eric. Not only did he forgive me, but this morning I awoke to the delicious smell of bacon and eggs – a real treat. A French *petit-déjeuner* tends to be very sweet and although, in general, I much prefer French *cuisine* to English, I do love a traditional English breakfast. It wasn't our anniversary or anything, he was just being nice. Being Eric.

Ben had a fun time helping me clear my plate, popping the egg yolks with his fingers and making off with the toast. He didn't seem too keen on actually eating anything; he scampered onto Eric's lap to help him polish off his hot-chocolate and *croissant*. His French half dominates at breakfast, but you can still tell he is half English. He likes Marmite.

I drove off to school on country roads which have been destroyed by lorries trying to avoid the road blocks. Their surface was cracked, the verges churned up and the ditches collapsing. The heavy loads have done untold damage, and I saw more than one farmer shaking his fist at a lorry. It is strange and frightening to see forty ton trucks trying to manoeuvre on farm tracks around the vines.

I got to school as the children arrived, and I could hardly believe my eyes when I saw them arriving not only on foot but also on bikes, scooters, roller skates and even on a pony. Six children came in a trailer pulled by a tractor. There was no petrol left, so they had to take whatever form of transport was at their disposal.

I had a great time at school, as usual, and just as I finished my last lesson the headmistress came bursting in. "The strike's over!" she said, with a smile of relief.

On the way home I realised I hadn't asked whether the strike had been 'successful'. The problem is that so many ordinary people have been suffering the consequences of the dispute that our sympathy has worn thin. Once I have had our gas delivered and taken a hot bath with Ben I will get interested in the strike settlement. Right now I'm just glad it is over.

When I got home it was lunchtime, and although I wasn't exactly hungry (having consumed about three million calories at breakfast) I was curious to see what was on the menu. It was a good thing I'd eaten well in the morning as the boys had already eaten... the pair of them had guzzled the rest of the eggs and bacon. *Décidement* they did like an English breakfast – for lunch.

Home. Saturday, 29th November.

Virginie has petrol, and we have gas. Not *that* kind of gas... I mean the cylinder in the garden is full, so our radiator and water are back on. It feels *fantastique*. Thank heavens the strike is over.

Tonight I ran the hottest, deepest bath I've ever had, and I was lying there quite fancying myself as a mermaid when Eric came in. "What are you up to?" he said, as I splashed about (rather alluringly, I thought). "Let me guess, are you being a whale?"

I threw the flannel at him, which sent him racing out of the bathroom.

227

I could almost forgive him, except he keeps laughing and yelling, 'thar she blows' at me. Hrmph.

Home. Sunday, 30th November.

This cold weather is very galling. I know it's practically December, but it feels as though we're in the midst of a Siberian winter. The temperature is at a record low, and the leaves have frozen off the trees. It's annoying because I love the autumn colours, and also because I bet Eric 100 francs that they wouldn't fall until December 15th this year. With the weather centres recording night-time temperature of minus ten, I'm beginning to think I could win my money back by betting on a white Christmas. The chances of it happening are virtually nil, but with the weird weather we're having you never know.

Although it was bitingly cold when we woke up this morning, we didn't want to stay indoors all day. It was such a relief to have a full tank of petrol that we thought we'd use it to visit the junk fair in Bordeaux. It did seem wise, however, to dress as warmly as possible, so we ended up donning most of our wardrobe. All three of us looked like multi-coloured snowmen, but at least we were snug. Sadly, I think it was only the pressure of all our clothes pushing against the inside of our wardrobe that was keeping it upright. Once we'd emptied it of its woolly support our pack-flat number collapsed. That's pack-flat for you. As the little plastic plugs and screws all pulled out, I'm not sure we'll be able to revive it.

Outside it was still below freezing, and our breath formed little fluffy clouds which Ben found delightful; he made himself quite breathless puffing in and out. We all went to milk the goats, and they seemed quite warm and happy in the barn. The chickens and the geese had also decided to stay indoors, and they sat up high on our bales of hay, fluffing up their homegrown eiderdowns.

We left the animals and drove off to Bordeaux, through a strange white landscape. The fields, hedges and vines were heavily powdered with frost, and just watching the cattle graze made my teeth ache. Once we got into town it was a little warmer; the central heating and log fires of the Bordelais had raised the temperature by a couple of degrees.

The junk fair was on Bordeaux's (and Europe's) biggest square, La Place des Quinconces. You can find just about anything for sale, from antique statues to books and china. I was particularly keen to have a look round the stalls as I am now a collector of antique porcelain coffee cups. Well, maybe 'collector' is exaggerating a little. Let's just say I acquired two of them in a car boot sale last year for a grand total of fifty pence, and I wouldn't mind having a few more.

As soon as we started wandering around the square it became obvious that this was no car boot sale. The Castanet family were the only ones wearing all their clothes (regardless of such trivial matters as colour coordination or taste) whereas the Bordelais were wearing soft layers of cashmere. They had not come with their loose change, but had come armed with cheque books and Gold Cards. The 'junk' was of the Louis 14th variety, although there were a few interesting bargains to be had.

Eric pushed Ben off to a book stall while I hunted for my cups. I couldn't find one for under 200 francs, and they were usually part of a pricey set. I did find one which was splendid, but as the dealer was drinking her coffee out of it I didn't ask whether it was for sale.

It took me an hour to find what I was looking for... a tiny colourful cup which was so delicate that it reminded me of a Fabergé egg. And it was only 10 francs. It was then that I realised that Eric had all the money on him. I set off in pursuit of the Castanet men, but trying to look for someone in over an acre of crowds is pretty much impossible. I hunted for what seemed like hours, getting colder and colder and increasingly panicked. We had arranged to meet beside a stuffed cow, but someone must have bought it because I couldn't find it again. Either that or it had come back to life and pottered off into the crowd.

After some very long time I went back to where we'd parked the car, and found them both sitting inside. They were scoffing *pains au chocolat* and looking a bit too comfortable, considering how miserable I was feeling. I was about to get cross when Eric handed me a plastic cup and a thermos of hot coffee. I decided then and there that a cup doesn't have to be antique to be very, very welcome.

I didn't want to go all the way back to the fair as I couldn't feel my toes any more, and I didn't want Ben to get frostbite either. Instead we drove home at a gentle pace, stopping to admire the frozen scenery. I read passages out loud to Eric from a book he'd bought, a French classic called *Le Petit Prince*. It was a book he introduced me to when we first met, and I still find it intensely moving. Despite the sub-zero temperature it warmed my heart.

229

DÉCEMBRE

Home. Monday, 1st December.

Woke up this morning and found myself singing 'Jingle Bells.' December! Christmas! I bounded about getting dressed, only pausing to cover Eric and Ben with Big Kisses. Eric was dumbfounded, and asked what had got into me. He was none the wiser when I kissed him again and sang "Tis the season to be jolly, fa la la la la, la la la la."

I have to be careful about Christmas. Eric, for some reason I have never quite fathomed, hates it. He once told me that it's because there is no cycling on TV, just repeats of tear-wrenching films like *The Little Matchgirl*. That can't really be the reason can it? Surely not??? Anyway, he usually sulks from December 1st to January, although his worse sulks can last into the spring. If it's not the cycling thing maybe the problem is less to do with Christmas itself than with the winter weather. He hates the cold and the lost hours of sunshine. He saw a programme on telly (in the days when the telly still worked) about SAD syndrome, showing people who suffer depression in winter due to the decreased amount of UV light. He thought maybe he was a sufferer. I agreed he was a Sad Case.

Once we'd finished breakfast the sun was shining, and I thought that would cheer him up. It didn't. I was disappointed but not surprised... I met Eric during the run-up to Christmas and spent a long time trying to convince him of the merits of holly, carols and stockings – the kind Santa's interested in, that is. Despite all my efforts he was unimpressed, and up until now all our Christmases have been half-heartedly celebrated. Eric grits his teeth and lets me put up a couple of strands of tinsel, and I feel upset that we can't have a few dozen more. Once they do go up, usually on about Christmas Eve, they don't have time to gather any dust... Eric has them put away by Boxing Day. He is a total Christmas pooper.

Now, I come from a family of Christmas fanatics; everyone goes barmy about the yuletide thing in the Franklin household. Ian loves decorations so much that rumour has it that he sticks tinsel around his TV and his shaving mirror. David does Tasteful, but he adores Christmas – especially mince pies. Anna is CRAZY about it, and once bought a ten foot high Christmas tree which wouldn't even fit into her flat. She had to lop off its topmost branches which were pressing against the ceiling. Did she throw those boughs away? Nope, like all true Christmas fanatics she sprayed them with fake snow and arranged them in the remaining space (which was Seriously Limited) in her living room. She couldn't move around her flat for three weeks, but she was perfectly content.

And my parents. My parents! They take Christmas more seriously than Santa himself. Mum rings bells on Christmas Eve, pretending they are the bells on the sleigh. She makes clip-clopping noises when she comes in to fill our stockings (yup, we still get stockings, see how into Christmas we are?) just to fool us into thinking that there are reindeer in the house. Every year Dad plants another baby Christmas tree in the garden after Christmas, and as they can't quite face the fact it's all over they leave fairy lights about the place until June. They are potty and quite wonderful. Anyway, we should all take Christmas seriously – otherwise Santa might not come.

I'm not giving up. Eric WILL get to like it. I am going to make another huge effort this year to convert him. There is Ben to think of, after all, so I'm going to do my utmost to succeed. The thought of Ben with no stocking is too tragic to bear. It's worse than *The Little Matchgirl*.

Home. Tuesday, 2nd December.

Clouds today looked like overfull pillows, ready to burst and scatter snow all over Bordeaux. I'm dreaming of a white Christmas...

Sang Christmas carols with conversation group, and discussed Christmas recipes. Good time had by all.

Eric still gloomy.

Home. Wednesday, 3rd December.

Off for a little shopping trip in the village. Old Grumpy in the general store said it was a good thing Ben was wearing a woolly hat. I thought I'd actually had the last word on Such Things, but it wasn't to be. He told me he should also have a pair of mittens.

While we were in the store I was rooting about for some candles and firelighters when I noticed Eric and Ben were gazing at the window display. It took me a while to find what I wanted, to pay and pack my things, and during all that time the boys' attention remained fixed. I walked over to see what they were looking at; it was an electronic Santa, programmed to climb up and down a ladder. Ben and Eric were totally captivated.

This evening Eric said gruffly that maybe Christmas decorations might be quite fun this year. For the sake of our son, of course...

Home. Thursday, 4th December.

Eric and Ben went out together this morning, on a Mysterious Outing. Usually such sorties are to the bike shop, and involve buying some expensive gadget for Eric's bike in my absence. I feared the worst.

They got back at noon, with loads of carrier bags from the supermarket. Lovely Eric (although that wasn't what I'd called him all morning) had done all the shopping.

I unpacked the usual loo roll, nappies, pasta etc, etc, and was not expecting to find anything out of the ordinary. I couldn't have been more wrong – the last two bags were stuffed full of Christmas decorations. Hooray!

We are now in proud possession of twelve strands of tinsel, a set of fairy lights, six bulbuls and a large (and delightfully tacky) plastic reindeer. Eric said he was tempted by another electronic Santa, this time (rather incongruously) riding a bike, but that our budget wouldn't stretch to it. Never mind, the main thing is that our Scrooge has seen the (fairy) light. We shall have Christmas after all!

Home. Friday, 5th December.

Mum rang just before I set off to school. My siblings and grand-mothers are flying down for an early Christmas on the weekend of the 13th to 14th. We are all gathering at my parents' house on the coast – I am desperately looking forward to it. I'd better think about Christmas shopping, though...

School was *sympa*, and (having checked with the teachers first) got all my children excited by promising a Christmas party during the afternoon on Friday 19th. There will be mince pies, crackers, musical bumps and balloons.

I feel quite excited myself.

Home. Saturday, 6th December.

Spent much of today reading manuscripts for the competition. Some are not *passionant*, such as one guy's detailed description of Germany's motorway network. Others are brilliant, and I think saying one is 'better' than another is going to be an impossible task. Perhaps we should consider more small prizes?

Anna rang this evening to confirm the time of their flight. A Franklin invasion is imminent!

Home. Sunday, 7th December.

4pm. Market as usual in Libourne. It felt really Christmassy; the stalls were decorated with holly and mistletoe and there were carols playing on the loud-speaker system. The only thing I found slightly sinister were the Father Christmases on most of the buildings. They were life-sized mannequins dressed in Santa gear, which had been tied to the façades. Some were climbing over balconies, and looked alarmingly like burglars. Another had slipped and was dangling by a rope around his neck – it was disconcertingly like a public hanging. All in all I'm not sure the Santas were a success.

I bought a nice pair of earrings for Anna, and we came home for lunch. I've been trying to tidy the house this afternoon, but the huge heap of clothes in our bedroom is too depressing. Since our wardrobe collapsed just getting in and out of the room has not been something to be taken for granted... we have to wade through shirts and trousers, and to get to bed we have to leap over skirts and sweaters. The annoying thing is that even with such vast quantities of garbs we still don't have anything nice to wear. I once heard that when you dig a pond you obtain a pile of earth five times bigger than the hole, and I think the same thing is true when you empty a wardrobe. Something has to be done.

10pm. We did something! We ferried all the broken bits of pack-flat out to the barn, and Eric, after much scooting around, managed to find a broom handle and the handle of a rusty old rake. With a good deal of determined DIY (and a ball of string) we fixed up two hanging rails, one slightly higher than the other. They are so sturdy that I'm sure Olga Korbet could have done her warm-ups on them. Instead of folding our clothes we have hung everything up, so our wardrobe problem is temporarily solved. It is not a thing of beauty, but it will do for now.

The enormous pile of clothes is now down to the few odds and ends which won't fit on hangers. We have made a molehill out of a mountain.

Home. Monday, 8th December.

Dog was weird this morning. She often goes out running with Eric, and as soon as he starts putting on his trainers she usually wags her tail and gets ready to leave. Today she didn't as look enthusiastic. He'd planned to drive to the local stadium and run a few laps there with her, but she was strangely reluctant to get into Virginie. I had to tempt her inside with a dog biscuit – she'd follow a biscuit anywhere, even over a cliff.

Perhaps Dog just fancied going for a gentle walk. Walks with Eric, however, are not really the 'twice round the block whilst carrying newspaper in mouth' kind of walks which many of the canine species tend to favour. Just to give you an idea, he runs with a pulse-rate meter.

Eric said Dog started to whimper in the car. She sat there miserably with her eyes closed, while Eric tried to cheer her up by telling her how fit she was getting. She put her paws over her ears when he had a few words with her about her Body Odour.

Once at the stadium she followed him for two laps, but not for the full ten kilometres. She spotted a runner who was running at a slower pace, and thought she'd run with him instead. Unfortunately her plan backfired, because when the poor man saw an enormous, salivating hound bearing down him he broke into a sprint. Dog gave up, and just walked back and forwards across the stadium rather than running around it.

After an hour Eric had finished. Dog needed no encouragement to get back into the car – although Eric said all the way back she glared at him accusingly, her nose twitching slightly, as though to say, 'now who smells?'

She has spent the rest of today in front of the fire. I don't think it's anything serious, she's probably just a bit off colour. I'll keep an eye on her though.

Home. Tuesday, 9th December.

Dog still inside, lying on the floor looking like a big yellow hay bale. She is eating well, her eyes are clear and her nose damp, so I will hang on before taking her to see the vet. She has already had 500 francs of vet's fees spent on her due to her misdemeanour, and we can't afford much more.

The conversation class went well tonight. We had a hilarious time doing a crossword; it was all about sport, and our ignorance of the subject made us all laugh. Marie-Thérèse won the overall "I don't know a thing about this prize" when she insisted that an the alternative name for table-tennis is "bing bong ball."

Getting all excited about seeing the family!

Home. Wednesday, 10th December.

Did a tad more Christmas shopping today. Eric wanted to buy everyone a wooden solitaire game each, but I crushed that as being a Sad and Lonely idea. Instead we bought candles for Ian, David, and for David's girlfriend, Sarah. Eric is copying photos of Ben to give to his parents, my parents and the Grans. Phew, having kids really does get you out of a tight spot as far as Christmas shopping is concerned.

The president of the library committee (Gladys) telephoned this evening to call us to an 'emergency' meeting tonight. I asked her what it was all about... you've guessed it, they have a shelving crisis. I can't face it, so I've asked Eric to go instead. He's my scapegoat, or sacrificial lamb, or whatever...

Home. Thursday, 11th December.

Hmmm. They may have talked about shelving last night, but they also discussed other things. Apparently they are planning a small Christmas party in the library for the children in the village. For a man who hated Christmas Eric has certainly done an about-turn; Gladys telephoned today just to confirm his appearance as Santa. Ho ho ho.

Home. Friday, 12 December.

Taught the children at school to sing "Jingle Bells", so now I'm not the only one in France singing it. They are all looking forward to their party next week, especially since the teachers suggested it be fancy dress. The headmistress gave me 400 francs to buy some mince pies in Marks and Spencer in Bordeaux, and to cover the other costs (balloons, orange juice etc) so now I'll be able to do it properly.

Dad telephoned this evening to say that all the family had arrived safely, and that they are expecting us tomorrow. Eric, Ben and I are going over there together in the morning, but Eric is going to have to drive home in the evening for the milking. He will come back to the coast on Monday to pick us up.

I spent this evening wrapping presents, and packing our things. It will be fantastic to have 'Christmas' all together.

Bassin D'Arcachon. Saturday, 13th December.

Up at an ungodly hour to get everything done on the farm before we left. Dog still looked lethargic, so we left her in the stable where she'd be cosy in the straw.

We packed up the car, put Ben in his little seat and headed for the coast. Although it was horribly early it was impossible not to be struck by the beauty of Bordeaux at Christmas. All the streets were glittering with lights and decorations, and the brightly lit stone bridges, churches and squares looked magical. The cobbled streets of the Old Quarter were frozen and shining with frost, but the rich smell of fresh, doughy *baguettes* somehow created an illusion of warmth. I'm still not good at mornings, despite the training programme Ben has put me through, but this morning was so special that it made me burst into a full-length rendition of "Hark the Herald".

We got to my parents in time for breakfast, and after we'd hugged our hellos we gathered around the Christmas tree. It was beautiful, and also brought back many memories – we still have all the decorations we made as children. Under it there was a great stack of presents which we thought we'd open before lunch.

Dad poured us all a drink (hooray for 10am. Christmas gins) and we opened our presents. We were all thoroughly spoilt, and Ben was particularly appreciative of Father Christmas' offerings – well, of the wrapping paper, anyway.

Lunchtime was a perfect *mélange* of French and English tradition. We had seafood, as people always do in France, but we also had turkey and cranberry sauce. The latter baffles most French people, who think that the *anglais* spread their meat with jam, and are (therefore) completely insane.

The highlight of the meal was provided by David and Sarah. They announced their Engagement. There wasn't a dry eye at the table; hearing them say they are getting married in July produced a great rush of happy emotion, and I wasn't the only one who expressed it by bursting into tears. Good luck to them, we love them and wish them well.

After lunch we all had an urge to blow away the cobwebs, so we set off down to the sea. Unfortunately, the weather had taken a violent turn for the worse, and gale force winds were howling around the bay. The pine trees were shedding so many branches that it was too dangerous to hang around for long. As is often the case, I was relieved to be a confirmed landlubber as we watched the local sailing enthusiasts desperately trying to secure their expensive toys.

We didn't want to stay outside all afternoon, as it was far too cold for Ben. By four o'clock we'd managed to stall Mum (she is well known for her Tremendously Energetic beach walks) and turn back for home. I couldn't wait to play with my new presents, and besides, the call of the hearth and mince pies was too strong to resist.

It was a good thing we'd given so many candles, because when we got home the electricity was off. It took four hours to come back on again (branch damage to cables is common here) so we were thankful for their warm glow. It made everyone realise what smashing presents they were! (Even Eric came round to thinking that I'd been right about candles, I mean wooden Solitaire games would have been of no help whatsoever.)

Ben and I said our farewells to Eric after tea, and then we all settled down to watch a video. Well, obviously we had to argue a bit first about what to watch. In the end we opted for *Titanic*, and all I can say is that I have never, ever seen my family cry so many tears in one day. We'd cried with happiness at lunch, but now tragedy struck. I cried for all the children lost in the ship's corridors, Anna cried for Leonardo di Caprio and

Granny cried for the broken china. That made for a lot of tears. (Only David blinked his back, because he's a bit snooty about James Cameron.)

Now my tears are dried and I'm tucked up in bed with Ben next to me. We have both had a lovely day – a perfect 'Christmas.' It's a pity Eric couldn't have been with us, but he's promised me he'll be fine. It's Sunday tomorrow and he's going to Libourne market to spend some of his Christmas money. Now he's all by himself he's going to buy a Solitaire game.

Bassin d'Arcachon. Sunday, 14th December. 'Boxing Day'!

It was brilliantly sunny today; the storm had blown itself out and left a pale-washed blue sky. While we waited for the temperature to climb above freezing we sat inside around the woodstove and chatted. Mum and Dad had put the playpen up for Ben, and he made us all laugh by

BASSIN D'ARCACHON NOEL

pulling himself up to standing and then shaking the bars of his 'cage', King Kong style. It's strange to think that next Christmas he'll not only be trotting around, but he'll also have some words. This year he ate Christmas dinner, and next year he'll be doing the washing up afterwards.

Once it was warm enough we went down to the beach again. There were several wrecked boats on the tide-line, and various oars, bits of rope and buoys strewn around. Dad wanted to bring home tons of junk which he thought might come in useful. He thought he could use a piece of fishing net to make a climbing frame for Ben,

238

arguing that he'll be needing one any day now. Well, we wouldn't want him to be deprived... Mum wanted a broken section of aluminium mast, which she reckoned they could add to the climbing frame to make a fireman's pole. We made a gigantic pile of their finds, and vowed to come back later with the (40 ton?) trailer.

Once we'd done with beachcombing we all sat down together at a wooden picnic table under the pine trees. It was great to catch up on everyone's news in such an idyllic setting. Nibbling Christmas cake in the sun and sipping Bordeaux just a few kilometres away from the *château* where it was made was simply *magnifique*. As I said before, I LOVE Christmas, and nothing but nothing beats Christmas in Bordeaux.

Home. Monday, 15th December.

Eric came over at 9.30. We had only been separated for one whole day, but I'd missed him tons. He said he'd been too busy playing Solitaire to miss me, but (I hope) he was joking.

He had a coffee and a mince pie, and watched Ben walking around the outside of his playpen. Eric thinks he's going to be an athlete.

We had a little celebration for my paternal grandmother before we left; it is her birthday a week before (real) Christmas. We'd bought her some delicious chocolates made in Bordeaux, which are filled with red wine. She seemed very pleased with them – in fact I'm not sure whether there will be any left to take back to England when she leaves on Wednesday.

The good-byes were hard, but I am lucky that everyone comes out here fairly often, so we will be saying our hellos again soon. The trip back soon jerked me out of my melancholy – Bordeaux was packed with traffic and the ride was memorable, to say the least. Driving just isn't the same in France as in England. Traffic lights, for instance, are not respected in the same way. Green means go, amber means go quicker, and red means streak across the junction. Horns are not things to be used gingerly, they are to be enjoyed as a percussion instrument, honking away in a great concert of city noise. Buses change lanes without warning, mopeds buzz in and out and cars bump each other like dodgems. We were glad to get home in one piece.

I made a fuss of Dog and Miu Miu when we arrived, and they both wolfed down the remains of the turkey. Dog is eating more than ever, but Eric said she had hardly left the fireside during Ben and my absence. If she is no better tomorrow I will take her to the vet's.

Once I'd done my tour of the goats and the poultry (all accounted for) I made a cup of tea, and then started unpacking. It was good fun, as there were so many nice gifts slotted into my suitcase. Ben played with his new foam bricks as I put the fleecy sweatshirt from Anna and the jacket from Mum onto hangers. As I went to hang them up on our Asymmetrical bars disaster struck; the string broke and the whole thing crashed to the ground.

Eric heard the noise, and came in to see what had happened. We were both depressed that our handiwork had come to naught, but then what goes up must come down. We sat on the bed and had a counsel of war about what to do – neither of us wanted to go back to just having a heap of clothes on the floor, but the broomsticks and string structure was not looking like a lasting solution to the problem. It didn't take long to decide that we'd put our Christmas money from Gran and Nana towards a new wardrobe. We are now on the brink of acquiring a Real Item of Furniture, and we're feeling very grown-up indeed.

So now the only cloud on the horizon is Dog. We are terribly fond of the old thing, and I can't help worrying about her.

Home. Tuesday, 16th December.

Woken up at 5 am by a peculiar noise from the end room, where Dog was sleeping by the fire. I thought she might be having some sort of fit as I could hear a high pitched squealing. Eric snapped the light on, and I raced over to her basket.

She was curled up around a tiny, wriggly puppy, which was yelping with all its might. Astonished as I was I helped it to its first feed, and the yelps turned to quiet suckling. Dog blinked with contentment, but then she started shifting uncomfortably. Another pup was on its way.

Eric was still shaking his head in disbelief, saying "where did that come from?" when I got on the phone to Véro. She's a good person to know in a crisis, and she sounded totally calm when I told her what was happening. She told me all about what to do if it was a breech birth, and that the mother should have a calcium injection. She said lots of other things, too – in fact by the time she'd finished all six puppies had been born. That was that, without so much as an epidural or my holding her paw.

Eric and I had a coffee and tried to work out what had happened. Yeah, yeah, we do know about the birds and the bees (although how a bird and a bee manage to have babies is still a mystery to me) but we were still amazed that Dog was now a mother. For starters, we had thought that as it is almost impossible to tell which end is her head and which is her tail (fur really being her only feature) the chances of her successfully mating were very much reduced. Nature, apparently, is not so easily fooled.

We speculated about who the father might be. He is certainly a dark horse (although, on second thoughts, that isn't very likely.) All the pups are chocolate brown, and Cathérine's Labrador is black. But then he's the honest dog-next-door sort of dog! (But then again, there we were thinking Dog wasn't 'that kind of girl'.) We had thought the two were Just Good Friends, but maybe dogs are incapable of platonic friendships. Plutonic, maybe.

We finished up our coffee just as Dog came padding into the kitchen. She'd shaken the puppies out of her fur and come looking for breakfast – I couldn't believe she'd got over a multiple birth so fast. Once she'd eaten a slap-up meal she went back to her basket to take care of her new family.

The babies are unutterably cute; dark and silky and seal-like. I'm sure we'll have no problems finding homes for them, but I can't help feeling Irresponsible. A dog isn't just for Christmas, and here we are with six puppies. Help.

A little light was shed during our conversation class. Marie-Thérèse lost her old dog last year, and she has reserved one of our pups. So that's one down, five to go.

Home. Wednesday, 17th December.

Tried to concentrate on planning the party, but spent all day playing with the puppies. I've been trying to think up names for them, but so far I have been lacking in inspiration. I haven't got much further than 'Eenie, Meanie, Miny and Mo.' That's pretty dire (who'd want a dog called 'Meanie' for a start) and it also fails to take two of the pups into account. I think maybe I was on the right track with Sleepy, Sneezy, Doc etc... but there we are one pup short. Blow. Why couldn't there have been six dwarfs?

Home. Thursday, 18th December.

Left the dogs to it today and went to Bordeaux with Eric and Ben. It's the party at school tomorrow, and I had to get all the shopping for it. It seemed like a long way to go for a few mince pies, but I had promised something typically English. I have a nasty feeling the kids won't like them, but never mind – a promise is a promise. See what a dedicated teacher I'm turning in to?!

I felt a bit disorientated in Bordeaux as it's still so Christmassy. Obviously there is good reason for this – the rest of the world hasn't had Christmas yet. There I was just getting that flat after-Christmas feeling, and now I find it hasn't even happened. I'm not sure I have the energy to do another one.

Found what we needed for the party, plus we bought a teddy for Ben and gifts for each other. I'm not sure what Eric has got for me, but I found something nice for him. I'm not writing it down here as he's perfectly capable of going through my diary looking for clues. That's the sort of fiend he is.

Tonight I'm panicking slightly. I will have to look after ninety kids for three whole hours tomorrow. I know parties should be fun, but the prospect of tomorrow is still a touch Daunting.

Can't sleep so I'm up talking my problems over to Dog. She always listens and understands... She blinked her friendly eyes at me, but I suppose she really had other things to think about, what with becoming a Mum and everything. She's making a good job of it – I just hope her milk supply remains adequate. Giving night-time bottles to canine sextuplets doesn't bear thinking about.

Home. Friday, 19th December.

9am. Oh god! SO much to do, so little time. Must go to village store and buy disposable cups and plates.

10am. Can't believe I forgot it's fancy dress. What the hell can I go as? 'Addled English woman' ?

Eric just pointed out a spot on the end of my nose, and suggested I go as Rudolph the red-nosed reindeer. He is such a help. No, I must do better than that. I have a cape and some boots, so I think I'll go as a musketeer. Will get dressed at 12, as too much to do before then. (Music –

where are Christmas tapes? Oh God, where oh where are the balloons?)

10.30am. Eric just back from the village store with Ben. Second visit this morning – old Grumps is going to think we're mad. Especially as Eric purchased a three foot long plastic sword from the toy section. Grumps said he thought Ben was a bit young for it, so Eric told him that it was for his wife, who's a musketeer...

10.30pm. Ooooooooouuuuuuuuuuuuuuuuuuhhhhhhhh. That was a long sigh of relief. It's over. I'm alive.

Here's a rundown of events...

Got dressed at the last minute, dabbed foundation on my nose and painted a black moustache under it while I was stuck in traffic on the way to the party. Got some Very Odd Looks from the driver behind. Oh well, a girl's gotta do what a girl's gotta do.

When I arrived I ran around panicking, trying to fix up the hifi system while simultaneously laying out the food on tables. The secret of success is delegation, so I got another teacher to help me string up some decorations. Wearing a large sword on my hip wasn't an asset; I fell over it twice. It's jolly tricky being a musketeer.

At half past one the children were shown in. There were karate kids and footballers, ballerinas, ghosts and princesses – one little girl had come dressed as a bottle of wine from her family's *château*. Another small boy had come dressed as An English Punk. His get-up was great, but I did find the way he kept hitting his head against the wall a little alarming. He'd yell *'je suis un punk!'* and then crash his head. His older brother failed to set my mind at rest, saying "Last time he went to a fancy dress party he ended up in Casualty." I had to make him 'chief orange-juice pourer', just to get him to do something else.

I had planned to play party games for an hour, and then watch a Christmas video in English. Yes, the latter was a cop-out, but then I was desperate. The kids, however, didn't let me wriggle out of my 'animatrice' role quite so easily. They loved musical bumps, and they just didn't want to stop playing. After an hour of intensive play I realised they were going to mutiny if I suggested doing anything else. They wouldn't even swap to musical statues, so we ended up playing bumps for three hours. Now I feel as about exhausted as it's possible to feel, but at least I know they had a great time.

I have a big bruise on my bottom to show for my afternoon... the kids wanted me to join in. I'm not complaining, I quite like musical bumps really. On the kitchen table there is another reminder of the party: a tray of ninety (slightly nibbled and rejected) mince pies.

Home. Saturday, 20th December.

Mince pies for breakfast. And lunch. And for Dog's breakfast. And her lunch and tea. Now we only have fifty-seven left.

Mum and Dad telephoned and I invited them over for Christmas Day. They were not at all put out by my offer of 'good-as-new' mince pies, so I am going to put them in the freezer until the twenty fifth. I'm not sure I could face another one before then anyway.

The one thing that worried me about their coming was the clothes all over our bedroom again. There was just no sweeping them under the carpet, so we took matters in hand: It was time to buy the Definitive Wardrobe. I was worried about fitting it into the car, but Eric said all these put-together things come in fairly small packages. We set out with a cheque book and light hearts.

I have always been a big fan of *The Lion, the Witch and the Wardrobe*, and had dreams of finding a big, solid looking item of furniture, preferably with a magic land behind it. Eric, on the other and, wanted something convenient and modern, all handy shelves, mirrors and slick sliding doors. He sent me into fits of laughter by saying he wanted it to look *sportif*. I said that was ridiculous, and he said no more-so than a Narnia wardrobe, so we sat in angry silence all the way to the furniture store.

The store was called 'But', which is a dumb name for anything. We found ourselves looking at the furniture and saying, "well, that's sort of OK. But..." They would have done better to call the shop "No Buts" or even, "Let's make a quick decision here, folks." More long-winded, perhaps, but more convincing.

I found a huge wardrobe, large enough for twelve people's clothes. Eric looked at the price and muttered something about it needing twelve people's salaries to purchase it, so we moved on. In the end it wasn't hard to make a decision – there was only one wardrobe we could afford. It was a big formica effort, somewhat similar to a white elephant. Not a thing of beauty, but Eric said it would be *très solide* and we'd be able to put all our clothes in it. I said I'd make it look nicer with stencils. (I could paint a pair of large ears on it and a trunk, I suppose.)

Fifteen minutes later the cheque was signed, and the wardrobe was in the car. Well, almost in. The long side sections were poking through the roof, much to Ben's amusement.

Now it is home, and we are leaving it in its (many) boxes until tomorrow. We have already had Cross Words once today, and neither of us can face the sort of row that putting furniture together can produce. For the moment we're letting sleeping wardrobes lie.

Home. Sunday, 21st December.

Ben came out with me to do the milking this morning. The stable must have been many degrees below the temperature in the house, but the animals and the golden coloured straw made it feel warmer somehow. The sun slanted in through a gap in the shutter, and dust was dancing in the bright white beam. It's extraordinary how beautiful something as simple as dust can be.

Back inside Eric was unpacking the wardrobe boxes, and Miu Miu was batting wood screws around the floor. Eric was looking tense, amidst the plastic bits and the wood-glue, so I decided to take Ben out and keep well away. Sometimes a Man is best left Alone with his Twiddlybits.

I wrapped Ben in a blanket and took him out for an hour in the pushchair. When we came back I was surprised to see that although the wardrobe was more or less standing, Eric was nowhere to be seen. I was even more surprised when I heard a muffled cry from within.

Eric, it turned out, had got so sick of trying to hold the doors on while he screwed in the hinges that he'd turned the wardrobe round to face the wall, and screwed on the doors from the inside. Unfortunately, once he'd fixed on the doors he hadn't been able to open them again. What's more, it was so dark inside he hadn't been able to locate the screws to undo them. He'd been stuck in there for half an hour.

I would have been sympathetic, but... but it's not in my nature. No, not really, but I couldn't help remembering how horrid Eric had been to me when I'd got stuck in the loo in the flat in Bordeaux. This reeked deliciously of revenge.

I helped Eric out, and I was Very Nice about it – keeping to a minimum my comments about whether he'd seen all of Narnia or just the outskirts. We finished off the assembly together without any row of Nuclear Proportions. That's love for you – the Real Thing, not just cupboard love.

Home. Monday, 22nd December.

An important day for Ben and for Eric today. For Ben it was his nine-month check, for Eric it was his appearance as Father Christmas.

The check for Ben was an important one – I looked in his Health Book beforehand and saw that there were two pages of questions to go through. His first exam! He got did tons of revision in the waiting room (sitting, standing up, hanging on to a chair etc...) so I was quite confident he'd do well.

When we got into the surgery Mr Badger said a friendly "hello" and gave Ben a big kiss. He examined Ben, then he weighed and measured him. As we chatted he ticked his way through the form, and in just a quarter of an hour he'd passed his 'exam' with flying colours. His next official test is at aged two, so we can relax for a bit...

Eric had a tougher day than Ben and myself. The library party was at two in the afternoon, and all the children from the village had been invited. Eric had to be there at half past one, to give him time to get into his Santa costume. He was worried about the latter, and all yesterday he kept asking me what I thought it was going to be like. My vague, "er, red, I suppose" didn't seem to be the answer he was looking for.

Well, at one thirty all was revealed. The library committee had put the costume on a mannequin, covered by a sheet. They explained to Eric that they had made it themselves, and with great ceremony they ripped off the sheet. Yes, it was red, but it was also crocheted. There was a thick woolly red cape and matching trousers, which were fringed by something which looked and felt like fibreglass.

There was no backing out. The ladies left him to get changed, and he sound found out that the costume was so tight that he couldn't wear anything under it except underpants. It was boiling hot to wear, and so itchy that he couldn't stop himself grimacing with pain. Gladys came in once he was dressed, and asked him whether he had a toothache. He almost had a sense of humour failure when she glued a thick beard to his chin, made of the same fibreglassy material as the fringe. Within minutes Eric realised he was physically allergic to being Father Christmas.

Once the party started things got even worse. The library had the heating full on for the children, and within minutes he was dripping with sweat. It made the suit even itchier, and he couldn't bear anyone to touch him; he had to grit his teeth before any of the littler children could sit on his knee.

He said it was Extremely Hard to keep a smile on his face, and say 'ho, ho, ho' when he was expiring from heat. Two hours of it was about as much as he could stand. He thought his torture would stop when the party ended and he got changed out of his costume. He'd reckoned without Gladys. She came in once he was changed, and offered to give him a hand with his false beard. He sat there waiting for her to produce some kind of solvent for the glue, but she just got hold of the end of the beard and yanked it hard. It came off in one painful rip, like strip wax, leaving a patch of bleeding stubble and Eric screaming.

Tonight, despite having a long cool bath with camomile drops in it, he is still covered with itchy urticaria. The slightest mention of the party makes him groan. He said that being Father Christmas is so awful that it's not surprising the poor man can only face it once a year.

Home. Tuesday, 23rd December.

Quiet day today. There is always lots of work to do here (what with milking and cheese-making and everything) but at least neither of us had Christmas parties to contend with. It was nice to have a play with Ben and get things ready for tomorrow at a gentle pace. Mum and Dad are coming for (another) Christmas, so we've made up a spare bed and done a bit of shopping.

In the afternoon we put up our Christmas tree, and decorated it with our new decorations – it is Quite Splendiferous. We have put our presents to each other and to Ben under it, and all three parcels look very tempting. I'm so relieved that Eric's unfortunate experience yesterday hasn't put him off Christmas altogether.

The puppies are a week old today, and we admired them in our conversation class. Marie-Thérèse has decided to call hers Neptune, and has offered to put an advert in the village paper to find homes for the others. It will be a relief when I am sure they all have a family to go to.

11.00pm. Dany just called. I was a bit befuddled as I'd fallen asleep, but she said they have found three lambs we can adopt. Do we want to come down tomorrow??

Well, my parents will be here, and I'm sure they won't mind looking after the farm and Ben until we get back. Eric says we will leave after lunch, and come back late in the evening. Sounds exciting.

Home. Christmas Eve.

Mum and Dad arrived in the middle of the morning, and said they were more than happy to take care of everything. They said they knew how to manage our animals, and that if they had any doubts at all they would ask Ben...

We had a clear run down to the Pyrenees, only stopping off in a Point Vert shop to buy some powdered milk for lambs. They also had a sort of bucket with four teats coming out of it, so that you can feed four lambs at the same time. You just fill it up with milk and hang it up in the stable, and the lambs do the rest themselves. I wonder why they don't make a similar thing for human babies to help with night feeds?!

When we got to the mountains it was getting dark. Dany had given us precise directions to the farm, but even then it took some finding. We drove around for hours along snowy tracks which hairpinned up and down seemingly vertical slopes. When we reached the fold it was pitch dark and freezing, but it was so beautiful we didn't mind. This was the stuff Christmas cards are made of; luminous white crags silhouetted against a navy blue, star-filled sky. The zodiacal bears were out, even if the Pyrenean ones were snuggled up in their winter dens.

When we stepped into the old stone building I was amazed at the blast of hot air. There were over three hundred ewes inside, lying quietly on their bed of dried bracken. The air smelt of lanolin, wool, milk and of the paraffin lamps which bathed the *bergerie* in a warm glow. The shepherd was kind and welcoming, and we leant against the wooden gate beside him and watched the sheep. It was such a peaceful and fitting place to be on Christmas eve that we were in no hurry to leave.

We picked out three orphaned lambs, wrapped them in blankets and took them out to the car. The shepherd filled the boot with bracken, and they settled down happily in their new bed. We only paid a few francs for them, but we both agreed we had given ourselves the best Christmas present we'd ever had.

The trip home started off peacefully, but the baby ram began bleating after a few kilometres. I took him out of the boot and sat him on my lap, where he snuggled down and went to sleep. His tiny, knobbly head butted against my tummy as he slept, and I really felt that he'd adopted me.

We filled up with petrol near Langon, and as Eric went off to get us coffees an old lady peered in to the car and rapped on my window. *"Excusez-moi, Madame,"* she said, hesitantly, "I just have to know, you're not going to eat them are you?" I promised her that they were going to finish up in an orchard, not in our freezer. She went away relieved, calling out a cheerful *joyeux noël* over her shoulder.

The petrol attendant also looked at us closely. When Eric produced his cheque book to pay for the fuel he said not to bother showing his identity card: "You must be Mary and Joseph" he grinned.

Now we are home, and we have tucked the lambs into the straw alongside the goats. Before we left them we gave them a feed of warm milk, and were astonished when they gulped down a litre and a half each in about thirty seconds. They suck it down like vacuum cleaners.

We had a hot shower to wash off the sheep smell, chatted a little bit to Mum and Dad and gave Ben a kiss before turning in. We are so tired that it's as much as I can do to write this. I am looking forward to undisturbed sleep.

1am. Just woken up by a clip clopping noise. In my dream I thought the goats had escaped, but no... it's just Mum pretending to be a reindeer...

Home. Christmas Day.

Ben woke at six, ready to open his stocking. We discovered that Mum and Dad had brought stockings for us as well – hooray!

After we'd unpacked our goodies (including spanners for Eric's bike and water colours for me, they are great at choosing presents) we set about feeding all our animal stock. There was hay for the goats and the rabbits, corn for the chickens and the geese, meat for Dog, fish heads for Miu Miu and milk for the lambs. Actually feeding all the animals took less time than Ben took to eat his Gigantic bowl of baby cereal. He likes to take his time at the table, and savours every meal – it must be the French half of him.

After breakfast we opened our presents. Ben loved his bear, and Eric was very keen on the Survival book which I'd bought for him. He'd bought me some nice jars of face cream, but spoilt things a bit by saying he wasn't sure whether to buy the anti-spot or anti-wrinkle variety, so he'd bought both. I said if he really felt that way he should just have put the money in a kitty to pay for some plastic surgery. Perhaps there should be a system of plastic surgery vouchers, so that we could offer our nearest and dearest their face-lift by little instalments? Hmmm.

After a lunch of twenty oysters each (kindly opened by Eric) we had chicken and sprouts from our garden, followed by mince pies. We had a gentle walk along the lane to get rid of about twenty of the six thousand calories we'd consumed, and then came home to read by the fire – it's seven o'clock and we still haven't moved! Ben has been playing with his new bear and some of the toys from his stocking, Mum and Dad are reading and I am writing this. Everything was Warm and Friendly and Christmassy. Only Eric is a bit off colour, the poor thing says he isn't feeling very well and has gone off to bed.

10.30pm. You can forget the 'poor thing.' I have just found out why he's feeling 'off-colour.' He has been blaming it on a 'bad oyster', but apparently when he opened the oysters he ate the top half of all of them – eighty in all. Not only that; it seems Lucienne sent a box of chocolates for Christmas, which I never even set my eyes on. Eric ate it ALL in the kitchen this morning. Someone told him that if you eat chocolate in a sandwich your stomach can't 'see' it, so you can't absorb the calories. Following this advice to the letter he'd made himself a sandwich of the entire box. It seems his stomach has better 'eyesight' than he thought, so now he's suffering from a Gargantuan *crise de foie*.

Serves him right.

Home. Boxing Day.

Mum and Dad went home this morning. Eric just about managed to get up to say good-bye, but he was a peculiar shade of green. He stayed in bed while I did the milking, and refused my offer of breakfast in bed.

Well, I've been on my own all day with Ben. We've had a great time messing about with our presents, and as it's still Christmas I have been indulging in more mince pies, cake and chocolate. Hang the diet plan, Christmas is the time of year when a few extra pounds are entirely in keeping with the general spirit of things. Look at all those plump snowmen, rotund robins and, frankly, obese Santa Clauses.

Still, reasoning aside I have to admit that I'm feeling just a teeny, weeny bit sick tonight. Somewhere along the line I also must have swallowed a bad oyster...

Home. Saturday 27th December.

Lucienne rang today to wish us all the joys of Christmas. Eric's sister, Sandra, and her two little girls, Cassandre and Léana are staying with them at the moment, and they are all having a happy and busy time. Sandra lives in Germany, and they all love it when it's the holidays and she can come back 'home'.

Lucienne said that they were having a great Christmas, with only one fly in the soup... They have two dogs which they adore, but the Wicked Hounds have done a Terrible Deed and are consequently in disgrace. Lucienne is a practising Catholic, and is proud of the nativity scene which she sets up under the Christmas tree every year. On the night of the twenty-fourth she placed Baby Jesus with Great Ceremony in the miniature manger. On Christmas Day the family awoke to find that the *crèche* had been raided by the dogs, and that the pair of them had eaten the donkey and half of the herd of sheep. And as for Baby Jesus... they have examined every dog poo since, but there's still no sign of him.

Home. Sunday 28th December.

9.30 am. Another phone call from Lucienne. The unfortunate babe has been 'born' again. She has scrubbed him in bleach and popped him back in the manger, but she's taken the precaution of putting the crèche up on a high shelf...

Lunchtime. Just got out Anna's present to Ben. It is a model Spitfire. I know he's a genius, but it is still a bit hard for him. There are little plastic bits and stickers and glue galore; it looks difficult, but I think I'll put it together and then hang it up above his cot.

Home. Monday, 29th December.

Well, thanks sis. Your "Spitfire: Beginner's Level" took me a day and a half to put together. Once I'd stuck all the plastic bits (and believe me assembling a real plane couldn't have been more complex) there were thirty-five transfer stickers to do. They had to be stuck on a plane which was three inches long, which was tricky to say the least. We (although admittedly Ben wasn't much help) had to boil up daft amounts of water, dip the transfers in it and stick them on such places as the inside of the wheels. Microsurgery is nothing compared to what I achieved on that

251

plane. There were moments when I nearly gave up, particularly on the true-to-life camouflage painting, but I got there in the end. I'm quite proud, actually, but I do hope she doesn't buy any more models...

Home. Tuesday, 30th December.

Had our conversation class tonight, and swapped Christmas stories. Mostly spent our time playing with the puppies – they have opened their eyes! Marie-Thérèse tried to teach Neptune some basic commands in English, but we've persuaded her to wait until he can walk.

Good News during the class; Martine has also reserved a puppy, and Françoise said that her neighbour would like to come round next week to choose one. It is great to know that half the litter have homes to go to.

Three down, three to go!

Home. New Year's Eve.

10 pm. I HATE New Year's Eve. I have a real thing about it, it's worse than Eric with Christmas. I freely admit that I have been Gloomy and Morose since this morning, with a sort of underlying feeling of panic. New Year's Eve is like teetering on the edge of a cliff, and I can't stand it.

Still, I suppose I should do some sort of summary of the year. Don't ask me to make any kind of Resolutions, because that will get me even more depressed. Here goes with the summary:

Had Ben. (Important Event, life changing, should have made International News.)

Eric left job. (Hooray!)

Moved house. (More hoorays.)

Got chickens

And geese

And goats

And cat

And rabbits

And puppies

And sheep

There, that's about it.

Right, it's half past ten. We're pretending it isn't *La fête du Saint*

Sylvèstre. We're going to bed.
Good Night.

JANVIER

Home. Thursday, 1st January.

Had an early night, as planned. I had hoped to sleep peacefully through the celebrations, but it wasn't to be. At twelve o'clock Anna rang to wish us a Happy New Year, and despite my unfriendly grunts she told me all about the (admittedly wonderful) man in her life; Neil. She was full of joy, love and, er, champagne. After a couple of minutes she asked me whether I was ill, as I sounded funny.

"No, I'm NOT ill. I'm asleep," I explained. Anna sounded shocked, and asked me whether I'd had oysters and champagne for New Year, French style. "Um, I had a Very Large Hot Chocolate instead." I replied. That must have alarmed her, because after she hung up five separate members of my family rang to see if I was OK. It was really nice of them to be concerned, but the only thing wrong with me was a Severe Sleep Deficit.

We gave up on our early night and got up. We made ourselves some toast which we munched by the fire, and then we went to look at Ben. I stroked his silky blond hair back from his forehead and gave him a kiss on his cheek, so round and warm. His dear little hands were relaxed and his fingers were spread like stars. There is nothing so lovely as our son asleep.

At about half past one we went back to bed, but half an hour later Véro and Stephan called. They had been trying to get us since midnight but our 'phone had been engaged. They wished us a *"bonne année,"* adding, *"on ne vous dérange pas, quand même?! Vous faites la fête, non?"*

We dropped off at two, and slept like Very Exhausted Logs until four, when Jean-Pierre rang. He was drunk and in tears, and wanted to speak to Miu Miu. Through clenched teeth I wished him a Happy New Year, and thought he'd get the message when I said Miu Miu was asleep, as it *was* 4am. Jean-Pierre wouldn't listen, saying adamantly "just wake her up and put her on the line."

Eventually got to sleep at quarter to five, and Ben got up an hour and a half later.

I hate New Year.

Home. Friday, 2nd January.

Still a bit groggy from yesterday, but we went out for a walk today to blow some fresh air through our heads. We put Ben inside an old sleeping bag to keep him warm, and then set out along the old towpath flanking the river.

It was very cold – crunchy ice under foot and brittle, frozen vegetation all around. Everything was stiff and still, and the only movement was the river; quick and lively in the sharp sunshine. Ben pointed to it and made lots of noises – he seems very keen on learning to talk! We said "river" and *"rivière"* very carefully to him, but he giggled and said "Ba." Well, it's a start.

We wandered along to Monsieur Beau's farm, and thought we'd drop in to say Happy New Year and to tell him about our lambs. He has quite a big flock of sheep, so we thought he could give us some advice.

He was pleased to see us, and interested to hear about us rearing orphan lambs. He said they were a pain for a 'real' farmer to look after, in fact he had a couple of lambs that he wasn't sure he'd have the time to bottle feed...

It was too tempting to resist, and we followed him out to his little wooden sheep shelter. Inside there were two lambs, penned in a corner with hay bales. They were skinny little things – knock-kneed and fragile – but full of bounce. As soon as I stretched my hand down towards them they sprang forward, licking my fingers as though they could coax milk out of them. They were gorgeous. They were free. They were ours.

We turned back home, rushing as we were so looking forward to welcoming the new arrivals. Monsieur Beau followed in his car, the lambs on the passenger seat. When we got home he and Eric carried them through to the stable, and I brought Ben.

255

Monsieur Beau looked over our three Pyrenean lambs, and said they were fine specimens. They were a completely different shape from the Bordeaux ones – it's weird how unalike sheep can look! They looked almost like different species, and for a second I was anxious about whether they would mix. I needn't have worried; when we put the two little ones in with them they made instant friends. They nuzzled each other and then started playing. It's true what they say about lambs skipping – they really do hop, skip and jump.

We left them to it and showed Monsieur Beau around the farm. We took him to see Dog's puppies first, and he said they would probably inherit their Mum's sheepdog instincts. I'm not sure if this will be a big selling point, but it's good to know. After that we went to look at our (large) family of rabbits, and then he stopped off to check the banana palm on the edge of the veggie patch. He said Eric had been wise to cover it with straw to protect in from the frost. "I can see you're serious about your bananas," he said, with a twinkle in his eye.

When he left we fed the lambs. The powdered milk is Horribly Expensive, about 250 francs a big bag, so we decided to feed them half powdered and half goat's milk. The cocktail must have been tasty, because they drained the bucket in record time. Afterwards they looked almost drunk and sagged down to sleep on the straw, knobbly heads resting on knobbly knees.

Eric sat down to study in the afternoon. He is getting a bit stressed about his work assignments – he has a huge landscape plan to finish. I helped him do some of the colouring, and it was good fun messing about with the coloured pencils. I LOVE colouring: I wonder how old Ben has to be before I can buy him a colouring book and felt-tips? Maybe I should come out of the closet and buy myself one of my very own.

Home. Saturday, 3rd January.

Familiar sound of a moped outside this morning; it was Jean-Pierre, here to wish us a Happy New Year and to apologise for the other night. He explained he'd just had the blues and been missing Miu Miu. But no, he didn't want her back. I was secretly relieved, as we've got very attached to her.

He thought Dog's puppies were delightful, but I told him they all had homes to go to. I know it was dishonest, but sometimes white lies are in everybody's interest. And I didn't dare show him the lambs in case he started fantasising about training one of them to tight-rope walk or ride a uni-cycle or something.

Ben went to have his sleep, Eric sat down to study and I set about cleaning the kitchen stove. Jean-Pierre sat on the step in the doorway – he wanted to smoke but I didn't want him to inside because of Ben, so he had to exhale each lungful of smoke through a crack in the door. It looked like an uncomfortable business. I thought he'd give up after one cigarette, but he instantly lit another one when it was finished, and then used the stub of that one to light a third. His hands were shaking and he looked worried and unhappy.

I asked him what was wrong, and he looked a bit embarrassed. He said that the problem was his New Year's Resolution. I was very impressed that he'd made one, because I haven't bothered this year (actually it's because I'm Perfect in Mind and Body and can think of no improvements). Well, it took a fourth cigarette for him to explain. He'd resolved to stop smoking, but the idea of stopping was so terrible that ever since he'd been chain-smoking. Stress had pushed him up to six packets in three days – twice his normal dose.

I had to be sympathetic because he looked so awful, but talk about a resolution back-firing! I cheered him up with coffee and biscuits, but couldn't think of any sound advice until he was leaving. Just as he was getting on to his moped I told him to make a resolution to START smoking – if *that* backfires then he'll be laughing. He looked puzzled but as though light was dawning somewhere, somehow. *"Ah oui, je vois!"* he said, streaking off with a smile. As he vanished into to the distance, his moped wobbling wildly, I really wished I'd got him to resolve to wear (or not wear?) a crash-helmet.

Home. Sunday, 4th January.

Market as usual this morning. The Christmas decorations were still all there, but the emphasis was on the next *fête*: Epiphany. On the sixth it will be time to *"tirer les rois"* – all in honour of the Three Kings. What we actually do in Bordeaux for Epiphany is eat a special cake, called a crown or a *couronne des rois*. The cake is cut into slices, and everyone hopes to find the miniature figurine which is concealed in the soft pastry. The figurine is called a *fève*, literally a bean, which was used in times of old. Anyway, the winner gets to wear the golden cardboard crown which comes with the cake. Half the stalls in the market seemed to be selling Epiphany cakes.

We are on an economy drive, so we only bought essentials. Couldn't help feeling a bit sad. Ben *would* look cute in a crown.

Home. Monday, 5th January.

Eric studied while I took care of the animals today. The lambs are so sweet – I can't wait until it's warmer and we can let them out of the stable. Monsieur Beau said that adopted lambs are often frailer as they haven't received their mother's antibodies in the milk, so we should cosset them. They look healthy enough – they were practically pinging off the walls in the stable this morning. The two older goats ignored them, but Houdini took an enthusiastic interest. Ever since they arrived she's been even more lively than usual, leaping over the partition fences in the stable and up into the mangers. I hope she's just showing off, and not actually starting a training program to teach the sheep how to become escape artists.

Home. Tuesday, 6th January. Epiphany.

Magnifique surprise in the conversation class – Martine and Marie-Thérèse brought *couronne* cakes. Hooray! We put one cake aside in the kitchen, but we polished off the other one during the class. It was yummy and I won the crown – but I was very generous and let Ben have it. He chewed the corner off it (no respect for Royalty) and I had an anxious fifteen minutes looking for the staple which had fastened it together. Fortunately it turned up on the floor, so we were spared a trip to the doctor's.

Françoise told us about her cake. She has four children, and every year she ends up buying four cakes to avoid squabbles about the *fève* – which is probably why *pâtissiers* had the idea of putting just one in each cake in the first place. Anyway, up until now her kids have argued over the *fève*, but as they don't really like the cake itself she ends up eating all four of them and feeling sick afterwards. So this year she has bought one small cake and has slotted three extra figurines into it. Brilliant.

During the lesson we had a cup of tea and Martine and Marie-Thérèse played with their puppies. Isabelle looked on enviously – she'd love one but she lives in a flat. The puppies are growing fast, and I have been worrying about finding homes for all of them, so I was relieved when Françoise's neighbour came round at the end of the lesson to choose one. She picked out the smallest pup, which has a tiny white mark on its forehead. I had (very imaginatively) been calling it 'Spot', which she decided to keep. She said the name was *très anglais* and *très sophistiqué*. Oh well.

When the lesson was over I went into the kitchen to get tea. Ben had already had his at six o'clock, but Eric and I usually eat once my teaching is over at eight o'clock. I was famished, and was glad to see that Eric had heated up a big tin of *cassoulet* on the stove. We tipped it into our bowls and started eating it hungrily, but we were both disappointed to see that this *cassoulet* was all beans; there were no sausages or pieces of meat. Eric said grumpily that he was going to complain to the supermarket. I tried to boost his morale by saying we had a nice big *couronne* cake to look forward to, and as soon as he finished his last mouthful of beans he dashed off to the sitting room to get it.

He came back empty-handed. I told him that I had brought the cake through to the kitchen, so there hadn't been any point looking for it in the sitting room. The odd thing was that it was nowhere to be seen in the kitchen, either. We looked high and low, accusing each other of putting it somewhere strange. After many minutes of searching I saw our table cloth twitch, and lifted up the corner. Dog was under the table, her whiskers covered in bean juice and icing sugar. She'd eaten our sausages and all the cake.

It was unutterably gross to think that we'd eaten out of the same saucepan as Dog, and had what she'd *rejected*. Yuck. Both of us raced to the bathroom and brushed our teeth three times, and then I went back into the kitchen and chased Dog outside. There was a terrible mess of beans and pastry under the table, and I set about cleaning up. As I swept up I trod on something small and hard, and reached down to see what it was.

All I can say is that Dog isn't All Bad. She'd left me the *fève*.

Home. Wednesday, 7th January.

Still very chilly, but we spent most of the day outside anyway. We planted our Christmas tree in the garden, and then worked on the veggie patch. I raked off all the old vegetable stalks and leaves while Eric dug it over; it's a large area so it was hard work, and we were both pretty tired when Cathérine came round in the afternoon. She was just coming to say *Bonne Année,* but when she saw how we were struggling to turn over the clay clods and break them up she said she would go home and fetch something to help us.

She came back half an hour later with a trailer. Sitting on it was a *motoculteur,* a sort of motorised rotavator. She and Eric got it off the trailer, and she started it as you would a lawnmower. Instantly there was a powerful roar, which sent Ben into floods of tears. I comforted him while Cathérine showed Eric how to use the new toy.

He is good at mechanical things, and needed to be to use this machine. It went off at a rapid pace over the lumps, leaping about on the uneven ground like some sort of bucking bronco. Eric had to hold on to its two handles for all his was worth stop it tipping up or running away. Despite the cold he soon had sweat pouring down his face; he had to struggle to control the machine, while at the same time use some of his concentration to stop the blades chopping off his feet. I was glad I wasn't the one using it – this was the sort of machine those Reader's Digest 'ordeal' articles are written about.

It was a Nightmare, but also very efficient. Within an hour the whole patch was beautifully turned over, and we went inside to pour all three of us a large *apéritif (*Ben stuck with orange juice.) We warmed our bottoms against the stove and chatted... it's nice to have friends.

Cathérine said we'd done well to do our garden today, as rain is forecast for tomorrow. Oh no, I don't like rain. I hope it misses us: Rain, rain, go to Spain...

Home. Thursday, 8th January.

Ooops, what did I say about Spain? I hope the rain doesn't go there now because that's where *we're* going. Mum and Dad are coming this weekend to look after the animals (I Strongly Suspect they want to play with the lambs) and Eric, Ben and myself are going to whip down to the Pyrenees for the weekend. Mum and Dad are going back to the UK for a month on the 22nd, so this is our last chance to get them to farmsit. They are Useful People to have around, and we'll miss them!

This is the first time we're going to the mountains for the snow. I have made Eric promise he won't bully me into skiing... I love tobogganing and we've decided we'll do that instead. Mum and Dad said that they kept the toboggan I had as a child, so we won't have to buy a new one. I'm secretly rather glad they never throw anything away.

Rang Dany to check we can stay with her – she was really pleased we're coming. She has got to work on Saturday, but she will drive up to the slope with us on Sunday, and teach Ben how to toboggan like a Pyrenean native.

Home. Friday, 9th January.

Back to School. Usual rush of little children, coming to greet me at the school gate. They gave me two kisses each – so I received nearly two hundred kisses within five minutes. That's a warm welcome. I wonder whether schoolchildren are that nice in England?!

The children were eager to tell me about their Christmas. One boy in the youngest class asked me whether I believed in Father Christmas, and I wasn't sure what to say. If he still believed in Santa I didn't want to spoil it for him.

He saw me trying to make up my mind, and laughed. "You're just like *maman,*" he said, "she still believes in *Père Noël.* I found it was all just a story ages ago – when I started school – but I haven't told Mum because she believes in him. She even makes me write a *letter* to him every year..."

The Pyrenees, Saturday, 10th January.

Mum and Dad arrived at eight o'clock, so we set off to the mountains nice and early. When we left my parents were heading for the stable with the bucket of milk for the lambs – they looked as excited as two kids at the children's zoo...

We had only done thirty kilometres when we had to stop and stretch our aching muscles. Virginie was stuffed full of bags and the amazing amount of equipment an (almost) ten-month-old child needs. It isn't easy travelling with your head twisted to one side to avoid a toboggan that's poking forward from the back seat, or with your feet higher than your ears because the foot-well is full of snow-boots, the pushchair and a pack

261

of nappies. Eric bought us a chocolate ice-cream in the service station to cheer us up – and we had to stop again twenty kilometres further on as Ben was sick.

When we got to the mountains it was the afternoon, and we had to put snow-chains on the wheels for the last slippery climb up to the Pierre Saint Martin. 'La Pierre' (as it's known here) is a fairly basic ski resort, not very beautiful but it holds sentimental memories for Eric. He used to go there as a boy, and as we got closer and closer I could see him craning his neck to get his first view of it. We had to go up through a thick layer of cloud to reach it, and then suddenly we broke through into brilliant sunshine. We could see the resort against a perfect blue sky, and gorgeous great dollops of snow all around. It had snowed heavily the day before, and the wind had sculpted the drifts into huge Mr Whippy cone shapes. It was good enough to eat.

We played for nearly two hours in the snow. Ben, of course, didn't toboggan by himself, but he yelled with delight as he rocketed down the mountain on my or Eric's lap. It was exhilaratingly, madly fun and put the roses back into our cheeks.

We stopped for a snack before we drove down to Dany's, and went into a *Bistrot* where seasoned skiers, Spanish and French, propped up the bar. They had all the gear, and we felt a little out of place in our anoraks and sodden jeans. Taking off our woolly gloves we picked up the menu and tried to decide what to have.

The barman came over to our table before we'd made our minds up, and he stood there looking impatient. After about a minute of heavy sighing he asked us how the skiing was. Eric shrugged, and said we weren't skiing, we were tobogganing. The barman looked us up and down before saying, with another (heavily sarcastic) sigh, *"chacun fait ce qu'il peut."* We all do what we can.

It's quite a relief to be at Dany's tonight, far from the skiing crowd. I don't know why they are so snobbish. They take it all so seriously! They are so intent on getting their parallel turns right that they don't even PLAY with the snow. They don't even make snowmen! How weird can you get...

Home. Sunday, 11th January.

Fabulous day with Dany. We stayed on the lower slopes and tobogganed, and also made snowmen, snow cats, snow whales and snow otters. It was wonderful.

Quite sad to leave the mountains and go home, but Dany said she'll come and visit soon. She promised to come for my birthday next month.

Sleepy ride home – I was tired out by the snow, as was Ben. He slept the whole way. Despite having the pushchair poking in my ear I also found it hard to stay awake. Thank heavens Eric was with-it and able to drive.

When we got back we found Mum and Dad had managed splendidly. All the animals had been fed and watered, and Dad had even rigged up a heater for the lambs, made out of "a bit of this and that."

Three cheers for Wombles!

Home. Monday, 12th January.

Mum and Dad left and the rain began this morning, and it hasn't stopped raining since. It's really chucking it down – the ditch along the front of the house was full at midday, and the river is swelling up to the top of its banks.

Eric put on his cycling cape when he went to tend to the animals, and came back with a big smile. He'd been to see the rabbits, and they'd had ANOTHER litter. Honestly, rabbits really do breed like rabbits. We will have to see about separating them, or else we'll be overrun. We would like to vary our diet with rabbit meat occasionally, but I don't want to start a large scale rabbit farm. It's a bit like The Magic Porridge Pot scenario; it was handy to have a bowl of free porridge now and then, but then it went on and on producing the stuff until not just the house but the entire village were flooded, because no one in town could remember the magic words to stop it. Actually I never quite got that tale... all they had to say was, "stop, Magic Porridge Pot, stop" but no one thought of that. They must have been utter dimwits.

I wonder what the magic formula is to stop rabbit production...

Home. Tuesday, 13th January.

I think we can start the drum roll: Eric's birthday is on Friday. I bought him a present in the market on Sunday, but as was the case with his Christmas present I can't write what it is here. Secrets are not safe in diaries, you never know who might read them.

Well, it poured with rain all day. Cats and dogs tumbled down in front of our windows and plopped into the river – it was boringly monotonous.

The conversation class brightened things up somewhat. Isabelle made my day by saying her Mum wants to adopt one of the pups. She is chuffed because she will see it often, and I'm happy to have another one off our hands. I only have two more to place now.

At the end of the class Marie-Thérèse cast a little shadow by saying the river was high, and she thought our road would be under water before long. She suggested we park Virginie in the lane along the top of our hill, just in case. Eric went out and had a look, and said he thought we'd be fine for another couple of days. It will probably stop raining anyway. Besides, I'm sure floods don't rise *that* fast.

Home. Wednesday, 14th January.

They do.

Woke up this morning to the sound of birds I couldn't place. Their call was incredibly familiar, but totally at odds with our surroundings. What on earth were *seagulls* doing here?

We got up and opened the shutters. As far as we could see there was a silver lake, it had completely covered the fields, and most of the hedges were under water. As for the road – it had disappeared beneath the waves.

Not quite believing our eyes we wrapped Ben in a warm blanket, and then climbed up our hill together. There was water, water, everywhere. The land looked like it must have done thousands of years ago, when the flat meadows were at the bottom of the sea, and the limestone bumps were islands. Thank heavens we live on one of the latter! Ducks, geese and seagulls were swimming about on the vast expanse of water, calling excitedly to one another like kids in a school yard. They were having a *great* time.

We walked slowly back to the house, both feeling a little frightened. We had been very wrong to ignore Marie-Thérèse's warning. Eric realised that when he'd checked the river level it had been low tide – another silly mistake. Now we were stuck.

Eric suggested Ben and I have breakfast and do the milking, while he tried to find a solution. He was sure the water couldn't be very deep on the road. He thought Virginie would make it along to Mr Beau's farm, where he could use his track to get up to the lane at the top of the hill. Then he would drive along to our part of the hill, and walk back down to the farm. It sounded simple.

VIRGINIE SWIMMING

He left at nine, about an hour after low tide, but he didn't get back until gone twelve. Poor Virginie stalled a couple of hundred metres up the road, and Eric had had to push her through knee deep water all the way to Monsieur Beau's. He was marvellous, making Eric hot coffee and helping him to dry the spark plugs. He said he thought Eric was wise to get Virginie out today, as the floods are set to last a few days. Virginie is a Good and Trusty car, she started again first time. A 2CV is the best car to have in such situations; cars with complicated electrics would have been Doomed. Once again we were relieved we'd chosen Virginie instead of a Porsche or a Jaguar.

Eric was going to come straight home, but he wisely went to the village to stock up on basics. He struggled down the hill with a big pack of potatoes, umpteen bags of flour, tins galore and a bumper pack of nappies. He was a real hero.

Tonight he's drawing up plans for the next few days – I think he's secretly pleased to be putting his survival training to the test. He's got many lists of things to do, including making fish traps and 'secondary shelters.' I'm supposed to be doing something clever with all the flour he's bought. Oh dear, when should I tell him I haven't the faintest idea how to bake bread?

Home. Thursday, 15th January.

My Robinson Crusoe was up with the sun, checking on the floods. I have hardly seen him since this morning, as he has been whizzing around chopping up bits of wood, and working on a construction which looks suspiciously like a raft.

Well, Girl Friday (*moi même*) stayed inside (it's still raining) and rang Mum up to find out how to make bread. I was ashamed that I didn't have a clue. I can make a curry, chow mein and sushi, but somehow bread has never been on the menu.

Mum also sounded somewhat vague, but gave me some basic instructions. I did as she said, and was pretty hopeful about the result. It smelt so delicious when it was baking that I even fantasised about opening a bakery to rival the *boulangerie* in the village. When the allotted time was up I opened the oven, and found my loaf was not exactly as I expected. It looked like a sort of brown boulder, and weighed about as much. I hit it hard to get it out of the baking tin, and it fell onto the table with a loud crash.

The loaf was intact, but the table was marked, and the impact had knocked a glass onto the floor. I cleared up glumly, wondering where I went wrong. I had so wanted to impress Eric, but this loaf wasn't going to do the trick. If he was planning a long voyage on his raft it might just have done as biscuit, but it was not the soft farm loaf I was hoping for. We would have needed the chain saw to cut slices off it.

I rang Mum again, and asked for ideas. This time she came up trumps, and gave me a sound recipe for bread and butter pudding. Once I'd soaked the bread in milk and done a few clever things it became quite a delicious dessert, if I say so myself. Eric had three helpings.

In bed tonight Eric gave me a hug, and said how brilliant the pudding had been. He also said other people might have used the flour to make ordinary bread, but that I'd had much more imagination, and that he loved me for it. I'm so glad love is blind.

Home. Friday, 16th January. Eric's birthday!

Right, I'll just quickly say that my teaching went fine, even if I did have to climb up the hill to get to the car, and arrived muddy and bramble torn. Being 'shipwrecked' on our island is a novel experience, but it's beginning to pall. Anyway, this is all by the by, as obviously the main thing today was Belovèd's Birthday.

I brought him breakfast in bed, but this went a bit wrong as an Excited and Bouncy Ben leapt onto the tray, tipping the coffee all over the quilt. I mopped it up and we moved swiftly on to Present Opening.

Eric opened Ben's card first, which he'd made with just a little help from me. I had dipped his hand in poster paint, and we'd covered a piece of card with his handprint. It was actually quite a work of Art, his tiny paw print looked like some sort of exotic butterfly. Eric admired his blossoming artistic talent, and then moved on to my present.

I had bought him two tapes. One was of owls, so that he could learn to identify the different sorts that live in our region. The other was a natural relaxation tape, which I thought might help with the stress of his mock exams which are coming up soon.

We had our first full cup of coffee of the day in the kitchen. Afterwards I was busy putting wood in the stove when I heard a strangled scream which made the hair rise on the nape of my neck, and sent me rushing to Ben's playpen. Seconds later there was another screech, and a chuckle from Eric. We were listening to screech owls on the owl cassette. The whole of the first side was like that – long periods of silence and then a terrifying cry. I tentatively suggested we try the relaxation cassette.

On side A we listened to a raindrop becoming a stream, river, sea etc...etc...(the plot was quite predictable) and it utterly failed to relax us. It sounded just like what's been going on all around our farm for the last few days. We've had just about enough of the water cycle. Side B was more drippy than flowy, and sounded like someone had failed to flush the toilet properly. I couldn't believe it. The thought that I had paid over 50 francs for a cassette of rain and dodgy plumbing completely stressed me out. Relaxation *mon oeil.*

Well, the first birthday surprise (the present itself) was a flop, but despite that Eric had a good day. He messed about with his survival gear all afternoon, and this evening I gave him his second surprise: we had a candlelit dinner for two (boiled eggs, but it felt Romantic all the same.) Now we are snuggled in bed listening to side B of the owl cassette... asthmatic-sounding baby barn owls. I fear this will mess up the third surprise. All I'm saying is that the sound of owls hissing and snorting at each other is not exactly an aphrodisiac...

267

Home. Saturday, 17th January.

Couldn't be bothered to struggle up the hill today. We could have done with a bit of shopping, but we've made do with our own produce. Getting a bit sick of eggs, milk and potatoes.

Gladys telephoned this evening – the library had had a meeting in our absence and set a closing date for the competition on the 20th of February, with an awards ceremony on Saturday 28th. We still have an awful lot of stuff to get through, but I suppose having a fixed date to work towards will spur us on. At this point, though, we have nineteen joint winners...

Home. Sunday, 18th January.

Seventeen peaceful days without any Resolutions, and today Eric spoilt it all by choosing one for both of us. I thought he was going to suggest we give up sugar in our morning coffee or somesuch but sadly it was nothing so trivial. His (our! Oh no!) Resolution was to give up practically everything we enjoy eating. The New Year Diet Plan was born.

The flooding, of course, means we can't go near any *pâtisseries,* and this has got the dieting off to a good start. When the floods go down the willpower will have to kick in, and that's when we'll have to worry. I wasn't even sure what the New Plan involved... Would this New Diet Plan be any different than the one he drew up last year, which we sort of forgot about? Would this plan actually implicate getting thinner, for instance? Eric said the New Plan would not only make us thinner, but that we would also be able to eat as much as we liked, whenever we liked. It sounded Suspicious, but Eric was so enthusiastic I said I'd test it. He said he would do the shopping for Day One, and set off up the hill to go to the market.

I got a bit nervous once he'd left. What would he come back with? Ben would surely get his usual nutritious and tasty grub – but what was in store for me? Eat all day long and not get any fatter???? Was I in for a nosebag of bran?????

I panicked and rang Dany, who failed to calm me down. Why is it that when you tell some people a disaster story they tell you an even more grotesque one? "Bran? A nose bag?!" she said, and laughed. "It's got to be something more radical than that... did I ever tell you about women who eat *live tapeworm eggs* to get thinner?" She went on to tell me all the gory details, and said that you can still find 'folk' remedies like this for sale in country markets. Heaven forbid he come back with tapeworm eggs.

Dany hadn't reassured me, so I rang Véro to see what she thought. "Tape worm eggs, they went out with crinolines and cast iron baths!" she said, but that didn't set my mind at rest. Our bath is made of cast iron, after all. She explained "no, tapeworm eggs are *de l'histoire ancienne* – stomach stapling is where it's at." She launched into a perfectly disgusting description of the operation ("your stomach is reduced to the size of a fountain pen filler") and told me all about the disastrous implications of over indulgence once the operation is over ("*eh bien,* you've seen the mess your average king-sized cartridge makes when it bursts...")

It was Horrible, and I had to make the excuse that Ben was crying so that I could hang up.

Eric came home soon after, with lots of bags. Happily there wasn't a tapeworm egg or a stomach stapler in any of them, just piles of green vegetables. Eric cooked up a delicious vegetable stew, and a fresh pineapple for dessert. We had organic orange juice with it, and I even spotted in the fridge a scrumptious looking low-fat cheese cake, destined for the evening meal.

All in all our New Year Diet Plan is looking positively rosy-but then whoever would complain about something so simple as going on a diet?!

Home. Monday, 19th January.

Floods down!!!! Hooray! Eric was so thrilled that he raced off to get Virginie. It was great to see her on the road again! I hope the flooding's over for this year.

After breakfast Eric looked at me with pleading eyes, and asked whether I'd mind terribly much if he went on a bike-ride. The floods had put a stop to cycling, and he was dying to get out on his bike again. Of course I didn't mind – in fact I was glad to be by myself with Ben, as I wanted to go to town and have a look at the sales. I still had a few francs of Christmas money to spend, and thought I'd try and get some new trousers for myself and my little boy. Especially as he was ten months old today.

I thought a spot of shopping would stop me dwelling on the diet. It isn't the most wretched of things to stick to, but I seem to be thinking about the next meal before I have even finished the one I'm eating. I think the effort it takes to chew up and digest all these vegetables is greater than their calorie content, so even if we're eating tons we're still hungry. More and more so, in fact.

The sales were disappointing, because unless you're built like the Green Giant there was nothing left in the shops. There were trousers two people (even of my size) could fit into, and I noticed that in the shoe shops the only shoes left were the size of large boats. I couldn't even have a *pain au chocolat* to cheer myself up, but Ben had the stickiest bun in the shop, so at least he had his birthday treat.

The thing which got me down more than sales were the pharmacies. In Libourne, which is a small town, there are about twenty of them, and today every single one of them had slimming aids in the window. I saw miracle slimming salts made of dried seaweed and there were special sachets full of god-knows-what that were guaranteed to dissolve cellulite. One shop window was particularly impressive: it featured three mannequins wearing quite startlingly unattractive rubber underwear. Apparently the nasty-looking girdle thingies are designed to squeeze that fat right out of your thighs like toothpaste out of a tube, which then disappears I know not where. I had horrible visions of fat running down my calves in yellow sticky rivulets. Deep down I was sure it wouldn't work, and that wearing one of those contraptions would not be Joyful. Even the mannequins looked uncomfortable.

Got home and found Eric had made vegetable stew for the third time running. He had also made a starter... the same vegetables as in the stew, but cut up and raw. Ben (lucky devil) had fish fingers and mash, and I was so hungry that I felt like stealing a fish finger of two off his place. I never thought I'd get to the point where Captain Birdseye would make me melt with desire.

Home. Tuesday, 20th January.

Diet Plan is going VERY well, in that we haven't cracked so far. I must admit I haven't lost much weight yet, but I'm feeling a bit less hungry. I suppose my stomach has shrunk on the inside, even if it doesn't look any smaller on the outside.

I have lost about 300 grams, according to our scales, and in the dieting game every gram counts. "Can you tell I've lost a third of a kilo?" I said to Eric this morning. *"Ah, oui!"* he replied. " But *how* can you tell?" I inquired, hoping to get a flattering reply. "By the way you keep pirouetting on the scales and grinning at me," he said. Great.

In fact I've since realised that I weighed myself while brushing my teeth, so really I should take off the weight of my toothbrush. Oh, and my contact lenses – that's probably about another kilo in all.

Anyway, we are being very healthy with our vegetables. It's just a pity there are no green veggies left in our garden; I prefer home-grown and it would have saved us some money. Never mind, I'm sure we're helping France's economics... if we keep on like this maybe French farmers will forget about subsidies, and just get rich growing veggies for dieting Anglo-French couples. Unless some new food scare happens (Mad Cabbage Disease... turns you into a vegetable) it seems we're going to live on green-stuff for some time to come.

The conversation group applauded our efforts, and said my cheeks looked hollow. Hooray! I've always wanted cheekbones! I'm going to stay on the dieting bandwagon.

Home. Wednesday, 21st January.

I don't know what happened today. We went to the supermarket to buy more veg, and a pizza sort of leapt into our trolley. Practically all by itself. I tried to hide it (only whipping it out for a micro-second at the checkout) because everyone knows we're on a diet and we didn't want to be caught out. I mean it wasn't even our fault... that pizza chose us, not vice versa...

We thought we'd got away with it, until we bumped into Marie-Thérèse in the car park. Little Ben was messing about in the bottom of the trolley, and just as she was congratulating us on sticking to the diet Ben pulled out the pizza from under a large lettuce. He brandished it above his head before deciding to use it as a steering wheel. Marie-Thérèse winked at us, and congratulated us once more on our Tremendous Will Power...

Home. Thursday, 22nd January.

Big Treat for me today. Mum and Dad turned up early in the morning, on their way back to the UK. Mum asked me all about the Diet, and I confessed we'd started straying from the Dieter's tough and stony path. She said our ordinary diet was perfectly OK, but if I wanted to get fitter I should do a bit more exercise. (Not that Mum is an exercise fanatic. She confesses that the last exercise she did was a bit of deck tennis on a boat bound for Australia in 1956.) Still, the idea of being able to eat normally again was too delicious to resist.

Eric wandered in on the conversation, and as Mum and Dad said they would look after Ben for the afternoon he suggested we go out together. He has an old friend who has riding stables nearby, and he thought we could go out for a ride this afternoon. Riding, he assured me, was brilliant exercise.

I've always liked horses. When I was a child I would spend hours and hours watching *Champion the Wonder Horse* – my dream was to have a horse of my own, and go galloping barefoot over hill and dale, my hair streaming in the wind. I thought my age (5) was the only thing stopping me.

My parents were never enthusiastic about horses – as doctors they were all too well aware of the damage a horse can do with its teeth and hooves. I think they were also a little put off by the fact that riding lessons, jodhpurs, the hat and all the other equipment you need to ride safely cost about a million quid. And needless to say, they were somewhat reticent about keeping a horse in the centre of Bristol – Mum banned me from ringing up about horses for sale in the *Evening Post.* Still, they weren't Completely Wicked, when I was about eleven they let me have a ride on a friend's pony.

It was a make or break thing, and sadly it was break. I turned out to be so alarmingly allergic to my Adored Animal that I had to have tons of treatment for asthma, and I was not allowed to go near them for a Very Long Time. I folded up all my horse posters and pony books, and put them quietly away (with a sniff or two, and not just of the allergic kind) in the back of my wardrobe. For the next few years I fantasised about riding hairless animals (seahorses, elephants) and put aside all thoughts of horses. Recently I've found I can go near them without Dramatic Consequences, and I was all too eager to try riding again.

I took a selection of tablets, nose sprays, eye drops and inhalers with me, and we set off to the stables. It was a fabulous place – not your usual muddy yard but a stunning medieval *château.* There was a large sign saying *centre hippique*; which means a riding centre, not a hippo reserve.

Eric and I said a big hello to his friend, who offered us an afternoon of riding for about fifteen pounds. He'd go trekking with us in the forest... it sounded fabulous.

He carefully chose our horses for us – a gleaming skittish horse for Eric (who rides well) and an ancient, moth-eaten and massive animal for me. He wasn't the kind of horse that streaks over hill and down dale, I can tell you.

My first problem was one of Considerable Size. Our teacher, having led our horses out into the yard, said (as though it was a mere trifle) "*allez-y, montez!*" My horse was so huge that it was blocking out the sun, and I had no idea how to get on it. Eric did some kind of vertical leap up into the saddle, while I stood there in the shadow of my mount, peering up at the stirrups which were dangling around my head.

"It's all a question of will;" I told myself, and not wanting to be shown up I somehow managed to scramble my way up. Three seconds later my horse decided it was time to go, and we were off on our ride.

It *was* lovely. We could see over all the hedges, and that high-up, top-of-the-world feeling was wonderful. Once we were in the woods rabbits popped in and out of burrows, seemingly unafraid of the horses. Everything was quite delightful until we were made to trot.

Eric, sickeningly, was brilliant at it, grinning away and letting out great whoops of pleasure. He could teach horse riding tricks to Zorro, he's that good. I, on the other hand, bounced around from side to side and up and down, hanging on for dear life. When we slowed down again my old horse was wheezing heavily. "You don't seem to be allergic any more, but I think your horse is allergic to *you*," said Eric, sweetly.

As though trotting wasn't punishment enough, it transpired that galloping was the next thing on the agenda. Eric raced off, while I threw both my arms round my steed's neck and prayed. Not only was I horribly, horribly, high off the ground, there was also NOTHING to hold me onto the horse. Don't they ever come with seatbelts?

The teacher seemed to understand that enough was enough, and we walked our horses back to the stables. It was nice just to be able to scratch my horse's ears and chat to it – it was the nicest part of the ride, actually.

On the way home in the car I did sneeze and wheeze a bit, but not enough to stop me riding again. And as for galloping... if I can't find a saddle with a seatbelt, then I'll choose a horse with shorter legs...

Home. Friday, 23rd January.

I ache all over today. Ughh. I also feel really miserable for some reason – Mum and Dad went, so maybe it's that. I had to struggle through my afternoon's teaching, which I usually love. Perhaps the aching is from the horse riding... I don't really know what's causing it, but it feels Awful.

Home. Saturday, 24th January.

Still feel bad. Telephoned Big Brother Doctor Ian to see whether he could come up with a medical explanation. He told me that if I was aching AND everyone around me was being irritating and stupid then I was probably going down with a cold.

Oh dear, Eric and I have been quarrelling all day, but that surely can't be because I'm getting a cold. He really has been irritating, after all. And stupid. And I don't care if he reads this.

Home. Sunday, 25th January.

11am. I've got a cold.

I could do with some sympathy, but I was so Horrid to Eric yesterday that he's hardly talking to me. I'm coughing and spluttering all alone, drowning in a lake of tears and misery.

12.30pm. Apologised for yesterday.

1pm. Eric brought me hot lemon and honey. Love him so much.

5pm. *Le grog* he brought me had rum in it. I've only just woken up. Eric keeps looking at me and making helpful comments like '*Merde*, you look Terrible."

8pm. Thank heavens Eric's there to take care of Ben. I'm having an early night. Not that I've actually got up today. Hope things are better tomorrow – although I can't see how they could get any worse.

Home. Monday, 26th January.

Things have got worse. Eric has got the cold as well.

Now, I may be a bit sexist, but I'm sure most women will agree that there are few things on earth more Atrocious than a man suffering from a common cold. Forget all that stuff about PMT – men with colds are far,

far worse. Eric isn't a feet-in-hot-water-towel-over-the-head kind of chap, but let's say he does turn a cold into galloping bronchitis. He has been taking his temperature every thirty minutes all day, and he's munched his way through most of our stock of medicines. He won't stop moaning and groaning, and even Ben's antics have failed to make him smile. I am up and about today (doing all the milking, animal feeding, childcare and generally being a martyr) but Eric says he 'physically can't move.'

If the cold doesn't kill him I will.

Home. Tuesday, 27th January.

10.30am. I can stand it no longer. I'm ringing the doctor's to see if he can prescribe some sort of Magic Potion for Eric. Or just put him out of his misery.

11am. The phone rang for ages, and I was surprised when a woman answered it. *"Désolé,"* she said, and introduced herself as the doctor's new secretary. She said she would have answered the phone before, but she was in the middle of a sneezing fit. "Aha!" I cried, "That's what we've got. Hasn't the doctor anything for that?"

There was a splutter on the other end of the line, which sounded more scornful than viral. "No, he hasn't. Between you and me doctors are bloody useless."

Just what I needed. I thought I ought to give the doctor a chance to do his stuff, so I asked her if it would be possible to make an appointment. "No, it's not." she said, quite firmly. "He's away all afternoon. At a funeral." After that there was a prolonged pause while she coughed like someone on their last legs with tuberculosis. It went on so long that I was tempted to hang up, but she sounded so bad that I wanted to make sure she survived.

Minutes later her voice came back, sounding faint and somewhat surprised. "Oh, are you still there?" she asked. "If you're feeling really bad then you ought to be in bed. Make yourself a grog. You can have an appointment for Friday, if you like, but you'll be better by then."

Looks like the doctor's isn't the solution then. We'll just have to weather this Alone.

Home. Wednesday, 28th January.

Marie-Thérèse, Martine, Françoise and Isabelle all rang this morning to see how we were. I had to cancel last night's class as I'd lost my voice, and it was comforting to see that they were genuinely concerned. We have real friends here now.

We are still ill, and I have just been to the pharmacy in the village. It was bedecked with slimming paraphernalia, but at least there was a little space on the shelves for cold cures.

The chemist said that everyone in the village seemed to have the Dreaded Cold, *la crève par excellence.* "Still," she remarked, "I haven't got it myself, and if sales carry on like this I'll be booking myself a holiday in the French Caribbean this year." I smiled, albeit wryly. She sold me a giant bag of remedies, and warned me to stay indoors. "It's the weather that's doing it. The fog after the floods – all that damp in the air. You must be used to it, of course."

Fog, you see, is what most French people think England is veiled with all the time. The *'purée de pois'* – pea purée, not just soup, is so notorious that it features in almost every French program about England. I remember watching TV when I was pregnant with Ben – every morning there was a murder mystery in which I always thought it was quite a miracle that the detective managed to find his way home, let alone find the murderer. Thick fog covered up everything except the bad acting.

In the past I tried to persuade people that England isn't all that foggy. I remember once trying to convince an old friend of Eric's – though admittedly without success. "I went to England on the ferry" he said, disbelievingly, "and there was so much fog that the Captain couldn't find the place, so we turned round and came home." You can see why I gave up.

Well, I drove home through a very, very light mist, and now that Ben is safely in bed we have eaten, drunk and sniffed cold remedies until it really has gone foggy. Now we are lying on the settee (romantically enveloped in metres of loo roll and the aroma of Vick) and we're listening to Bordeaux thrash Marseilles at football. Eric, smiling anew, has forgotten his sore throat, and keeps yelling, "This isn't football! It's History!" I am also feeling much more mellow, having left the honey and lemon out of the grog and just drunk a Comforting Quantity of rum.

Oops, the phone just rang. It was my sister Anna, ringing from England. "Excuse me if I sound terrible," she said, coughing so hard that the receiver shook, "but we've got the most terrible cold going around over here..."

Home. Thursday, 29th January.

Both Much Much better today. It is great to be back in the land of the living. I'm so relieved Ben didn't get it – I don't really understand why he didn't. He must be a strong little chap.

We all went out together to the barn this morning and this evening, and it we admired our livestock. The goats are glossy and healthy, the lambs look twice the size they did, and the poultry and rabbits are thriving. We feel quite proud of our little farm.

Home. Friday, 30th January.

Enjoyed teaching now my cold has gone! The children are fabulous, and I also like all the teachers. I got my first invitation today – apparently a bus-load of English people are coming over next month on an exchange scheme. The English school children will be staying with families, and on one of the days their teachers plus the French teachers from the village will all go out together, and I've been asked to go with them. It should be a great day, and I feel quite chuffed that they thought to include me. I think I've been accepted here!

Home. Friday, 31st January.

Monsieur Beau called round today, and he congratulated us on our animals. He said the lambs look as big and strong as the ones which had sheep mothers. He said we could let them out now the rain has stopped, so we opened the doors and they went out to play on the hillside. They looked adorable, springing around on the grassy tussocks, and dodging in an out of the goats' legs. We have our own proper flock!

After we'd let the lambs out we were surprised when he asked to see the puppies. We were even more astonished when he said he'd like one. He shrugged and explained once again that dogs often inherit the characteristics of their mother, so he thought the pup would be an excellent sheepdog.

I suppose he's right. And in that case I'd better warn him not to leave any *cassoulet* or cake hanging around....

FÉVRIER

Home. Sunday, 1st February.

Funny month February. Sort of stuck between winter and spring, and the weather is often weird. Last year it was warm enough to be in a tee-shirt, the year before I didn't take my woolly jacket off. Just when you're getting used to whatever weird weather is on offer, the month suddenly ends. I've never got used to it having just 28 days.

February is, of course, a special and cosmically important month because it's my birthday on the fifteenth. This year February has become even more enriched with meaning because today Ben took his FIRST STEP! He was hanging on to the sofa grinning with me, and the next second he was walking over to try and get at the buttons on the stereo. He is WALKING – not necessarily in the right direction, but his development has definitely taken a Big Step Forward.

Home. Monday, 2nd February.

There you are. Told you so. I said there was strange weather in February, and now everyone's talking about it on the radio. We have just been listening to accounts of avalanches all over the Alps and the Pyrenees, caused by freakish weather conditions. I'm glad we got our tobogganing in when we did.

It has been reasonably warm and sunny today – better than the February drizzle I was used to in England. Apart from taking care of the animals I spent lots of time indoors, doing my Motherly Duty. Ben practised his walking while I worked in the kitchen – it's *le chandeleur* today,

Pancake Day, and I spent all afternoon making *crèpes*. I used some of the mountain of flour Eric bought during the floods, and mixed up a batter with goat's milk and our own farm eggs. I cooked the *crèpes* on a cast-iron pan on the stove, and (miraculously for me) they turned out just fine.

Eric and Ben must have liked them, because twenty-four vanished at teatime. Eric said how nice it was to make them with our own produce, and said that next year they'll be even better as he'll be able to put his favourite filling in them...he's banking on having *crèpes à la banane*.

Home. Tuesday, 3rd February.

Just after my conversation class the telephone rang. It was Véro, and I'm still hopping around with joy because her call made my day. She said she was SURE this year was going to be a great one. I asked her why, and she said, "because Stephan, Théo, myself and the pregnancy test are Positive."

Oooooh! I'm so excited! She said she is only about ten minutes pregnant (those pregnancy tests let you know the Good News practically before the baby's heart starts beating) but she has started eating healthily, stroking her tummy and going up to complete strangers in the street and telling them to stop smoking. That's my girl.

Home. Wednesday, 4th February.

Still can't believe Véro's news . She sounds so full of bubbling enthusiasm, and she said how lovely it will be for Théo to have a little brother or sister. I quite agree with her, but I'm not sure that I personally would have the energy to cope with two little ones simultaneously.

I talked to Eric about it this afternoon, but he was listening to the radio and was in an Uncommunicative Mood. When I talked about Another Addition he said we should concentrate on the next batch of births – the goats – before we consider any more livestock. I screeched with indignation, and yelled that I was talking about a BABY, not another ungulate. Eric looked at me, finally taking on board what I meant, and went pale. He retreated into the bathroom with the portable radio.

Had a chat to Ben about having a baby, and he didn't stop grinning. I'm sure he's on my side. He wouldn't stop walking up and down all the time I was talking to him... all this exercise should help him to sleep

Soundly and Long. Maybe once I recover from the sleep-loss incurred during the rearing of Ben I will be really ready for a second round.

Home. Thursday, 5th February.

A lady rang about the sixth (and last) puppy today. She'd seen the ad in the local paper and had contacted us straight away. She was looking for a mongrel (*un méga mix* as she put it) and she said ours sounded Just Right.

She came over and had a look, and fell for the last puppy. She has asked us to keep him for her, and she will come back next week to collect him. She said she already has a dog, but is more than happy to see her 'family' grow.

Everyone's family is increasing in size except ours. Sniff, sniff.

Home. Friday, 6th February. Anna's Birthday.

Big sis's birthday today. I sent her a nice little pot of make-up, which is supposed to make you look suntanned. She's been complaining about the British weather, saying that she's the colour of an aspirin (it's a good thing she isn't a soluble one, or else she would have dissolved in the never-ending rain). Anyway, now she will look Delectable and Sun-kissed.

I drove though sunshine to school, and flipped the window up on Virginie so that the bottom half of my face could tan – I'm going for the Real Thing, here. Unfortunately it was still quite cold, so instead of getting a tan I only really succeeded in giving myself a stiff neck. Well, you have to suffer to be beautiful.

The teaching was fun, but it will be my last session until the end of the month; there are two weeks of holiday coming up. It seems a bit daft to have a long holiday so soon – Christmas was only five minutes ago. Oh well, I have a feeling it will be all hands on deck once the baby goats are born, so perhaps it would be better if I were at home.

Home. Saturday, 7th February.

I don't know why I was moaning the other day about our family decreasing in size. Ben takes up 110% of my time, adorable though he is, and it is hard to lavish enough attention on all the baby animals we have about the place. The puppies are now weaned and are eating us out of house and home, and if I think logically about it then I'm not sorry they're about to leave us. Although I'll miss them like mad.

Omelette has gone broody, and despite her odd timing I think she will soon have a family of chicks of her own. The rest of the farmyard is also growing; we haven't separated the rabbits yet, so if we're not careful they'll not only have babies again, but their babies will be having babies of their own. We are going to have to muster up some courage and despatch a few of them to the freezer one of these days.

As for our hoofed friends – we spent a long time in the stable tonight with them, playing with the lambs and fussing around the goats. All three goats have the most enormous bellies – they look just about ready to give birth. I'm sure at least two of them will have twins, and this evening we are both scouring our goat books for information on how to deal with multiple births. It's nail-biting stuff. The poor loves haven't even been to an ante-natal class, so they are not very well prepared. We are doing the reading for them in case of difficulty.

Oh, and just a little note about Little Ben: He is not just walking now – he learning to potter. He has been pushing his wooden trolley around the house, just observing what there is to observe. He seems perfectly content – I wonder what he makes of all the animals outside? Soon it will be warm enough for him to play out, and I'm sure he'll love that. Before long he'll be bounding about on the hill with the lambs and the new kids. It's what this is all about.

Home. Sunday, 8th February.

Beautiful day today. It was marvellously spring-like, and instead of coming straight home from the market we went for a little tour around. As we passed through tiny hamlets I thought how lovely they looked. I've always thought that one of the most delightful things about France is the sight of red-tiled roofs in the sunshine.

We went through hamlet a that we've always called 'chez-Eric'. Eric spent every summer there when he was a little boy. The school holidays were long – three months or more – from the warm days of June until the grape harvest in September. As a child he would help with the *vendanges*; when he was only eight he learned how to drive the tractor, towing trailer loads of grapes back to the wine-house. He loved it. *La belle saison* was long and happy.

Eric used to stay with his grandparents for the entire summer. There were, in fact, only two houses in the village; his family's rambling house, and another huge farmhouse in which several generations of another family lived. The latter was very mysterious, the kind of place any child dreams of living in. The floors were made of beaten earth, chickens clucked under an oak dining table which nearly filled the kitchen, and in the thick stone walls there were priest holes. The cellars beneath it seemed endless, filled with bottles, ancient furniture, mouldering leather-bound books and even a human skeleton. Archaeologists from Bordeaux once visited the house in the 1960s, but the family, worried that they were really from the Inland Revenue, bolted the iron-studded doors and refused to let them in. The archaeologists huffed and puffed but ended up going back to Bordeaux empty-handed.

His grandparents' house was also special. There were no mod-cons; the bathroom was a trough and a pump in the kitchen garden, and the toilet was a shack at the bottom of the field. There were so many holes in the walls of the privy that Eric's grandfather pasted posters of pop-stars of the day over them. His great grandma, who visited from time to time and was well advanced in years, never liked it. "Whenever I go in there's already someone there," she used to say. The 'someone', in fact, was a life-sized poster of Johnny Halliday.

The privy used to make Eric laugh (except at night, when he dreaded braving the Dark Shadows to visit it) but it was the kitchen he loved most. It was outside, and ran the whole length of the house. Its roof was a wooden trellis, which creaked under the weight of a hundred-year-old vine, intertwined with wisteria. There was a stone sink, a heavy table and just one gas ring. As his granny cooked she would pluck fresh herbs and spices for the meal from the crumbling limestone wall of the house.

It was always perfectly quiet, just the noise of bees buzzing in the wisteria and the distant crowing of a cockerel. In the 1960s and early '70s the only cars were the postman's and the country doctor's, and there was no reason for anyone else to drive to the country. Tourism was unheard of.

Eric was at his happiest when he crossed the farm track to the neighbour's house. There were four boys at the farm; boys who had grown up in the country and knew how to tickle a trout from a stream. Eric lived in town during term time, and he was more than eager to be initiated into country life. Armed with a penknife and a catapult he scrambled after the bigger boys, across the fields and through the woods. When he went back to school in the autumn he would invent stories to impress his city friends: for instance, a tiny cut on his arm was where a buzzard had attacked him and he'd fought it off with his penknife... He also had them all believe he spoke the country patois. He didn't understand a word of it, but the boys back home all learnt Eric's invented language. Thirty years later he has friends who can still remember his gibberish...

It was not all play in the country – Eric and the boy closest to him in age had jobs to do. In the afternoons they had to look after the elderly cows, cows which were bullied by the younger ones in the herd, and which the boys took to graze in peace in the ditches around the vine-yards. Often they would spend their time firing pebbles at each other with the catapults, or catching grasshoppers with their hands. Sometimes they would just lie in the warm grass with their hands behind their heads, gazing up at larks in the blue, blue sky. Weary from the heat and heads buzzing with the wine they had stolen from the family barrel, they would fall asleep and wake hours later. Then it would be a race to find the cows and round them up before night fell.

Eric is now deeply against hunting, but when he was a child he had an airgun like all the country boys. It was their job to fire at the sparrows when they landed on the pile of corn cobs destined for the chickens. His granny would roast them on a spit over the fire – any hunting trophies were cooked with great ceremony for the 'hunters.'

Eric's granddad died and his gran moved to Bordeaux. She was sad to leave the country, but needed the shops and all the other amenities the town has to offer, especially as she couldn't drive. Eric went into the Navy, and when he returned he felt too awkward to go back to the ham-let. Chez-Eric was no longer his home. He knew that if he knocked on the heavy door of the farm he wouldn't be greeted with a bun and a glass of lemonade, which as a child he would have wolfed down, in a hurry to be with the boys. He probably wouldn't have been shown into the kitchen at all, but in to the parlour, reserved for grown-up visitors.

Going back is hard. We stopped in the hamlet, and his eyes filled with tears when he saw his grandparents' house. The trellis has fallen down, the windows are broken and many tiles have slipped off the roof into the long grass which was the kitchen floor. He felt terrible until he saw Ben, gambolling across the road to see another toddler in the garden of the farm opposite. The past has its regrets and treasures, but the future is also rich with possibilities.

Home. Monday, 9th February.

Sunny again today, but we had our own little avalanche here. I reached up to the top of our wardrobe to get the folder of entries for the writing competition (I'm having to put precious things up higher and higher so Ben can't get at them) and the whole thing emptied out onto my head. There were so many pieces of paper that it took me two hours to get everything straight. Ben was NOT a help; he kept trotting off with the papers I'd sorted through. I had to have quite a tug of war to get some of them back, and I'm not sure how I'm going to explain to wear and tear to the writers. I'll have to just tell them that their fans fought over their work.

I have gone through most of papers again today, but Eric and I still can't decide on a winner. I wish we had someone to help us. At present I think we're going to have to create lots of categories (best poem, best junior entry etc...) so that every good piece can win something, somewhere.

Home. Tuesday, 10th February.

12.30pm. Have started dropping Huge Hints to Eric about my birthday. I would love to let him choose whatever he wants for me, but I've been down that path in the past and it leads Nowhere. Last year he bought me a pocket calculator. As I'm allergic to maths it wasn't the best present, and the Nasty Suspicious Side of me thought he'd done it on purpose. The day after my birthday my calculator was in his briefcase. I'm going to be tough this year and give either/or instructions, in case he buys me something else he really fancies for himself. I'm worried that if I don't I'll end up with new handlebar ribbon or cycling shoes – size 42.

8.30pm. Where are the Kleenex? The conversation class is over, and Marie-Thérèse, Martine and Isabelle all went home with a puppy each. Little Spot left in Françoise's arms, to be delivered to her neighbour. She said she felt like a stork...

It suppose it's a happy time because all four pups are off to loving homes, but I am more than a little woebegone tonight. We have two left

284

– until tomorrow – and I suppose that will be when the final wrench will come. At least all Dog's babes will be local, so she can see them whenever she wants.

10.30pm. I don't know why I was worrying about Dog – she seems relieved to have the pups out of her hair. She is stretched out on her side tonight, dozing in front of the fire and ignoring the last two puppies. Maybe twins would have been enough (or more than enough) for her. Still, I suppose she might get depressed once the last two go. We'll have to think of something to cheer her up.

Home. Wednesday, 11th February.

The lady who answered the advert in the paper came for her puppy today, closely followed by Monsieur Beau. It is for the best, but I'm down and missing the pups already.

Eric thought we should do something for Dog, so we took her out on a Great Long Walk. It did her good, and she seemed quite pleased to be puppy-free. She kept streaking off across the fields, and didn't want to be called back to heel. The poor hound hadn't been out for two months, and was full of energy.

Eric said that if I really wanted to be nice to Dog I'd take her for a run instead of a walk. He has been trying to persuade me again tonight, saying the running will do us both good. Hmm. I've told him I'm going to sleep on it. Maybe he will have forgotten the idea by tomorrow morning.

Home. Thursday, February 12th.

Eric woke me up at seven o'clock, asking me if I wanted to go running before or after breakfast. *Quel horreur.*

I dreamt of running all night, especially of school cross-country runs. I have miserable memories of slogging round the school playing-fields and into Ashton Court in Bristol, always running against the rain and away from the games teachers who yelled at us from various strategic points. Curiously, all my dreams of those ghastly games afternoons are in black and white, like films about the war. It was a long time ago – this was back in the days when I would wear leg-warmers (crocheted by granny) to try and make my thighs look less spindly. Believe me, that was many moons ago.

I have better memories of running when I was at school in France. For a start cross-countries were in the autumn, when it was still warm enough to enjoy running around outside. Enjoyment was considered to be important, sport was fun: there was none of that British sado-masochistic public school thing about it. We had a short circuit around the vineyards, which I loved. There was always a grape or two left on the vines, which could be picked and eaten as we ran. At the end of the vineyard there was a small orchard of apples trees, where we would stop and crunch the small, wrinkled but extraordinarily sweet apples before racing back to where the teacher could see us. There was no cheating on the distance; the way the vines are planted means that it's impossible to cut a corner. Oddly no one ever tried to cheat, it was so lovely to be out of doors, to smell the earth and the heady smell of the grape skins, scraped off the press and heaped in piles around the vineyard. It was like breathing wine.

Over breakfast I talked to Eric about those French cross-countries, and he said that there was no reason why I shouldn't like running again. The English school system had done its best to make me hate sport forever, but there was still a little spark of enthusiasm in me.

I waited until I'd digested my breakfast, and then I put on a pair of Eric's running shorts (hideous to behold on me), a sweat shirt and a pair of trainers so old that they date from the days when trainers were plimsolls. Ben giggled, but Dog got up with a happy woof, and went over to the front door. Eric held Ben and they waved goodbye from the kitchen door, and the Dog and I were off. Well, I didn't get very far, and I didn't break any records. But I did enjoy it...

Home. Friday, 13th February.

This running thing has really got to me – I was out there this morning before breakfast, trotting along the towpath with a big smile on my face. The countryside had looked rather grey and bleak from inside the house, but outside it was fine. As I ran I saw rabbits hopping off into the grass, and blue tits bobbing in and out of the catkins. When you're in a car you never get any of this, and it was a whole new world. Also I was without Ben, and had a strange, free, on-my-own feeling (like Dog without her pups, I suppose). I suddenly found myself streaking along, full of spring and racing for joy. I fancied myself to be like a racehorse in a field which gallops just for the fun of it, but I must say I don't have a great deal in common with a racehorse (well, except hairy legs.) Anyway, I only managed to sprint for about a minute, but it was great. I think I have become a runner! I belong to *le monde sportif*!

Véro rang in the afternoon, and read me extracts from her baby book. She told me her little one is about the size of a kangaroo foetus when it crawls into its mother's pouch, which is a weird thing to know. She said she was wanting to go out and buy a babygro, but she couldn't really visualise it on her new Little Person – she said ever since she read the baby book this morning she's been imagining her baby with kangaroo ears and a great long tail...

Home. Saturday, 14th February. Valentine's Day.

Oh Eric, love of my life. He bought me an absolutely superlative present. I was getting ready to go running this morning when he gave me a box, and said Happy Valentine's. It looked remarkably like a shoe box, but I thought there might be flowers or undies inside. When I opened it I had a fantastic surprise: He'd bought me a pair of running shoes! Modern, ultra-light and comfortable trainers!

They had an explanatory leaflet with them, but Eric said there wasn't really anything to explain. He said that if I want to run for an hour every other day then I need the right equipment, and these shoes will stop me from getting stress fractures etc...

I read the leaflet anyway, and it said that these shoes were for regular training, but also for distances of 40 kms and more. I tried them and they were brilliant, it was like bouncing on air. It was still hard work running, though. I'm fine on short distances, but if my shoes want to go 40 kms they'll have to go without me.

Home. Sunday, 15th February. My BIRTHDAY!

Well, I'd been moaning all week about getting older and wider, but Eric announced a surprise outing this morning in honour of my birthday, and told me to smile and look enthusiastic. Thoroughly shamed I helped him pack a picnic, and as soon as the milking was over we were off. Dog was also allowed to come, now that she is puppy-free.

We drove through a sleepy Bordeaux to the beach, singing traditional French songs all the way, such as the Postman Pat theme song and Bob the Builder. Let's face it, *Alouette* and *Frère Jacques* could never hope to compare with such musical masterpieces. Well, we'd just launched into one or the other of the two tunes for the thousandth time when we rounded the last bend and were at the beach.

We poured out of the car and onto the sand, Ben and Dog chasing each other in and out of the boats and the driftwood. Dog found a crab under an anchor and played with it, whilst Ben listened to the sound of the sea in a shell for the first time. It was a pity we couldn't find one that would play 'Happy Birthday.'

At lunchtime we ate our lunch on the sand, sheltering behind a big wooden boat. Our sandwiches were more sand than wich, but they tasted lovely all the same. Eric had also bought me a birthday cake, complete with candles. It was a thoughtful and delicious touch; the cherry on the cake and the cake from my *chéri*.

Once lunch was over I was whisked back in the car, and driven back to Bordeaux. I was sad because I thought the day was over, but there was more in store. Eric said he wanted to go to a garden centre to buy my present – it was a Little Something for my fishtank...

If I'm honest then I'll have to admit that my fishtank has only really been a tank up until now, being devoid of fish of any kind. Since the move it's been empty, gathering the dust while I try and decide where to put it. I've thought about having useful fish, like sardines or trout (lacking the necessary space for tuna) or even a dozen oysters. I did buy a couple of tropical fish when we lived in Bordeaux, but one ate the other within thirty seconds of being put into the aquarium. It would have been only half a disaster if had successfully swallowed its victim, but it swam around for an entire day with the deceased's head sticking out of its mouth before giving up the ghost and dying of indigestion. No wonder fish don't rule the world.

Eric had decided to buy me guppies, which he claims are indestructible. When we got to the garden centre we found dozens of varieties of them, and the poor sales assistant looked a little panicky when I tried to select individual fish in tanks of a hundred or more. "We want the *petit vert* behind the rock, oh now it's behind the filter, no, not that one..." In the end she persuaded me to take two females and six males. *"Trois males pour une femelle, c'est très bien,"* she said, in a voice so prim that it was quite impossible to detect any trace of sexual innuendo. Still, I agreed heartily.

We got home at the end of the afternoon, and immediately installed the fish. I put one of the sea shells in the water that I'd picked up on the beach, so that they could hear the sound of the sea. They looked pleased with their new abode, and up to now no one has eaten anyone.

Now we're sitting round the fire and sipping *tisane*, and I realised that I was daft to worry about having another birthday. I have had a smashing time. As Eric said, the song's not called 'Happy Birthday' for nothing, you know.

Home. Monday, 16th February.

The running went much better today, and despite suffering from cramps, stitches and a near heart attack I managed to run 5 kms.

I was warming down when a teacher from the primary school drove past. He said I looked as though I was blooming with health, and added lots of other nice things which he probably would have been sued for in America. He asked me if I'd just come back from skiing, as I looked so fit...

Wow, maybe exercise is the answer. It would be amazing if I could have fun, improve my health and get slim all at the same time. I would have settled for just one of those three, but to knock three nails on the head at once is nothing short of a miracle.

Home. Tuesday, 17th February.

Postman Patrice brought us a great stack of letters this morning, all from the health department and family allowance. They were weighty forms to fill in, and I thought I would slog through them while Eric was on his bike ride.

I was half way through the first form (four pages into it) and was crossly ticking boxes and penning in 'it depends' after each yes/no question when I got a nasty shock. It was just after question twenty seven... a horrible phrase saying, "you have given your details as the chief of the household, now tell us about your wife."

Bloody cheek. Honestly.

France is so sexist sometimes that it makes me purple with rage. Lecturers at university had warned me that the masculine dominates the language (_il faut, il pleut_ etc...) and that the French male dominates society, but this really was too much. I felt like sending the form straight back to them, stamped with "the chief of the family is out on his bike. Will a daft female response do?"

I know France has already had one Revolution where heads rolled, but I think it's about time we had another one. France could really do with lopping the heads off a few of these mad sexist bureaucrats. Some people would see that as being a bit harsh, but I can assure you that something needs to be done. We could always go half way... it doesn't necessarily need to be their heads we cut off.

We should act now. *Elle le faut!*

Thought I discuss this with my conversation group tonight, but they stalled me by giving me a huge, fragrant bouquet of roses for my birthday. It was so kind of them that the rest just went out of my mind, and after we'd admired the roses the conversation had changed. We talked about the pups for an hour and a half. I think we may as well call the class the 'Canine Conversation Club.'

Home. Wednesday, 18th February.

A new experience today.

We went into Libourne this morning to buy some exercise books and paper for Eric. We came out of the shop and saw a queue of people outside the town hall. This isn't terribly unusual; the *mairie* is really important in France, every time you take an administrative step you have to pay a visit, so the place is often crowded. What was strange was that no one waiting looked grumpy or impatient, they were positively beaming.

We soon discovered the reason for the smiles. These people weren't there to fill in official forms but to give blood. Blood-doning is seen as an act of *solidarité*, which explained the atmosphere of *bonhomie*.

As I'm officially a French resident I thought I'd give a drop or two while Eric looked after Ben, especially as I'm sure that my blood is healthy these days. I've been running about three times so I'm now a seasoned athlete. I was also curious to see whether blood doning is the same in France as in England. It isn't.

To start with, there was (of course) a form to fill in. Not an epic male-oriented form; this one was all about recent body piercing, tattoos and scintillating sexual activity. I was allowed to complete it all by myself like a Big Girl. It was much more fun than the Family Allowance form.

The blood giving itself was much the same as in England, but the doctor was different. Like the locum GP last summer he was Italian, and was so stunning that I'm sure every female donor felt tempted to faint into his arms. I don't know why so many French people complain about an influx of Italian doctors, I'm all for it myself. (Ooops, maybe I'll sound sexist if I treat my doctor like a sex object, but five minutes of sexism is probably OK as we've had it the other way round for several thousand years. Don't complain too much, guys.)

Well, he took my blood, and asked me whether I wanted to lie down for a while. I could hear my heart thumping in my ears, and blushed madly.

Eric and Ben came back from their little walk at that point, and put an end to my fantasy. Eric pointed out a table near the exit, where there was food laid out. In England I'd have been offered a cup of tea, but this was a real *expérience gastronomique*. There was *pâté*, bread, fruit, biscuits, olives, slices of ham and slabs of apple pie. I was even offered a glass of *rouge*. I took the time to fill myself up; the food was delicious, the atmosphere friendly plus I'd just lost four hundred grams... all good reasons to enjoy the meal to the full.

Giving blood was fun, and I'll definitely do it again. Especially if that doctor's there.

Home. Thursday, 19th February.

Just rang Mum to say we've had twins. She gasped with shock and asked whether I'm on some sort of fertility drug, but I set her mind at rest and said that the proud mother is Marguerite, the goat.

Eric went out to milk them this morning, and got a huge shock when he saw Houdini, Rose and the lambs nibbling the hay, and Marguerite standing quietly in a corner, licking two babies. They were already taking their first steps on shaky legs.

Eric came back inside and called me, and I raced out to the stable with Ben. The babies were snow white, and were quite different from lambs. They looked tough and hardy already, but also very dinky and cute. They are both females, which is a relief as we'll be able to keep them. One male would be good for the herd, but we couldn't possibly house two. Billy goats can be fierce and are a pain to look after.

We were delighted that Marguerite had delivered the babies so easily, without us having to call the vet out or anything. Births are all new to us, and we rang everyone we knew to tell them about the latest babes. I was pleased that even the country folk were excited. Marie-Thérèse, Monsieur Beau and Cathérine have all been round to see the kids, despite the fact they're all from farming families and have seen baby animals many times before.

Monsieur Beau said both kids were a good weight and looked like excellent future milkers. It was a bit weird when he left... he clapped Eric on the shoulder and said, *"c'est bien, mon petit, c'est bien"* as though he were congratulating a new father.

Is there something Eric isn't telling me?!

Home. Friday, 20th February.

So caught up with the new births that we forgot Ben's birthday (again). He's eleven months old – nearly a whole year of Ben already! My little baby is fast becoming a Real Boy – he is not only walking, he's RUNNING about the place. I have a job to keep up with him, and I'm seriously thinking about using those trainers for everyday wear. I may not get up to marathon standards, but I'm going to have to improve my sprint.

Home. Saturday, 21st February.

12.30pm Oh GOD!!!!! We were supposed to give the results of the competition YESTERDAY! Gladys just rang, and I lied my head off and said we were just going through the entries again. Actually I was reading something about caesareans for goats.

Called Eric in from the stable, and we've sat down with the entries one more time. We'll ring Gladys back at four.

5pm. The writing competition is in the bag. We have six winners in different categories, and lots of runners-up. We are impressed with how many excellent writers there are locally, and despite how hard it's been to judge everything we're going to organise another competition in the autumn. Gladys said she has enjoyed it, but I'm not sure at what level. She hasn't read a single entry!

7.30pm. Guess what?! Houdini has just had twins as well!

Eric went out to the stable to check on Marguerite's kids, and found

Houdini was having her first baby. As soon as it had hit the hay she walked over to the manger for a feed, as though it were all over. Even Houdini couldn't escape from this, though, and the second twin was soon on its way. She had to break off her feed to have it, glaring all the while at Eric with her piratical stare.

The second twin is the spitting image of her. The first is an all-white male, but the second is a female who has inherited her mum's black eye-patch. I've just been out to try and have a closer look at this little one, but as I bent forward to pick her up she went leaping off. In a split second she'd run under the fence that divides the stable.

She takes after her mum, all right. It looks like we're in for more trouble.

Houdini et al

Home. Sunday, 22nd February.

We were setting off to the market this morning, and for once I suggested I drove. I like driving, I have never had an accident and Virginie is, after all, my car. All perfectly good reasons for my taking the wheel.

Eric looked grumpy, and I for the first time in ages I just lost it. I don't know if it was really because I was still cross about the stupid, sexist forms I filled in on Tuesday, but whatever it was I was Mad. I quoted statistics at him of how many crashes are caused by men as opposed to women – the number of collisions women provoke is Piddling. That didn't sway him, so instead I accused him of being a macho, pig-headed pig (not the best use of language but I was angry) and then I just stood there, mouth opening and closing, desperately searching for cutting adjectives.

I have never seen my parents quarrel (well, only about Scrabble scores and that doesn't really count). I don't know how to do Fights, as I haven't had the training. For the first few years when Eric and I were together I would completely avoid all dispute, even resorting to locking myself in the bathroom until the Hot Air had dispersed. Eric, on the other hand, knows how to argue. His parents have blazing Latin rows, where they yell at each other and fire accusations back and forth. It's quite entertaining, really. For days afterwards they only communicate with each other through other family members, until one of them apologises. Then they are all cuddly again, except that they will each individually claim to have been right.

Well, I thought Eric would come back at me with his side of things, and that we would have a proper Barney. I was quite looking forward to it. Then he spoilt it all by saying *"si c'est comme ça, je m'en vais. Au revoir!"* He stomped off in the direction of the field, and vaulted over the barbed wire fence. That's where his Escape Plan went wrong.

Somehow he messed up his vault, and ended up painfully astride the wire, the spiky bit stuck into the crutch of his trousers. He was stuck and screaming in agony, and shouted at me to come over. I went and stood beside him, and once he'd taken his weight on my shoulders he was able to unwind the prong from his Naughty Bits. He had to look a bit apologetic, as I literally had him by the balls. His child producing days were not in danger, but his pride had taken a severe knock.

We went back in the house, still angry. WHY did he object to my driving?!! It was infuriating. It's been proven time and time again that women are better drivers than men.

Eric said he'd explain, and now – at bedtime – he's done just that. The only reason he prefers to drive is because of his wretched travel sickness; if he's not driving he feels awful. He also hates admitting to it, and it makes him grizzly.

Well... now I know why he always wants to drive. He is insisting that travel sickness is a perfectly sane and decent excuse, and that any argument I try to use will be flawed. We've apologised to each other now, so I suppose he's had the last word.

Hrmph. Between you and me, I was right really.

Home. Monday, 23rd February.

I've been writing 'February' for twenty three days now and the word still doesn't feel quite right. It's that 'br' in the middle that spoils it. I remember in infant school our teacher spelling out fe-bru-ary, just so we never forgot the 'r'. Unfortunately, I never quite learnt how to pronounce my 'r's, and I always get stuck slap-bag in the middle of the word. But I can spell it, honest. Oh well, who cares? – It's March soon...

More happy news today; Rose produced twin nanny kids at midday. That's a hat-trick of twins! So far we've had zero mortalities, so we are very chuffed. We now have five sheep and nine goats – our stable is full!

Home. Tuesday, 24th February.

No more milk for us now, as the goats need to feed their babies. It's good that the little sheep are now supplementing their diet with hay. We've been able to reduce the amount of powdered milk we're giving them, and stop the goat's milk altogether. (It will be great when we don't have to give any powdered milk at all... we're poorer than ever at the moment.)

We are really missing our fresh milk supply. Although neither of us was keen on goat's milk to start with, we both love it now. It's delicious to drink in the morning, warmed on the stove and with a vanilla pod in it. We also rely on it for making flans and omelettes... buying cow's milk from the supermarket feels like treason!

I made cups of tea in the conversation class tonight, and even 'the girls' said they'd preferred it with goat's milk. One thing led to another, and within seconds they were talking about weaning their puppies... Another Canine Conversation Club meeting!

At the end of the lesson the 'phone rang – it was the primary school where I work, asking me if I would come on the exchange outing tomorrow. I had forgotten all about it, but I said I'd love to come. It will be interesting to meet some people from England, and I'm curious to see what they make of us...

Home. Wednesday. 25th Feb (R!) uary.

I handed Ben to Eric this morning (they both looked extremely jolly) and drove off to meet the teachers for the trip. They were all in good spirits, and explained we were heading north to the Charente Maritime for the day, to discover the town of Cognac and taste 'pineau', a fortified wine similar to sherry. All we were waiting for were the English teachers.

They turned up at about half past nine, and we set off in a convoy of ten cars. There were seven English teachers from the Bristol area, and eight French teachers from 'my' school, all of whom were there for Strictly Cultural Reasons. There was also Bill the Bus Driver (from Bristol, too) and Frank (who was Frank???) who kept telling us (oddly) about his dislike of South Americans. Apart from one Anonymous Brit who went on and on about the state of the seams of her shoes, all was well.

We drove along country lanes through pine and oak forests, past lush green meadows where cows the colour of butter-cream grazed. I was happy when we stopped at a beautiful sun-washed *château* to visit its vineyards and cellars. The vineyards were gorgeous – less immaculately groomed than the ones in Saint Emilion, and full of spring flowers, almost like an old-fashioned cottage garden. The cellars were also impressive, especially the shining copper still used to make cognac.

After the tour we got down to the serious business of tasting pineau (the cognac itself was reserved for another outing, as we feared the consequences of foolhardy mixing...) It seemed a little alarming to be tasting pineau at such an early hour, but a couple of *carafes* of the stuff soon settled things. At midday we still couldn't decide whether we preferred the red or the white, so we decided to give up and go to a restaurant in a neighbouring village.

The restaurant was typically French *paysan*, and a feast was swiftly rustled up. Tapioca soup and delicious wholemeal rolls, duck in *confit*, cured sausage and ham all washed down with several litres of the house red. I was glad I'd left Virginie parked outside the school.

I was completely full when I realised that this was just the starter. The waitress then brought roast beef with potatoes and garlic, which was so succulent that I managed to put away a Respectable Quantity of it. My seams were splitting even more than the English teacher's shoes, but I nonetheless attacked the following cheese course with gusto. At this point Frank had forgotten his grudge against South Americans, and Bill the Bus Driver had fallen for a sixty-year-old Mrs Robinson look-alike at the next table. She had a wine *château* of her own, and visibly untapped sources of Sexual Energy.

Blackcurrant sorbets came next, accompanied by nectar-sweet Sauternes. The bill was brought in with a weighty glass of amber cognac each, as though this would soften the blow. There wasn't much danger of us being too put out – the whole lot came to just 80 francs a head.

When the monies were dealt with we staggered out into a slightly drizzly afternoon. I could feel the drops steaming on my flushed forehead. Bill then revealed the entire cooked duck which he had somehow hidden in his coat hood. "I gets hungry at nights,' he said, with a leer, and went on to describe how he was going to warm it up on the hotel radiator.

I found myself a place in a battered Renault 4 belonging to one of the French teachers (or so I hoped). Fortunately, this was confirmed when I found that the back seat was already occupied – by a student teacher. She had gone to lie down after the first course, but no-one had noticed. "I never claimed to be able to hold my drink..."she said, weakly.

We went on to see a Stone Age monument near Montguyon, which was something nice and solid to lean against. The Brits admired it and the French watered it, and the thought did cross my mind that this was, perhaps, what it was originally for. Was this one gigantic *urinoire néolithique*?!

We all gave up on going to Cognac, as the exertions of the day were taking their toll. We went home via the ruins of the medieval *château* in the heart of Montguyon, which had recently been restored. It was a pity that the restoration hadn't been carried out before half of it fell down in the 1980s, but it was an interesting and historically powerful place to visit all the same.

We returned back to the village school full of the *cameraderie* brought about by a good day in good company with good food and good wine. Next year we've all promised we'll do Culture and not just Alcohol, but that remains to be seen. In any case, we all had a great time, and new friendships were made. And that is what the exchange is for...

Home. Thursday, 26th February.

I had an early night last night after my tiring day (my liver had worked ten times as hard as usual.) I was snoring away at half past eight, so it wasn't surprising that I was up at six this morning. I put on my new go-faster trainers and went for a run. It was still inky dark, and I thought that this added bit of martyrdom would help me get rid of some of the excesses of yesterday. I had a few thousand calories and Uncountable units of alcohol still jiggling around uncomfortably inside me, and I thought a long run would burn off some of this horrible cocktail.

I'm not sure if it did, but at least I felt like I'd done something. When I got home the boys were having breakfast, and I joined them. I only ate half a grapefruit, and sat and looked at Eric's *pain au chocolat* with a holier-than-thou, disdainful expression. He sighed and said that it was no use pretending – he'd flipped through my diary when I was out running, and he'd read all about yesterday. There he was looking all nice, yet underneath it all he's a fiend. Yuck, yuck, I can't stand hypocrisy...

After breakfast the sun came up, and it turned out to be a fabulous day. Eric hid his true wolfish self in sheep's clothing again, and asked me if I'd like to go for a walk with him. He had lots of studying to do, but he had an hour to spare.

We put Ben up on Eric's shoulders and wandered down the Castanet track. We saw Henri and Huguette, who were taking their cows from one meadow to another, and stopped to chat to them. Huguette told us that the beautiful weather was going to last; she could tell because the snails had come out of hibernation. I hope she's right – I could do with an early spring.

We looked at the buds bursting into leaves on the willows, and examined the yellow crocuses and bright pink primroses on the river bank. It felt like spring, even though it is technically still winter – I think we've said goodbye to the cold now.

We were near Monsieur Beau's farm when I spotted him in his top meadow. He was walking along behind his sheep with his stick in hand, and for just a second I thought there was some kind of brown wild animal at his feet. It was Little Dog, of course, out in the spring sunshine, learning to be a sheepdog. I had a flash of happiness, a sort of sudden, bright hopeful feeling. We may be sorely lacking in money, but I know deep-down that we are all right, and that life is being good to us. This is what life has to offer.

Home. Friday, 27th February.

School hols over today, and I was pleased to see that the children were full of energy and as keen to learn as ever. We sang the Muffin Man, and one of the children asked me how to make muffins. I didn't have a clue, of course, but I've promised to look it up. I'll have to be careful not to launch another cookery competition – I'm not sure my waistline has recovered from the last time.

Incidentally, Eric and I were chatting tonight about our diet plan, ie: whatever happened to it. It was there, looming over us like a tidal wave of vegetables, and then it retreated gently like a falling tide. I'm not sure why. Maybe it just got swallowed up by Pancake Day, or perhaps it was my birthday cake that did the trick. Either way, we haven't been following it for ages.

I'm glad. I hate having to give up Nice Things, and I am too busy calculating the overdraft at the moment to even consider totting up calories. A girl can't do too much maths in one day..

Home. Saturday, 28th February.

Bingo! Here we are at the end of the month. I wasn't caught out by February this year. Although my bank manager was – I promised him some more funds on the 30th of the month and he didn't say a word...

We had a Big library meeting today; it was the prize ceremony. All the competitors were there, plus the library committee (smiling as though they'd had something to do with the competition) and the mayor, complete with his dangling chain.

It was quite fun really, although Eric said afterwards that he thought he was going to have to physically restrain me during Gladys' speech. She said something about "her" competition, and about having had a bit of help from "new people in the village." She even dared to say that she had proof that "farmers do (occasionally) have brains." *Mon dieu.*

We ignored Gladys and talked to the competitors, and over tea and cake got to know some of them. I chatted to a ten-year-old boy called Hugo, who had submitted a collection of remarkably polished and mature poetry. He spoke with such sensitivity that I could hardly believe he was only ten. He told me he was working on a novel, and I was mightily impressed. I was still playing with my Tiny Tears when I was his age.

Eric was Very Clever at the end of the meeting, and got everyone to swear they'd take part next year. He persuaded the mayor and several other library committee members to sign a paper to become part of the official jury... as they all had to sign in front of each other they couldn't really say no. We now have a team of twelve judges – nice work, Eric.

Now it's bedtime, and Eric and I are snuggling down with Ben. March will come marching in while we sleep, and when we wake it will practically be spring.

MARS

Home. Sunday, 1st March.

I was just getting my diary out when Ben toddled in to see what I was doing. It is strange to think that this time last year he wasn't even born. He is so much a part of the family that it seems he's always been with us.

He's been here nearly a year – a whole year already. I have only just realised that my diary has turned a full circle, and that I have to buy another one. A year ago I had no idea that I would be leading this life, and I don't think I had any conception of how busy it would be! Taking care of a baby is hard enough, but running a small farm and fitting in some teaching fills my life to bursting. I love every second of it.

Home. Monday, 2nd March.

Eric spent his day in the garden, finishing the preparation of the vegetable patch and pruning trees. I'm not quite sure what he pruned... the trees looked like twigs when we planted them, and they haven't done any growing this winter. It's a good thing we left the picture of what they're supposed to turn into pinned to them... it gives our imagination something to work on!

Eric has taken all the straw away from the baby banana tree; he's sure the frosts are over and done with. He didn't dare prune it as it is so small, but he said it has survived the winter OK. Now it's almost spring he's expecting a big growth spurt.

Home. Tuesday, 3rd March.

I hope we haven't made a terrible mistake. We went to the supermarket this morning, and they had a special counter open where we were invited to taste fresh exotic fruit, chopped up in a fruit salad. It was delicious but very expensive, so we just bought a tiny amount as a special treat for Ben.

He wolfed it down at lunchtime – he loved every bite, and didn't leave anything. It looked so healthy that we didn't think twice about giving it to him. Tonight, though, he has a roaring temperature, diarrhoea and he keeps being sick. I don't know if it is some sort of reaction to the salad or whether he has something else, but it looks like we're in for a long night. He's had paracetamol and a cool bath, but he still looks terrible.

Home. Wednesday, 4th March.

8.00am. Off to the doctor's. Ben looks even worse – he is so pale and can't keep anything down, even water. I know it must just be a tummy bug, but I am so frightened.

11am. Back from the doctor's. He said he thinks he just has *gastro-enterite* of uncertain origin, and I have a big bagful of powders and potions to give him. I'm not sure how he's going to take them though – his tummy seems too wobbly to take anything. The doctor has told us to give him sips of water every few minutes, but that if he refuses to drink or looks any worse we must take him to Casualty in Bordeaux. Dehydration is a serious business, and he may need a drip and some tests.

6pm. We're going to Casualty. He won't drink at all, and his temperature is still going up.

More later.

Home. Thursday 5th March.

What a night.

We were terrified as we drove to the hospital. It was so awful to see Ben looking so poorly and not be able to help him. He was so bad that he didn't even have the energy to cry.

I was worried about having to wait for hours and hours in a crowded waiting room with a sick baby in my arms, but when we got there we were whisked straight in. Two nurses made him as comfortable as possible in a cot, and a doctor saw him a few minutes later. We were scared, but the hospital was efficient and modern and everyone we saw was friendly. They did everything to put our minds at rest.

The doctor examined him and said he had nothing serious like meningitis; it was just a simple bug which had led to dehydration. They would keep him for the night, and we were told to give him a syringe of Coca Cola to drink every twenty minutes. He said it was Excellent Stuff for re-hydrating kids... it was the first time I've ever heard anyone out here sing the praises of Coke, usually it's treated with undisguised contempt.

Anyway, Eric and I were reassured, but it was still a dreadful night. Ben hates Coke, and it was dreadful having to force it down him. I suppose it's not such a bad thing if it puts him off it for life.

Early this morning the doctor looked him over, and said he'd drunk enough to bring him out of his dehydration. We could take him home.

Well, I would like to have felt relieved, but even tonight Ben still looks like a very poorly boy. We're still having to force him to drink, and needless to say he can't eat anything. He is still being sick, so I'm not sure where we take it from here. If he's still as bad tomorrow we're going back to the hospital.

Bordeaux Hospital. Friday, 6th March.

Ben was just as ill this morning. We didn't even have to talk to each other to decide what to do. I packed an overnight bag and telephoned the school to cancel my lessons, while Eric went to see Monsieur Beau to ask him to take care of our animals. Then we set off to the hospital.

This time little Ben was put straight on a drip and admitted to a children's ward. He hasn't moved since – he has just slept soundly all day. I have sat by his bed stroking his little back, watching the drips go into his arm. We have been told that he'll stay a few days, so Eric has had to leave me and go back to the farm. I have asked him to bring some more clothes – I'll need a change as well.

If the medical staff weren't so fabulous I would be feeling Very Gloomy, but they have been cheerful and kind. They have told me that there are a lot of tummy bugs going round – the ward was full of little kids with dehydration. As the ward is actually made up of double rooms all joining onto a central space I hadn't even seen any other kids apart from his room-mate... a three-month-old baby who also has dehydration. There's a lot of it about.

It's bedtime now, and I have had a sandwich and the nurse has just given me an easy chair to sleep in; *'un fauteuil relax,'*, as its called in French. I'm not sure I'm going to do much relaxing tonight.

Bordeaux Hospital. Saturday, 7th March.

Spent all day by Ben's bed. He slept and I sat and bit my nails with worry. I've just telephoned Eric and told him what the doctors have said... they think he's improving and will probably start drinking tomorrow. Eric told me not to cry; he is in the best possible hands, and he's sure he will be all right. I'm too tired to think straight.

Bordeaux Hospital. Sunday, 8th March.

Ben woke me up this morning with a chuckle – he was sitting up in the cot and grinning at me. I was so relieved I burst into tears.

I called for the nurse and she gave him a drink – which he drank greedily and also managed to keep down. I gave him a kiss and rushed to ring Eric.

Eric also cried when he heard the good news. He said he was coming straight over, and thirty minutes later he walked into the ward. He had flowers for me and a new bear for Ben.

Ben stretched out his arms to his Daddy, and despite the drip we all managed to give each other a humungous hug. A few minutes later the doctor came and checked him over, and said he could have as much fluid as he could take today. If he isn't sick then the drip can come out tomorrow. He said we'll probably never know what bug he had, but the main thing is that he is getting over it.

Eric stayed all day, and just before he left he unpacked the bag of things he'd brought with him for us. There were some familiar toys for Ben, including the multi-coloured xylophone Anna had given him last Christmas. Dear Eric had tried to put in some things for me, but he isn't the world's best packer. He'd put in winter-weight jumpers (far too hot for the hospital) and a too-small Wonderbra that's been in the back of my underwear drawer for years. (" Well, you said you wanted a change, darling...")

The saga is not over yet as Ben is still in hospital, but if all goes well he could be tucked up at home this time tomorrow night.

Home. Monday, 9th March.

We are knackered and feel like we've been through major trauma, but we're home. Ben is in his cot beside us, and he has just fallen asleep after a large tea. I can hardly believe that we are together again, and that all is well. I don't know if it's just some weird response to stress, but I can't stop crying... Eric has just told me to put this diary down so he can cuddle me. He is feeling fragile too, and I think we could both do with a hug.

Home. Tuesday, 10th March.

This is my last entry in this diary. Eric presented me with a new one this morning, which he'd bought while I was in hospital with Ben. I'm so relieved that this journal can end on a happy, healthy note – Ben is bursting with smiles and energy today. I have never seen him looking so impish and well.

To celebrate his coming out of hospital we went on a family walk today. We didn't go too far, just up our hill to take in the splendid view. We wandered around the wood at the top, and were taken aback by the amount of work the badgers have been doing. They have dug out incredible quantities of sand – maybe they are expecting babies, because it looks as though they've added several bedrooms to their houses.

We came out of the wood and sat down in the grass, marvelling at how warm it was. We could see all the way to the spire of Saint Emilion's church; meadows and grape-vines stretched before us to the horizon. Cathérine's chimney was smoking, and we could see Henri and Huguette with their cows. Soon Mr Beau would be out with Little Brown Dog. On our slope the goats and sheep grazed, and the chickens pecked in the grass, excited by all the insects the sun had brought out. It was a lovely landscape to look at; the landscape of our Life.

Eric pointed out our vegetable patch, and said the sun was getting so hot that he was sure he could see the fronds of the banana palm unfurling in the sun. Perhaps we're dreaming when we imagine it heavy with bunches of ripe yellow fruit. Still, dreams are Powerful Things... so maybe sometime soon there will be Bananas In Bordeaux.

Keep up to date with the Léonie Press's latest books about France on our website: **www.leoniepress.com**

A BULL BY THE BACK DOOR

Written by ANNE LOADER and illustrated by PATRICIA KELSALL

An unexpected legacy enables the Loader family to buy an old stone farmhouse in the depths of the French countryside. It has been unoccupied for years but they are drawn to the charm and dignity lying under the grime and cobwebs.

Even before the purchase goes through 'Les Anglais' are welcomed with genuine affection by their new neighbours. From their very first day at St Paradis they begin to make close and lasting friendships in spite of the language barriers.

But it is not only their neighbours who welcome them. Soon they are aware that the spirit of the former owner seems delighted to see her family home being restored to life. Indeed, it appears uncannily almost as if she has chosen the Loaders for this task.

ISBN 1 901253 06 6   Price: £8.99

THE DUCK WITH A DIRTY LAUGH

Written by ANNE LOADER and illustrated by PATRICIA KELSALL

This much-requested sequel to "A Bull by the Back Door" continues the Loader family's story. Renovations to their old house are going well but slowly, as they tackle every aspect of the work themselves. The spirit of the former owner still seems to be with them as they get busy installing electricity, plumbing and drains – and doing the decorating. Old friendships prosper and new ones are made.

Just when it seems everything is perfect, tragedy strikes at home in England and they face a period when just 'hanging on and surviving' is the simple goal. Their first test at St Paradis is coping with the coldest weather in Europe for a century: it's –12°C outside and 1.6°C in the kitchen, the water is frozen, it's snowing hard and everyone in the hamlet is ill...

ISBN 1 901253 09 0   Price: £8.99

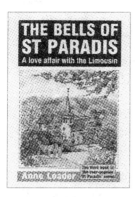

THE BELLS OF ST PARADIS

Written by ANNE LOADER and illustrated by PATRICIA KELSALL

'The Bells of St Paradis' covers the period from August 1998 to April 2000, in the Loader family story, introducing new characters and situations as well as describing old friends and familiar places.

While Anne and her husband Jack continue to work on the renovation of their 200-year-old French farmhouse, under the watchful eye of its late owner, Marguerite, they take time off to make more friendships and enjoy the social life of the community including the colourful medieval fair (where women in wimples use mobile phones) and the *sauerkraut* supper (where everyone has a good time but leaves the *sauerkraut*).

The animals, as always, take centre stage, too. Meet the gosling who starred at a wedding reception, the diabolical migratory *grues*, the donkeys confined by a 'psychological' electric fence, and Cédric – the turkey who sang the angelus.

ISBN 190125326 0   Price: £9.99

BON COURAGE, MES AMIS!

Written and illustrated by SHEILA WRIGHT

In 1994, primary school teacher Sheila Wright suddenly had the means to buy a house in the Creuse department of France but the amount of her legacy meant that she was looking at "the bottom end of the market". She found herself falling ridiculously in love with a very old stone house which had been abandoned for years and had an alarming 20ft crack up the front.

From these inauspicious beginnings, Sheila and her family worked hard to create a habitable holiday home full of happiness, music and laughter. Along the way she developed a passion for building with stone, constructing two granite staircases herself over a five-year period. French neighbours seeing the Wrights tackle the enormous task fervently wished them *"bon courage"* which could perhaps be loosely translated as "Good luck - you'll need it!"

ISBN 1901253 30 9   Price: £8.99

BUTTERFLIES ON MIMOSA

Written by
ELEANOR FRANCIS
and illustrated by
PATRICIA KELSALL

Owning a gîte in Charente-Maritime has been a far from humdrum experience for the author and her family – though they love their charming house dearly.

Surprises were the order of the day and they learned to expect the unexpected. The purchase took place around Black Wednesday, their money seemed to vanish into thin air after being paid over, they had trouble with caretakers and eventually became astonished onlookers as a tale of arson and murder unfolded. Wayward sewage and occasional difficult guests were the least of their problems...

ISBN 1901253236   Price £8.99

LILAC AND ROSES

by PEGGY ANDERSON
edited by JAN BEVAN

The late Peggy and Alan Anderson bought La Clède, a ruined farmhouse near the appropriately named town of Joyeuse in the Ardèche, in 1963 – long before Peter Mayle appeared on the scene and made such purchases fashionable. Set amidst vineyards and sweet chestnuts, it cost £900 and they spent the next ten years, and most of their savings, renovating it. Their friends thought they were mad.

Yet by the time the couple came to retire they had transformed the ruin into an enchanting home. A local newspaper article described them as being set for "a life of lilac and roses". This delightful book was written in 1975 and has been edited by Peggy's daughter Jan Bevan as a tribute to her mother. It contains 18 b&w and colour photographs.

Jan now lets out half the house as a summer holiday *gîte* and lives in the other part.

ISBN 1901253 22 8   Price: £7.99

All these books are available from Léonie Press, 13 Vale Road, Hartford, Northwich, Cheshire CW8 1PL (01606 75660). Please add £1.30 each for p+p.